THE PMLD AMBIGUITY

THE PMLD AMBIGUITY
Articulating the Life-Worlds of Children with Profound and Multiple Learning Disabilities

*Ben Simmons and
Debbie Watson*

KARNAC

Extract from Merleau-Ponty, M. (2002). *Phenomenology of Perception*. London: Routledge. Reproduced by permission of Taylor and Francis Books UK.

First published in 2014 by
Karnac Books Ltd
118 Finchley Road
London NW3 5HT

Copyright © 2014 by Ben Simmons and Debbie Watson

The rights of Ben Simmons and Debbie Watson to be identified as the authors of this work has been asserted in accordance with §§ 77 and 78 of the Copyright Design and Patents Act 1988.

All rights reserved. No part of this publication may be reproduced, stored in a retrieval system, or transmitted, in any form or by any means, electronic, mechanical, photocopying, recording, or otherwise, without the prior written permission of the publisher.

British Library Cataloguing in Publication Data

A C.I.P. for this book is available from the British Library

ISBN-13: 978-1-78049-034-2

Typeset by V Publishing Solutions Pvt Ltd., Chennai, India

Printed in Great Britain

www.karnacbooks.com

For Gillian, Rosalie, and Caleb—for enriching my life beyond measure and for the abundance of love and support

—BS

For Neil, Charlie, and Will—with love and thanks for your patience and support as ever

—DW

CONTENTS

ACKNOWLEDGEMENTS ix

ABOUT THE AUTHORS xi

PREFACE xiii

CHAPTER ONE
Exploring "PMLD" 1

CHAPTER TWO
Behaviourism 21

CHAPTER THREE
Cognitivism 51

CHAPTER FOUR
Phenomenology 87

CHAPTER FIVE
Interpreting Sam: the search for a sensitive methodology 131

CHAPTER SIX
Sam's life-worlds: subjectivities and intersubjectivities 159

CHAPTER SEVEN
Concluding discussion: negotiating ambiguity
    as a means to the life-world 197

REFERENCES 205

INDEX 235

ACKNOWLEDGEMENTS

This book is based on Ben Simmons' MSc and PhD work undertaken at the University of Exeter during 2005–2010. His thesis was supervised by Dr Phil Bayliss and Dr Debbie Watson, and examined by Prof Dan Goodley (external) and Dr Deborah Osberg (internal). His fieldwork (the observations of Sam in his different schools) was made possible because of an ongoing inclusive education project set up by Phil and Dr Glynis Pratchett (who was the headteacher of a Scope UK special school that Sam attended). We wish to acknowledge that this book would not have existed without Phil and Glynis, and thank Phil in particular, who has been a continuous mentor and friend. We also wish to thank Sam, his parents, teachers, and support staff for sharing their time with us and letting us participate in Sam's life at school.

Ben's MSc and PhD work was also made possible with the generous financial support of several organisations. We wish to thank Scope UK for funding Sam's inclusion and employing Ben as a research assistant, which made his fieldwork possible; the University of Exeter, which provided Ben with an MSc studentship, and the Economic and Social Science Research Council (ESRC), which provided a PhD studentship.

Finally, we would like to thank Karnac Books for providing us with the opportunity to tell Sam's story, Rod for his editorial guidance, and our critical friends who helped review the manuscript.

ABOUT THE AUTHORS

Dr Ben Simmons is a British Academy Postdoctoral Fellow at the Graduate School of Education, University of Bristol, UK. This book is based on his MSc and PhD work undertaken at the University of Exeter (2005–2010). His long-standing research interests involve developing understandings about the agency, lived experiences, and inclusion of children with PMLD. He is particularly interested in the application of phenomenology and consciousness studies to these issues. Before joining Bristol, Ben was a Qualitative Researcher at the Health Experiences Research Group, University of Oxford, where he developed an online information resource about arthritis in young people. Prior to this, Ben was a Research Assistant at the University of Exeter and Plymouth University, supporting projects in the fields of special education, inclusion, and outdoor pedagogy. He also worked as a Researcher and Support Worker for third-sector disability organisations, including Scope and Mencap.

Dr Debbie Watson is a Senior Lecturer in Childhood Studies in the School for Policy Studies at the University of Bristol, UK. She is a qualified secondary school teacher and has a PhD in Education from the University of Exeter (1998). Her research interests focus on understanding and improving children's wellbeing, particularly in school contexts; rights-based approaches to working with children and young people; diversity and children's identities; educational inclusion; and supporting children and families in inclusive services. Her current and recent research projects include projects developing postgraduate training for children's advocates in Egypt and Jordan, quality in family support provisions, services for young disadvantaged children, and post-adoption support. She has long-held interests in theorising children's experiences of diversity and in developing methodologies that enable children and young people's participation in research.

PREFACE

Children with profound and multiple learning disabilities (PMLD) are said to experience the severest of cognitive impairments which typically stem from extensive neurological damage (Carnaby, 2007). The abilities of such children are often compared to those of the neonate or infant insofar as children with PMLD are described as operating at the earliest, preverbal stages of development (Coupe O'Kane & Goldbart, 1998). It is argued that the profound developmental delay of children with PMLD precludes them from engaging in most social and educational environments (Foreman et al., 2004). Subsequently, such children are typically educated in special schools (Salt, 2010).

This book takes an alternative perspective which challenges the very idea of "PMLD" itself and, consequently, what constitutes appropriate educational provision for children described as having PMLD. We take the position that the dominant conceptual approaches used to understand children with PMLD (i.e., behaviourist psychology and cognitive psychology) are too simplistic, overly reductive, and (when used exclusively) essentially objectifying. These approaches privilege only a small cluster of behaviours said to be indicative of the presence or absence of children's conscious awareness of self, other, and surrounding world. By privileging only a limited number of behaviours deemed to be meaningful (or not), the PMLD literature overlooks the complex, dynamic, and varied forms of shared and personal experience.

In an attempt to address this situation, this book presents alternative ways of thinking about, experiencing, and engaging with children described as having PMLD. This aim is achieved through several steps. Chapter One explores the concept of PMLD, first through the introduction of contemporary terminology and definitions. We then provide a thematic review of the PMLD literature and identify key issues relating to how the concept of PMLD is described, constructed and understood, and how this relates to policy and practice for children described as having PMLD. We draw from a range of theoretical and empirical perspectives in order to grasp the main issues discussed, with the purpose of locating our approach to thinking about children with PMLD. During the literature review we also engage with research about adults with PMLD (particularly with regards to deinstitutionalisation and community participation). Whilst the focus of the book is on children with PMLD within educational contexts, the theme of exclusion identified in the adult literature is arguably just as important to children in light of minimal opportunities for educational inclusion.

In Chapters Two and Three we deconstruct the dominant psychological perspectives used by academics who conduct research with people with PMLD. We do this in order to illuminate the core ideas and presuppositions that guide interpretation of people with PMLD and shape specialist practice. In these chapters we use the term "people" instead of "children" as this is consistent with the literature we review. In Chapter Two we look at the core concepts found in behaviourism—that is, classical conditioning theory (Watson, 1913) and operant conditioning theory (Skinner, 1986). We then explore how these concepts have shaped several decades of research concerned with conditioning the behaviours of people with PMLD. During the review of the behaviourist literature we also identify how contemporary researchers have started moving away from a purely "externalist" ontology toward grasping how events theorised as "internal" to people with PMLD, such as behaviour states (Guess et al., 1993), mediate the efficacy of conditioning programmes. Further, we note growing interest in how operant conditioning procedures can lead to people with PMLD developing contingency awareness (or knowledge of cause-effect relationships) (Saunders et al., 2003b). We also describe how conditioning techniques have been used to increase the "happiness" of people with PMLD.

In Chapter Three we deconstruct the cognitivist literature as it relates to children with PMLD. Researchers influenced by cognitivism draw from a wealth of studies about infant–parent interactions (e.g., Bates et al., 1975; Schaffer, 1971a; Trevarthen, 1979) in order to map out the "normal" developmental trajectories of children without disabilities, and to illuminate the mechanisms through which children typically develop. We begin the chapter by exploring key ideas at the heart of this work. What we present is not a coherent theory of child development, but a range of perspectives which are in some respects radically opposed to each other, particularly with regard to the nature and emergence of intersubjectivity and joint attention. After identifying these tensions we then explore how the work has influenced school assessment strategies for children with PMLD—that is, the early communication assessment (Coupe O'Kane & Goldbart, 1998). We also look at how cognitivism has influenced intervention strategies, such as Intensive Interaction (Nind & Hewett, 1988; 1994; 2001) and responsive environments (Ware, 1994; 2003).

In Chapter Four we break away from traditional psychological approaches and critically engage with an alternative approach to thinking about consciousness and (embodied) cognition found in phenomenology (Merleau-Ponty, 1963; 2002). The purpose of this engagement is to explore the ways in which non-traditional concepts challenge traditional understandings and offer potential for rethinking the awareness and abilities of children with PMLD. In the chapter we describe the notion of the "life-world" (Husserl, 1970) as a level of awareness or experience that is not found in descriptions of children with PMLD informed by behaviourism and cognitivism. Following Lewis and Staehler (2010) we define the life-world initially as our pre-conceptual experience of the world. Through Lewis and Staehler (2010) we then explore Husserl's (1970) "mature" concept of the life-world, which holds that history and culture (including scientific activities such as psychological research) influence our immediate, pre-thematic, everyday experience. We explore how the life-world is actualised through the body in the world as the vehicle for perception and signification. Through explication of Merleau-Ponty's (2002) notions of the "pre-objective" body (p. 281), "organic thought" (p. 89), and "being-in-the-world" (p. 90), we bridge the mind-body (or rather, cognition-behaviour) dichotomy of cognitivism and behaviourism and locate children with PMLD in a philosophy that has the power to theorise the agency of children with PMLD in new ways. As a third way between reflex responses and explicit cognition, we find Merleau-Ponty's conceptualisations (1963; 2002) particularly exciting.

In Chapters Five and Six we present a novel research project about how inclusive education could support growth and learning in a young boy with PMLD, called Sam. Specifically, in Chapter Five we describe the research methodology and locate this in wider debates about accessing marginalised voices, particularly the voices of children with PMLD, who are described as having no point of view (Ware, 2004). Chapter Six presents the findings of the study. This presentation serves two purposes. First, the study demonstrates the ways in which freedom to engage with different social milieus allows for different expressions of ability and development. Second, the study "tests" the three perspectives (behaviourist, cognitivist, and phenomenological) by analysing the extent to which each perspective can make Sam's actions intelligible. Analysis demonstrates that a phenomenological perspective has the power to illuminate the research data in new ways. However, analysis also reveals that Sam makes the three different perspectives problematic. Sam resists being "read" from each, insofar as neither perspective can account for Sam's complex behaviours in their entirety. Further, Sam contradicts and obscures dominant understandings in many ways, leading to an ambiguous or shifting identity.

We conclude the book by considering the role of ambiguity in articulating the life-worlds of children with PMLD. At one level we revisit the idea that the actions of children with PMLD can have more than one meaning, and are thus open to different interpretations. This is evidenced by the competing understandings found in the psychological literature that the PMLD research overlooks. At a deeper level we describe ambiguity as an essential feature of the life-worlds of children with PMLD. Following on from the idea that Sam resisted being read from any individual perspective, we theorise the possibility that this is because consciousness and cognition are not capacities contained in the mind (or the brain), but are situated and enacted. In order to understand children with PMLD, we may need to see consciousness and agency as embodied and relational.

CHAPTER ONE

Exploring "PMLD"

The purpose of this chapter is to induct the reader to existing issues reported in the PMLD literature in order that we identify emergent themes that explore the lives of people with PMLD. This process provides valuable insights into the ways in which people with PMLD are regarded, the discourses that surround them, approaches to working with them, and the spaces and gaps within the reporting of people's lives that exist. How these gaps in the PMLD literature provided the space for the study reported here will be elicited as the issues are presented and critiqued.

Whilst we do not claim this to be a systematic review of the available PMLD literature, we explore both research (empirical/theoretical) and practice literatures, and the multiple perspectives contained within them. We also make reference to work published by disability advocacy groups. By surveying the literature in this way we situate this book in a broad context of understandings about children with PMLD and what is (or is not) in their best interests. Inevitably, we have had to make a selection of themes and topics that are included in this discussion, and the overriding concern has been to provide context for the study that is reported in Chapters Five and

Six. This results in some issues not having a robust consideration, such as abuse and neglect, which are important issues but not the focus of this book.

We first describe the terminology and definitions of PMLD operating in the literature. We briefly describe the demographics then discuss literature regarding physical health and mental health. Through this discussion we illuminate common themes such as health inequalities, difficulties with communication, problems accessing the experiences and perspectives of people with PMLD, and negative attitudes about quality or value of life. After exploring the position of families in this debate, we discuss issues related to the inclusive education movement and the extent to which it is realised for children with PMLD. In the educational literature we identify a distinct lack of concepts regarding what inclusion means for children with PMLD, partly stemming from difficulties accessing children's point of view, and partly stemming from a lack of research and opportunities for inclusion nationally. We describe the key theoretical perspectives that inform special educational practice for children with PMLD—that is, behaviourism and cognitivism. We critically analyse the notion of "identity" as it relates to children with PMLD, and how this shapes the way we think about, experience, and engage with such children. The chapter then concludes with a consideration of how concepts of quality of life and wellbeing have been constructed for people with PMLD and the extent to which a perspective emerging from capabilities theory offers a challenge to deficit-based assumptions of the lives of children with PMLD.

It is important to note that a great deal of the literature about people with PMLD is ambiguous in respect of whether it describes children or adults (and often literature refers to both). It is also not clear how children are defined in respect of age and this reflects the definitions explored in the next section whereby PMLD status is often associated with the developmental capacities of infants. For the purposes of this book we define children as encompassing nought to nineteen-year-olds and therefore refer to children and young people. We also attempt to direct the reader to the age group being discussed where it is possible to do so. This developmental definition challenges the identity of people with PMLD (of whatever age) and this is a discussion we return to later in this chapter.

Defining profound and multiple learning disabilities (PMLD)

Research and policy is often plagued with terminological inconsistencies when referring to people with PMLD (PMLD Network, 2001). For example, the UK government white paper *Valuing People* (Department of Health, 2001) contains nine different terms which refer to the population we wish to discuss, including "young people with complex and multiple disabilities" and "the most severely disabled". Researchers at the 12th World Congress of the International Association for the Scientific Study of Intellectual and Developmental Disabilities (IASSID) used eleven different terms, including "profound multiple disabilities" and "severe intellectual and motor disabilities" (Nakken & Vlaskamp, 2007). In this book we use the term "profound and multiple learning disabilities" because it is consistent with much of the contemporary literature in our home country (UK) (Dawkins, 2009; Lacey, 1998; Young & Lambe, 2011). However, we recognise that historically the UK has preferred to use the term "profound and multiple learning *difficulties*" (rather than disabilities) (Nind, 2007; Salt, 2010; Ware, 2003), and that various other terms are currently used in the UK such as "profound intellectual and multiple disabilities" (Mansell, 2010; Pawlyn & Carnaby, 2009).

Given the varying terminology, it is perhaps not surprising that there is also variation regarding the way "PMLD" is defined (Bellamy et al., 2010; Nakken & Vlaskamp, 2007). However, there are core descriptions common to the published literature. PMLD is a label given to children who are said to experience the severest of impairments to cognition resulting in significant developmental delay (Scope, 2013). The abilities of such children are often compared to those of the neonate or infant insofar as children with PMLD are described as operating at the pre-verbal stages of development (i.e., the earliest stages of development, which infants are said to pass through during their first year of life) (Burford, 1988; Carnaby, 2004; Coupe O'Kane & Goldbart, 1998; Nind & Hewett, 2001; 1994; Samuel & Pritchard, 2001). Consequently, a range of descriptors are used in the PMLD literature to indicate that such children typically fail to reach particular developmental milestones that some associate with later infancy. For example, children with PMLD are understood as being pre-volitional (they lack free will or agency and cannot move with intent) (Farrell, 2004; Mercieca, 2008); pre-contingency aware (they do not show awareness of cause-effect relationships) (Ware, 1994; 2003); pre-intersubjective (they do not represent other people as subjects "like me", and cannot differentiate between subject and object); pre-symbolic or pre-intentional (they do not intentionally communicate meaning to others) (Coupe O'Kane & Goldbart, 1998; Goldbart, 1994); stereotypic in behaviour (they display reflexive, non-volitional behaviour) (Tang et al., 2003), and who are at high risk of living in a world of confusion (Cartwright & Wind-Cowie, 2005; Ouvry, 1987).

In addition to profoundly delayed cognitive development, children with PMLD are also said to be prone to a range of other difficulties including physical impairments (Neilson et al., 2000), sensory impairments (Vlaskamp & Cuppen-Fonteine, 2007), mental health difficulties (Fergusson et al., 2008), and complex medical conditions (Pawlyn & Carnaby, 2009). They may also engage in challenging or self-injurious behaviour (Denis et al., 2011; Forster et al., 2011; Lacey, 1998). Against this backdrop, children with PMLD are described as being highly dependent on others for the most rudimentary care needs and are deemed to require a lifetime of support (Mansell, 2010; Petry & Maes, 2007; Tadema & Vlaskamp, 2010).

There are various estimates of the number of children with PMLD in the UK. One recent report suggested that there are 9,000 school-aged pupils identified as having PMLD (Salt, 2010). Another report suggested that there were 14,744 (Emerson, 2009). Despite varying estimates, there is agreement that the number of children with PMLD is rising because of advances in medical treatment (Carpenter, 2007). Between 2004 and 2009 it was estimated the number of children with PMLD rose by an average of 29.7% (DCSF, 2009, in Salt, 2010)—though clearly this estimate must be taken tentatively given the variation in original estimates. Between 2009 and 2026 it is estimated that the number of adults with PMLD in England alone will increase from 16,234 to 22,035 (Emerson, 2009).

Physical health

People with PMLD have "complex" healthcare needs (Bellamy, et al., 2010; Mansell, 2010; Pawlyn & Carnaby, 2009). The research literature describes a range of conditions that people with PMLD are said to be particularly prone to, including epilepsy (Arvio & Sillanpää, 2003; Hinder & Perry, 2000); respiratory problems (Wallis, 2009; Zijlstra & Vlaskamp, 2005); gastro-oesophageal reflux disease (Van Der Heide et al., 2009); sleep disorders (Jan & Freeman, 2004); fractured and broken bones

(Glick et al., 2005); pressure sores (Carnaby, 2004); malnourishment (Emerson, 2005; Ganesh et al., 1994); constipation (Veugelers, 2010); incontinence (Pawlyn & Budd, 2009), and dysphagia (Harding & Halai, 2009). People with PMLD may be technology-dependent and require oxygen, suctioning equipment, and nasogastric or gastrostomic tubes for feeding (Carnaby, 2004). Research has also suggested people with PMLD have poor oral health (Hulland & Sigal, 2000). Their lifestyles are described as being sedentary (Jones et al., 2007), leading to problems with posture, muscle strength, muscle tone, and bone metabolism (Lancioni et al., 1999; Pfister et al., 2003). Research has often reported that people with PMLD die significantly younger than people without learning disabilities. For example, a national study in the UK reported that people with PMLD are three times more likely to die as young adults than people without learning disabilities (Tyrer et al., 2007). A different study explored the premature deaths of people with learning disabilities in south west England and found that "the age at death decreased with increasing severity of learning disabilities … Essentially, the more severe a person's learning disabilities, the younger they were likely to die" (Heslop et al., 2013, p. 26).

Despite the growing literature documenting the aetiology and prevalence of medical conditions in the PMLD population, their lack of access to appropriate healthcare is a continuing concern. For example, treatable conditions sometimes go undiagnosed (Meehan, 1995). It has been suggested that this is partly because people with PMLD are denied access to screening services and check-ups (Burtner & Dicks, 1994; Hutchinson, 1998; PMLD Network, 2001). Problems also emerge when people with PMLD struggle to communicate their symptoms easily, such as the type and nature of pain (Davies & Evans, 2001). Behavioural expressions of pain can be idiosyncratic and unique to individuals (Van Der Putten & Vlaskamp, 2011). Consequently, the literature advocates that health professionals rely on non-verbal assessment (such as checklists) combined with expert judgement as well as carer intuition, though interpretation of symptoms can still be difficult for some, and it is believed that children may have learned to live with significant amounts of pain (Carter et al., 2002; Regnard et al., 2007). Another continuing concern is how to assess the sensory abilities of children with PMLD. Some researchers have attempted to use multisensory environments (MSEs) during assessment (Van Der Putten et al., 2011), whilst others combine behavioural and physiological measurement to assess the sensory responsiveness of children with PMLD (Lima et al., 2012). Checklists have been devised but sometimes their reliability is in doubt, and the intimate knowledge of familiar others such as teachers has proved more fruitful (Vlaskamp & Cuppen-Fonteine, 2007).

In addition to assessment, other major barriers to healthcare include the negative attitude of some health professionals and a lack of specialist skills and resources to care for people with PMLD. In the UK a series of reports has documented parents' experiences of the ways doctors question the quality and value of life for people with PMLD (Mansell, 2010; Mencap, 2001; 2004). It is argued that this has contributed towards delayed treatment, suffering, and premature deaths (Heslop et al., 2013; Mencap, 2007; Michael, 2008). By contrast, recent research has demonstrated how nurse specialists draw from medical knowledge, common sense and intuition to provide comfort for people with PMLD who experience terminal illness (Ng, 2011), and there has been a call for instigating reflexive practice in nurses with regards to interpreting the meaning of behaviour of people with PMLD (Phelvin, 2013).

Mental health

Depression is said to be a common problem for people with intellectual disabilities but the mental health of people with PMLD has often been overlooked (Carpenter, 2004; Hogg, 1999). Diagnosing conditions like depression in people with PMLD can be challenging since formal assessments typically require verbally articulate people who can self-report their symptoms. In the absence of self-reporting, a diagnosis has to be made based on behavioural manifestations of a mental health problem, but this may prove to be difficult if observers fail to grasp the meaning of behaviour and lack confidence to make inferences about mental health (Fergusson et al., 2008). Furthermore, behavioural expressions of depression are not recognised by many standard diagnostic manuals (Hermans & Evenhuis, 2010) meaning that health professionals may lack the necessary tools to make a diagnosis in the first place. Several observation schedules have been designed that aim to assess constructs such as mood in people with PMLD, but these have been criticised for lacking validity and reliability (Ross & Oliver, 2003) or they lack research into the robustness of the schedules by people not involved in their design (Liu, 2007). In the search for alternative methods to explore mental health problems, researchers have explored physiological change (e.g., endocrine output, vital signs, and temperature) to identify situations that people with PMLD may find stressful (Janssen et al., 2002). Other literature has advocated using interpersonal approaches to become familiar with the non-verbal behaviours of people with PMLD and to potentially "tune in" to their meaning and communicative intent (Sheehy & Nind, 2005). The role of carers who know people with PMLD intimately can be essential to the process of monitoring changes in behaviour indicative of mental health. However, there are reports that the observations of those who know people with PMLD best are not always taken seriously (Fergusson et al., 2008). Despite innovations in the field the complexity of personal, political, social and environmental factors of assessment are rarely recognised (Carnaby, 2007).

Children with PMLD are said to regularly engage in challenging, self-injurious behaviour, though in one study support staff were not inclined to rate such behaviours as a problem (Poppes et al., 2010). It has been suggested that such challenging behaviours result from the inability of people with PMLD to develop strategies to cope with stress (Janssen et al., 2002). One way of treating mental health disorders is to prescribe psychoactive medication (Lim, 2007; Kwok & Cheung, 2007). Some people with PMLD taking antipsychotic medications may experience adverse side effects such as akathisia (or "restless leg syndrome"). Akathisia is a movement disorder and the symptoms are said to include a sense of restlessness and a strong urge for motor activity. In the most severe cases people may experience uneasiness, anxiety, and irritability (Garcia & Matson, 2008). Non-medical interventions to improve the mental health of people with PMLD have also been explored. For example, research has suggested that exercise can reduce unhappiness in people with PMLD (Green & Reid, 1999b). Multisensory storytelling has also been used to help people with PMLD cope with sensitive issues (such as reducing fear of seizures or of equipment used by dentists) (Young et al., 2011).

The role of the family

The role and importance of the family of children with PMLD has been acknowledged in the literature. Children with PMLD can be heavily reliant on families, particularly parents, for basic care needs (e.g., eating, dressing, toileting) (Tadema & Vlaskamp, 2010). Historically, there has been criticism for the lack of support families receive given the sheer volume of physical and emotional demands that "parent carers" may experience (Mencap, 2001; 2003; 2006; Withers & Bennett, 2003). The ongoing care routines that parents engage in can prevent them from seeking and gaining employment (Gordon et al., 2007). Research has explored the emotional complexities and ambiguous sense of loss that parents experience when their children are placed in out-of-home care (Roper & Jackson, 2007). Parents may feel particularly anxious if authorities offer out-of-borough placements (Jaydeokar & Piachaud, 2004). Some want to see their older children living in their own home, perhaps with a companion, and with twenty-four hour care and support (Fitton et al., 1995).

Families are also described as rich sources of information regarding the needs and abilities of children with PMLD. Family members should work alongside, or at least inform, professionals involved in their children's education, support, and care (Brett, 2002; Jansen et al., 2012). The literature has increasingly positioned parents as central to their children's cognitive development (Kurani, 2009) and communication development (Wilder, 2008). Despite the acknowledgement of parental expertise in the literature, there is also a body of work concerned with improving the knowledge and skills of parents (De Geeter et al., 2002). For example, one study identified the difficulties that parents experienced when trying to identify "high points" in the narratives of children's lives (Grove, 2007). The researcher theorised that the difficulty may have emerged from the interplay between children's lack of verbalisation about past events, and parents focus on the mundane care routines which are said to be punctuated by painful memories. Thus, where this is the case, there is a need to foster engaging experiences, recording of narratives, and the development of collaborative storytelling skills involving parents.

Deinstitutionalisation and community participation

Research has explored different models of care and accommodation for people (mainly adults) with PMLD, particularly in light of the development of community-based services as alternatives to institutional care. This research is typically framed in relation to how alternative settings support different levels of engagement (e.g., leisure time and social interaction), how different settings afford opportunities for people with

PMLD to develop functional skills or reduce challenging behaviour, and the impact of staff training on these issues (Felce & Emerson, 2001; Hiemstra et al., 2007; Mansell, 2006; Vlaskamp et al., 2007a; 2007b). The costs of quality care have also been explored (Emerson et al., 2000; Hatton et al., 1995) and research has advocated the need to present and maintain subjective histories for people transitioning to community care, such as the continued production of life story books (Hewitt, 2000a).

A related issue concerns the extent to which people with PMLD are not just deinstitutionalised in the sense of residential relocation, but how such relocation brings with it richer forms of community participation. Literature reviews in the field have cast doubt on the extent to which such participation actually occurs, since most empirical work fails to define and theorise what community participation means for people with PMLD (Verdonschot et al., 2009). Friendship is said to be a key factor that differentiates community placement from community participation (Clement & Bigby, 2009), but questions have been raised about the meaning of friendship for people with PMLD, particularly when such individuals are denied agency and thus said to lack the capacity to interact with others in reciprocal ways (Hughes et al., 2011).

Education: schooling

In recent years the United Kingdom has witnessed a rise in children with special educational needs and disabilities attending mainstream schools—learners who have traditionally been educated in segregated, specialist schools and units. The impetus for such change has largely come from legislation in the form of the Special Educational Needs and Disability Act (SENDA) (OPSI, 2001). SENDA has enshrined children's access to mainstream provision and made the refusal of access on the grounds of a child's impairment difficult. However, a report to the House of Commons has supported the general view that inclusive education may only go so far and that full-time mainstream placements for some children are unrealistic (Education & Skills Committee, 2006). Similarly, Baroness Warnock has challenged the extent to which inclusion can be achieved for all, and has championed a future and ongoing role for special schools (Warnock, 2005). The views of the House of Commons Select Committee and of Baroness Warnock are continuous with the Special Educational Needs Code of Practice (SENCOP) (DfES,

2001). SENCOP falls into a familiar governmental policy pattern of emphasising the need for inclusive education for most children whilst reinforcing the segregation of a selected few (Croll & Moses, 2000). Specifically, SENCOP describes how local education authorities must comply with parents' preference of school unless the school is unsuitable to the child's ability or would be incompatible with the education of other children in that school.

Children with PMLD are part of the group for which inclusive education is sometimes deemed unsuitable and unrealistic. It is argued that such children do not have the cognitive capacity to meaningfully engage with standard learning environments; that mainstream teachers lack the knowledge and skills required to support the development of children with PMLD, and that only special schools house the appropriate infrastructure and resources that children with PMLD require (Ainscow & Haile-Giorgis, 1998; Chesley & Calaluce, 1997; Foreman et al., 2004). More recently, it has been reasserted that people with PMLD need separate and distinct pedagogies (Imray, 2012) and individualised curriculums (Rayner, 2011). Rather than being included within mainstream schools, a commonly proposed model for children with PMLD is one of "inclusion" in a mixed-ability class within existing special school provision (Ouvry, 1986; Pratchett, 2004; Simmons & Bayliss, 2007). Despite resistance to inclusion there are examples which buck the trend, such as the London Borough of Newham which closed down most of its special schools and offered full-time mainstream placements to children in the UK with PMLD (Alderson, 1999). Currently, the majority of children with PMLD (82%) attend special schools. The rest attend mainstream primary schools (15%) or secondary schools (3%) (Salt, 2010). However, these figures do not indicate whether placement is full-time or part-time and, as discussed previously, estimating the number of children and adults with PMLD in the UK is open to debate. It is also important to note parental perspectives of inclusion. Whilst there is a dearth of research on this topic, one older study reported that parents of children with severe learning disabilities (SLD) and PMLD were satisfied with their specialist provision and did not want their children placed elsewhere (Male, 1998).

Very little research has been published which sheds light on the nature of inclusive education for children with PMLD, perhaps owing to the fact that such children are typically educated in special schools. Studies have explored online modules for training inclusive teachers

(Jones, 2010); methods to increase the comfort levels of teachers toward inclusion (Smith, 2007b); the role of learning support in inclusive education (Lacey, 2001), and the need for collaborations between professionals (Strogilos et al., 2011). Whilst these issues are important in their own right there is a distinct lack of research which explores the meaning of inclusion from the perspective of children with PMLD (Whitehurst, 2007). Literature that discusses inclusion tends to do so from the point of view of school staff (Baker, 2009), trainee teachers (Bishop & Jones, 2003), or parents of pupils with PMLD (Cormany, 1994). The perspectives of children with PMLD themselves are rarely sought. This may be because appropriate methods for gleaning the views of children with PMLD have not been described, or it may be because some have questioned whether children with PMLD are capable of having a point of view at all (Lewis & Porter, 2004; Ware, 2004; Williams, 2005).

It has been recognised that mutually satisfying and reciprocal social interactions can serve as a vehicle for learning and development (Burford, 1988; Hostyn et al., 2010; 2011; Nind & Hewett, 1988; 1994; 2001) and is an important measure of quality of life (Petry et al., 2005; 2009a). A growing body of literature has explored how the inclusion of people with less profound learning disabilities can lead to increased social engagement, the development of communication skills, and the establishment of friendship (Carter & Hughes, 2005; Downing, 2005; Giangreco et al., 2001; Hakken & Pijl, 2002). However, it is unclear whether such benefits could accrue for people with PMLD. One study described how people with PMLD were happier when receiving instruction from non-disabled peers in specialist settings (Logan et al., 1998), whilst another described how children with PMLD were more alert and had higher levels of communicative engagement in mainstream school classes as opposed to their matched peers in special school classes (Foreman et al., 2004). Similar outcomes have been reported by research in early years or preschool settings (Cormany, 1994), though it was stressed that very young children without disabilities may need encouragement to initiate interactions and help them understand and respond to the idiosyncratic behaviours of peers with PMLD (Hanline, 1993).

Education: behaviourism and cognitivism

The majority of published literature regarding educational practice for people with PMLD is informed by either behaviourist psychology or cognitivist psychology. There is also a growing body of literature concerned with behaviour states. For example, a wealth of international research has explored the efficacy of training programmes to develop functional or adaptive skills in people with PMLD. Such skills are defined as behaviours which allow people to care for themselves and engage with the world around them (Reid et al., 1991). The training programmes are usually guided by behaviourist principals of learning, such as operant conditioning theory, and it is hoped that the presentation of a stimulus each time a discrete behaviour is performed will increase the likelihood of that behaviour reoccurring in the future (Saunders et al., 2003a). When this happens the stimulus is deemed to be a behavioural reinforcer. Much research has been published documenting strategies for identifying stimuli to act as reinforcers (Tullis et al., 2011), and reinforcers are often used to increase the occurrence of behaviours such as microswitch-pressing in people with PMLD (Lancioni et al., 2007a; 2011; Mechling, 2006). The idea here is that by learning to press microswitches people with PMLD may master a level of control over their environment and choose between items or events (Cannella et al., 2005).

An alternative to the functionalist approach described above is one that attempts to develop social cognition and symbolic communication in people with PMLD. This cognitivist approach is not concerned with controlling discrete behaviours through presentation of stimuli. Instead, it fosters the beginnings of social awareness so people with PMLD can begin to engage intentionally with those around them (Coupe O'Kane & Goldbart, 1998). For example, Intensive Interaction (Nind & Hewett, 1988; 1994; 2001) supports the simulation of interactive sequences described in studies of parent–infant communication (such as contingent responding, imitation, and turn-taking). The idea is that infants naturally develop intersubjectivity and communicative intent through preverbal, implicit social transactions with parents. By simulating what occurs between parents and infants, practitioners can engage with people with PMLD on a basic level which may lead to social learning. A different approach involves constructing contingency-sensitive or responsive environments (Ware, 1994; 2003). The idea here is that if the environment consistently responds to select behaviours then people with PMLD may discover that they can influence the world around them—that is, they develop contingency awareness. It is argued that people with PMLD first need to learn that their actions have consequences in the objective world before they learn that their actions can also be meaningful to others and thus influence the social world.

Behaviourist and cognitivist approaches are not mutually exclusive and research interests can overlap. For example, research into switch-based training programmes has explored how the presentation of preferred stimuli can lead to the emergence of contingency awareness (Lancioni et al., 2005a; Saunders et al., 2003b), and the purpose of some of these behavioural interventions is to support the development of communication, such as indicating choice (Lancioni, 2007b).

Another body of literature concerns the assessment of behaviour states in people with PMLD. Behaviour state assessment measures levels of engagement and responsiveness (e.g., awake, active-alert, crying and agitated, asleep, etc.), which in turn provides an indicator of whether or not somebody is in an optimal state conducive to learning (Arthur-Kelly et al., 2008; Guess et al., 1990). Research has explored the relationship between different environments and the behaviour states of people with PMLD. For example, one study explored the behaviour states between children with PMLD who attend a special school and children with PMLD who attend a mainstream school (Arthur-Kelly et al., 2007). Research has also explored how behaviour states can mediate the efficacy of microswitch training programmes (Mellstrom et al., 2005), and vice versa (Munde et al., 2012a; Munde et al., 2012b).

Published literature demonstrates how understandings derived from psychological approaches can be filtered down into practice. The literature describes how teachers can maximise the development of functional skills by tailoring switch-based programmes according to individual need (e.g., by describing optimal seating positions and procedures for identifying preferred stimuli, target behaviours, and switches) (Smith et al., 2001). These activities can be performed in classrooms and multisensory environments (Moir, 2010). The development of cognition and communication skills through subject-driven curriculums like literacy, numeracy, music and drama has also been explored (Ellis, 1997; Ockelford et al., 2005; Park, 1998; Porter, 2005; Young & Lambe, 2011) and so has the development of cognition through preschool play (Brodin, 2005).

Multisensory environments (MSEs) are also commonly used as a form of therapy through which people with PMLD can experience a range of visual, auditory, olfactory, and tactile stimulation. The environments are typically closed off from the outside world and contain soft furnishing such as beanbags and cushions, and a combination of low-tech and high-tech sensory items (e.g., mirrorballs, spotlights, projectors, bubble tubes, and vibrating mats). MSEs have aided assessment of the sensory abilities, stimuli preference, and behavioural reinforcement of children with PMLD (Fava & Strauss, 2010; Matson, 2004; Van Der Putten et al., 2011). Whilst it is claimed that such environments support the development of functional behaviours and/or cognitive abilities in people with PMLD, the value of MSEs has been questioned because of a distinct lack of empirical research to support such claims (Hogg et al., 2001; Mount & Cavet, 2007; Vlaskamp & Nakken, 2008).

Identity

The PMLD literature that concerns identity is relatively sparse and largely focuses on questions of provision for people with PMLD. There is an apparent discourse of "othering"—where their identity is constructed by others based on their impairments. This is seen in medical literature where there is a focus on functional assessments of awareness and staff training (Wilson et al., 2007); particularly in respect of knowledge and attitudes towards hospital patients with PMLD (Binney, 1992) and the impact of negative staff reactions on challenging behaviours exhibited by people with PMLD (Lambrechts et al., 2009). A study that explored learning disability nurses' understandings and practices of "advocacy" with patients with PMLD revealed a range of activities "underpinned by opposing ethical principles of autonomy and paternalism" (Blackmore, 2001, p. 231) whereby "autonomy" was represented more by nurse decision-making on behalf of patients than by true autonomous activity by the person with learning disabilities. Arguably, this provides medical practitioners with a great deal of power, and challenges "best interest" principles whereby "bodily integrity, sanctity of life, and freedom from coercion are cherished values that apply to all of us, regardless of the type or degree of disability we might have" (Diesfeld, 2001, p. 388). Parents report "oppression" on the part of professionals where professional attitudes towards them and their child (and their knowledge of their child's disability) act to further impact on their joint experience of disability and to disempower them in care decisions for their child (Brett, 2002). Other studies of professionals and parents' perspectives on support characteristics for people with PMLD reveal different foci even when asked to take on the perspective of the person with PMLD and focus on their needs specifically (Petry et al., 2007).

Whilst parents are reported to have little voice or partnership role in respect of powerful professional accounts of their children with PMLD; the child's voice is even more absent on questions of wellbeing and quality of life (Lyons & Cassebohm, 2012) or of experiences of disability (Connors & Stalker, 2007) and this further compounds the othering of children with PMLD as "disordered bodies" that require treatment. This appears to manifest, in particular, at the stage of adult transition where young intellectually disabled people are reported as not holding concepts of emergent adulthood and decision-making capabilities. Instead, these are decisions made by parents and professionals, often with quite polarised perspectives on qualities such as autonomy (Murphy et al., 2010). The ability of disabled children to exert agency was apparent in Connors and Stalker's (2007) study with disabled children who reported their reactions to other people's positioning of them; but this was largely conducted with physically disabled children.

There is also a body of literature regarding teachers' perspectives of their pupils with severe disabilities. One such study concerned with teacher attrition describes teachers of severe and profoundly disabled children according to whether they were "survivors" or "non-survivors" (Ware et al., 2005), and the authors comment on "the surprising picture" that emerges as "the majority of the teachers are stimulated rather than demoralized by working with children for whom progress is extremely slow" (p. 192). Other studies also reveal the positive attitudes of teachers towards their profoundly disabled pupils' learning progress; but also acknowledge that professionals usually hold far more deficit-based views of children with PMLD than do parents (Jones, 2005). Special needs teachers have more positive attitudes towards disabled children compared to mainstream school teachers (Jones, 2004), and this signals that there are still shifts to be made in order that disabled children are not stigmatised and problematised by educationalists (Bishop & Jones, 2003). Indeed, the discourse of "specialness" arguably focuses on an individualised and medical model of practice that constructs disabled children as "other" (Adams et al., 2000).

The language of difference, disability and labelling has been critiqued as not allowing opportunities to enter into the worlds of profoundly disabled people and relate to them as "fully human and encultured beings" (Klotz, 2004, p. 101). Instead, they are seen as people who lack "competency" (Vorhaus, 2005). Historically, such a perspective has permitted both euthanasia and surgical and hormonal treatments to stunt growth (Hogg, 2007) and to control learning disabled people's sexuality and fertility (Aylott, 1999). Such actions have been taken on the basis of arguments that people with PMLD "lack the capability of reason, of self-awareness, and of self-determination" (Hogg, 2007, p. 79) and this has resulted in many calls to have a broader conception of personhood (Hogg, 2007) and participation in society (Eriksson & Granlund, 2004). Indeed, it is argued that a repositioning of profoundly disabled people needs to occur that reveals their social and cultural engagement in the world and allows for their personhood to emerge, and this means services being responsive to the breadth of their needs that includes expression of their sexuality (Aylott, 1999). Indeed, there is a dearth of research specifically regarding the sexuality of children with PMLD (Downs & Craft, 1996), though guidelines about how to deal with masturbation have been published (Downs & Farrell, 1996). By not engaging in discussion about sexuality and putting into place sensitive plans we essentially deny sexuality as a valid dimension of personhood for maturing children with PMLD (Aylott, 1999).

Some researchers propose a phenomenological perspective for people with PMLD that is based on "acceptance theory" and the importance of reciprocal relationships with disabled people that allow for their disability to be secondary to their "humanness" (Bogdan & Taylor, 1989; Taylor & Bogdan, 1989). There is a need for "multi-situated understandings of the lives of disabled people which move away from this epistemological reductionism" (Simmons et al., 2008, p. 734), and this rests on close and personal knowledge about disabled people's lives (Eriksson & Granlund, 2004). Attempts to capture life history stories of people with PMLD (Hewitt, 2000b) echo this sentiment as care workers reported their experiences in the context of the disabled person's emergent identities, personhood and personality (ibid.); as people with histories, likes and dislikes: of individuals who inhabit a particular social and cultural space (Bogdan & Taylor, 1989). Studies about parents of children with PMLD also show little difference in interaction with their child and the display of emotions as compared to non-disabled control groups (Wilder et al., 2004).

Quality of life/wellbeing and capabilities

Achieving quality of life is sometimes judged as incompatible with the impairments of people with PMLD. Those making judgements do so from their own able-bodied situation (Richardson, 1997). Some have conducted literature reviews to identify domains of quality of life; for example, physical, material, social, developmental and emotional wellbeing (Petry et al., 2005), but these are largely based on proxy reporting by familiar others and have questionable validity and reliability. Such approaches are largely reliant upon questionnaires that parents and professionals complete on behalf of children with PMLD (Petry et al., 2009a; 2009b).

A different understanding of quality of life for people with PMLD involves identifying behaviours associated with "happiness" (or "unhappiness") (Petry & Maes, 2006) and quantifying them in relation to environmental variables (Dillon & Carr, 2007; Lancioni et al., 2005b). This has led to strategies involving environmental enrichment whereby stimuli associated with happiness are provided and are contingent upon people with PMLD pressing a microswitch (Lancioni et al., 2002b). Teaching staff have also been asked to become more reflective during social interactions with people with PMLD (Singh et al., 2004). Other researchers have attempted to move away from subjective measures of emotion in order to develop objective, physiological measures, including readings of the respiratory, cardiovascular, and electrodermal response systems (Vos et al., 2010).

Whilst the quality-of-life literature for people with PMLD focuses on the deficits and barriers to the "good life", increasingly there is a literature that seeks to challenge deficit-based othering perspectives on quality of life and wellbeing and rather focuses on the "capabilities" of disabled people using capabilities theory drawn from the works of Amartya Sen and Martha Nussbaum (Sen, 1985; 1993; Nussbaum, 1992; 2000; 2003; 2007; Nussbaum & Sen, 1993). Capabilities were initially defined by Sen and refer to "what people are actually able to do and to be" (Nussbaum, 2003, p. 33). As such "capability" is not based on actual abilities of a person, but as "practical opportunities" that need to be viewed alongside "functions" that describe "the actual achievement of an individual, what he or she actually achieves through being or doing" (Mitra, 2006, pp. 236–237). Sen's work on capabilities has largely focused on questions of social justice, particularly insofar as inequalities impact upon individual quality of life, wellbeing, poverty, freedom, and choice. He describes "agency achievement and freedom" and "wellbeing achievement and freedom" (Vorhaus, 2013) and sees these both incorporated in a theory of human justice where, at times, to achieve one may signal a decline in another. It is, however, essential that we not only focus on people's functioning (especially as deficits in function) but also their capabilities; whereby "liberation from disability is about having choices" (Burchardt, 2004, p. 742).

Nussbaum extended the ideas of Sen to questions of gender, particularly in development studies (Nussbaum, 2000). This has led to her defining the capabilities essential for quality of life as a list, as she has been vocal in critiquing the vagueness of Sen's concepts such as freedom (Nussbaum, 2003). Nussbaum's lists of capabilities provide a foundation for a rights-based approach that allows an assessment of quality of life. Whilst other writers and philosophers have attempted to define the "good life" (Parfit, 1984; Scanlon, 1993) in respect of goods and human needs, Nussbaum's approach has been more to define the essential human capabilities that incorporate (at the time of writing as they have evolved): "life, bodily health, bodily integrity, emotions, practical reason, affiliation, senses, imagination and thought, ability to live with regard to other species, to play and to have control over one's environment" (Nussbaum, 2003).

Nussbaum's theory of human development, in particular, provides a framework for assessing the extent to which capabilities have been hindered by factors outside of the person "leaving them with deficits of potential functioning" (Baylies, 2002, p. 734). Arguably, such an approach could provide a fuller understanding of human development whilst also acknowledging the variability of individual functioning (ibid.) and provide an alternative lens on disability that does not just focus on dualist understandings of the individual or society (Terzi, 2005a) but sees a genuine integration of both, along with the socioeconomic and individual circumstances that can also contribute to disabling individuals (Mitra, 2006). This has implications for the education of children with PMLD, as capability proponents argue for the relational aspects of human capabilities that do not support individualistic pedagogical practices—rather that a pedagogy focused on "cooperation and mutual support" (Terzi, 2005b, p. 221) might allow for the fuller participation of disabled learners (Morris, 2009) and acknowledge the reciprocal and relational basis of humanity founded on dependence and mutual respect (Vorhaus, 2013).

Chapter summary

This chapter has explored the impact of definitions and understandings on the ways in which children with PMLD are regarded in respect of their health, education, inclusion in educational systems, and the influence of family and professionals in constructing and facilitating a sense of autonomy and identity. It is evident that there are gaps in understandings and a range of perspectives on what is possible, achievable and desirable as educational and wider life outcomes for children identified as PMLD.

The reviewed literature presents people with PMLD in particular ways; often as objects of intervention and study, defined by the extent of their impairment and functioning. Whilst there is a literature that seeks to identify the strengths and capabilities of people with PMLD, traditional reporting has been deficit-based, reflecting a medicalised and objectified understanding of individuals with PMLD. Arguably, this is even more the case in the literature on children with PMLD, who are largely positioned as helpless and lacking in volition and intention (points we explore in detail in subsequent chapters). Such assumptions predicate the subjective reporting of experiences by children who are largely believed to have little agency, ability to voice experiences, or opportunity to participate in society. These inferences pose challenges to the rights of children with PMLD and to their quality of life experiences. How the child with PMLD is understood theoretically and in practice frames their subjective experience of being a *child* and being a *child with profound and multiple disabilities*.

In this book we explore both traditional and non-traditional approaches to developing understandings of children with PMLD, and how these shape research and practice. We import critiques of the literature reported in this chapter to the challenge of how the subjectivities of children with PMLD can be understood such that their identity is focused on them being *children* first and foremost. This is both a theoretical and a methodological challenge. We begin this journey in the next chapter by exploring how behaviourist psychology has shaped understanding of both children and adults with PMLD, and how this relates to research and practice in the PMLD field.

CHAPTER TWO

Behaviourism

This chapter discusses behaviourist psychology (also known as behaviourism). Behaviourism is one of the two main approaches found in the PMLD literature. Cognitive psychology (or cognitivism) is the second main approach and is explored in Chapter Three. We begin this chapter by describing the theoretical principles of behaviourism. We then explore how these principles shape research and practice as they relate to people with PMLD. Our review of the behaviourist literature leads to the identification of core concepts which inform a framework we apply to empirical data in Chapters Five and Six.

Whilst this book is primarily concerned with children with PMLD, behaviourist research sometimes includes both young children and adults in its sampling. Hence, during our review of the behaviourist literature we will use the term "people" with PMLD instead of "children" and/or "adults" with PMLD.

Part I

Summary of behaviourist theory

What is behaviourism?

Behaviourism, as the name suggests, is an approach in psychology concerned almost exclusively with the scientific study of observable behaviour. Behaviourism is an approach which privileges the external: it defines behaviour as a reflexive (i.e., non-volitional) response exclusively under the control of environmental variables, defined as stimuli. The aim of behaviourism is to learn about and uncover the lawful linkages or contiguities between stimuli and behavioural responses in order to predict and regulate behaviour. Concepts related to mind, such as thought, emotion and knowledge are deemed to refer to unobservable "internal" phenomena and are denied scientific legitimacy (and hence a place within behaviourist conclusions) (Baars, 1986; Skinner, 1986; Watson, 1913). As Gregory and Zangwill (1987) describe:

> The central tenet of behaviourism is that thoughts, feelings, and intentions, mental processes all, do no determine what we do. Our behaviour is the product of our conditioning. We are biological machines and do not consciously act; rather we *react* to stimuli. (p. 71)

Behaviourism achieved great popularity during the first half of the twentieth century. Contemporary textbooks documenting the history of modern psychology describe behaviourism as being virtually synonymous with psychology itself during this period, heavily influencing both empirical research and clinical intervention. Whilst behaviourism's dominance is said to have peaked in the 1950s, it still exerted a strong influence in mainstream psychology up until the 1970s (Brennan, 2003; Leahey, 1994; Robinson, 1981).

Nowadays cognitivism dominates most scientific work in psychology. Cognitivism is an approach that studies behaviour in order to make inferences about how the mind processes information (Baars, 1986; Bolton & Hill, 1996; Varela et al., 1991). Cognitivism is discussed in detail in the next chapter.

Despite its lack of popularity in mainstream psychology, behaviourism is still a choice methodology for some researchers and special educators. The purpose of this chapter is to present the core tenets of behaviourism and how they relate to interventions for people with PMLD. The behaviourist account given here is one which situates behaviourism in the context of evolving academic thought. Whilst behaviourism is broadly understood as a methodological approach to the study of behaviour, it is an approach which is, to a certain extent, non-unified in the sense that various "behaviourisms" have emerged over the course of history, each of which conceptualise behaviour in slightly different ways. This chapter discusses the two most dominant approaches: classical conditioning theory and operant conditioning theory. Whilst the former theory has informed several studies, the vast majority of behaviourist literature about people with PMLD is informed by the latter.

The rise of behaviourism

John B. Watson (1878–1958) is considered the founding figure of behaviourism (Baars, 1986; Reber, 1995). As Gregory and Zangwill (1987) note: "though it is now unfashionable to credit one man with a discovery, Watson was very much responsible for the initial success of behaviourism" (p. 71). The behaviourist movement is said to have been officially launched with Watson's (1913) seminal paper *Psychology as the Behaviorist Views it*. In this paper, Watson (1913) argued that psychology should move away from concepts related to consciousness towards scientifically observable behaviour.

> Psychology as the behaviorist views it is a purely objective experimental branch of natural science. Its theoretical goal is the prediction and control of behavior .... The behaviorist, in his efforts to get a unitary scheme of animal response, recognizes no dividing line between man and brute. The behavior of man, with all of its refinement and complexity, forms only a part of the behaviorist's total scheme of investigation. (p. 158)

Watson's (1913) behaviourism aimed to account for all psychological phenomena in terms of external behaviour without loss of meaning. Complex psychological phenomena were reduced to complex behaviours, and such behaviours were said to be composed of simpler behaviours. Motor habits (such as typing and walking) were portrayed as being built up from small movements in the arms, legs, fingers, toes, etc. Similarly, complex emotions were described as learned visceral bodily reactions, rather than affective qualities or feelings. Such visceral reactions were said to be built up from basic, innate, unlearned reactions. Speech was construed as a "Laryngeal habit" (Baars, 1986, p. 46). Laryngeal habits were said to consist of tiny movements in the vocal cords, which develop from random, unlearned vocalisation in the same way that complex motor habits are formed. By a process of conditioning, the child is said to acquire words, which are substitutes for concrete situations (Watson, 1930).

Watson (1930) placed much emphasis on learning, so much so that his work embodied a strict environmentalism in which genetic or inherent factors made little or no difference to the acquisition of complex behaviours.

> Give me a dozen healthy infants, well-formed and my own specified world to bring them up in and I'll guarantee to take any one at random and train him to become any type of specialist I might select—doctor, lawyer, artist, merchant-chief and yes, even beggar-man and thief, regardless of his talents, penchants, tendencies, abilities, vocations, and race of his ancestors. (cited in Baars, 1986, p. 48)

Whilst Watson (1913) has been recognised as the founding figure of behaviourism, it was Ivan Pavlov (1849–1936) who described the mechanism by which learning was supposed to take place. This mechanism is known today as classical conditioning theory.

Classical conditioning theory

Classical conditioning theory begins with a Russian physiology paradigm known as reflexology. Reflexology is the investigation of the physiological basis of behaviour. Such investigation is reductionist in its understanding of the relation between the mind and body, and this reduction translates into an attempt to explain the origins of behaviour in terms of biomechanical responses to environmental stimuli, rather than psychological agency (Brennan, 2003; Leahey, 1994; Robinson, 1981). The Russian physiologists attempted to expand their knowledge of the physiological to include processes that had traditionally been labelled as psychological. It was assumed that eventually all psychological processes could be explained in their entirety by reference to physiological mechanisms. Reflexology was the programme of research which attempted to discover such mechanisms (Brennan, 2003).

The first to articulate the research programme was Ivan Sechenov (1829–1905) (Brennan, 2003). It was his student, Vladimir Bekhterev (1857–1927), who coined the term "reflexology". Sechenov and Bekhterev hypothesised that all activity, including complex psychological (thought) and physiological (behavioural) activity, could be reduced to simple reflex actions to environmental events. Such reflexes were said to be centrally mediated at the cortical level. To use Bekhterev's term, both psychological and physiological processes involved the same "neural energies" (1965, cited in Brennan, 2003, p. 242). It was believed that with the discovery of the organic causal mechanisms psychology as a discipline would cease to exist. As Brennan (2003) notes, Russian reflexology was "a monistic interpretation of human activity, which equated psychological processes with essential neural processes" (p. 241).

The most famous and influential of the Russian reflexologists was Ivan Pavlov (1849–1936). Pavlov's work on the neural and glandular bases of digestion led him to the principles of associative reflex conditioning. These principles greatly inspired early behaviourism to the extent that Watson himself declared reflex conditioning as the core mechanism by which all learning took place (Baars, 1986; Brennan, 2003). Pavlov's investigations were partly concerned with differential quantities of saliva secretion. He devised a test-tube-like device which he inserted into the cheeks of dog subjects to collect their saliva. During his measurement, Pavlov noted that the dog subjects had not simply salivated at the presentation of food (an innate response which he later termed "unconditioned response"). Rather, the dog subjects were salivating when they were in the presence of the assistant who fed them. Pavlov called such salivation "psychic secretions". The discovery of psychic secretions led Pavlov on a programme of research into their acquisition, the findings of which form the basis of what is known today as classical or Pavlovian conditioning. Pavlov predicted that if a particular stimulus in the dog subjects' surroundings was presented with food then the stimulus would become associated with the food, resulting in the stimulus eliciting a salivation response from the dog subjects without any food being present. To test his hypothesis, Pavlov used a metronome to signal that food would shortly be arriving. Each time the metronome emitted a sound, food would be given to the dog subjects. Over time, the dog subjects began to salivate in response to the metronome. Thus, a neutral stimulus (metronome) became a conditioned stimulus as a result of pairing with the unconditioned stimulus (food). Pavlov referred to this learned relationship as a conditioned response (Baars, 1986; Brennan, 2003; Leahey, 1991; Reber, 1995).

Pavlov described the processes of conditioning as being contingent upon the following four events (taken from Brennan, 2003, p. 244):

- Unconditioned Stimulus (US): an environmental event (such as the presentation of food) that can elicit an organismic reflex.
- Conditioned Stimulus (CS): an environmental event (such as a tone) that is neutral with respect to the response prior to pairing with the US.
- Unconditioned Response (UR): the natural reflex (such as salivation) elicited involuntarily, by the US.
- Conditioned Response (CR): the acquired reflex (such as salivation) elicited by the CS after association with the US.

N.B.: The unconditioned response and the conditioned response are the same type. They differ only in their eliciting stimulus.

In addition to his studies on how conditioned reflexes were acquired, Pavlov also studied how they were lost. Central to Pavlovian conditioning is the role of *extinction*. Extinction of a conditioned reflex is said to occur as a consequence of inhibition, of which there are two types: external inhibition and internal inhibition. External inhibition occurs when an animal, conditioned in one way, is moved into a new environment or exposed to new stimuli before being fed. This form of inhibition results in new conditioning replacing the old conditioning. Internal inhibition refers to the gradual loss of the conditioned reflex if the food is withheld after the presentation of a conditioned stimulus; the conditioned reflex requires regular reinforcement by the unconditioned stimulus (Gregory & Zangwill, 1987).

In the development of behaviourism, Watson (1913) claimed that Pavlov had discovered the core mechanism by which all learning took place, and from here onwards North American behaviourism was informed by the concept of Pavlovian conditioning theory. This concept was the core explanatory device by which observable behaviour was supposed to adapt to the environment. It was not until some forty years later that Pavlovian or classical conditioning was challenged and replaced by an alternative form of conditioning, known as operant conditioning.

Operant conditioning theory

Operant conditioning theory begins with the radical behaviourism of Burrhus Frederic Skiner (1904–1990). Skinner's (1986) fame derives largely from his laboratory work in which he developed all the basic concepts of what he called operant conditioning (Baars, 1986). Operant conditioning theory was Skinner's (1986) alternative to Pavlov's classical conditioning theory. Skinner (1986) had grown dissatisfied with the behaviourist attempt to explain all behaviour in terms of automatic reflexes. Skinner (1986) had grown dissatisfied with the behaviourist attempt to explain all behaviour in terms of automatic reflexes, and proposed that behaviour operated on the environment to generate consequences. For example, if a rat is given food each time it presses a lever, it is *operating* on the environment to achieve food. Skinner (1986) therefore argued that most behaviour involved operant conditioning. We behave the way we do because of the consequences that past behaviour has generated.

It is important to point out that Skinner was not interested in volition. In fact, Skinner explicitly denied the value of speaking in terms of purpose or agency, and instead spoke of "environmental contingencies of reinforcement" (Baars, 1986, p. 63). To use Baars' (1986) example: whilst in everyday language we may say that the dog sniffing at his food bowl has the goal of eating, in Skinnerian language there is simply a conditional relationship in the environment between moving towards the bowl, opening the mouth, and eating the food. Food is just a reinforcing stimulus, which increases the probability of any preceding response. A reinforcing stimulus is not a purpose, a reward, or a source of pleasure—Skinner's view eschews such mentalistic terms. Skinner (1986) defines reinforcement circularly as any stimulus that will increase the likelihood of a response that precedes it (Baars, 1986). In this way, Skinner (1986) sidesteps consideration of agency and instead talks about the probability of response to environmental stimuli. Gregory and Zangwill (1987) describe how Skinner's examples of behaviour initially appear to be concerned with motives, feelings, intent and so forth, but are in fact oppositional to mental explanation.

> For Skinner, it is the history of reinforcements that determines behaviour. Consciousness is just an epiphenomenon, and feelings are not causes of actions but consequences. Behaviour can be predicted and controlled without reference to them. (p. 73)

Skinner (1986) understood behaviour in operant rather than classical terms. An operant is defined as a behaviour emitted by an organism characterised in terms of its effects upon the environment. An operant is a class of response, all of which share the same environmental effect. In experimental terms, the basic difference between the classical conditioning and operant conditioning is that in the former the outcome of a trial (the unconditioned stimulus) always occurs regardless of how the organism responds—Pavlov's dogs received food whether or not they salivated. In the latter, the outcome of a trial (the reinforcer) is contingent upon the organism making a specified response—Skinner's (1986) pigeons were not given food unless they pecked the prerequisite number of times under the proper stimulus conditions (Baars, 1986; Gregory & Zangwill, 1987; Reber, 1995).

Operant conditioning is said to occur when an operant is brought under stimulus control, and the operation through which such conditioning occurs is the presentation of *reinforcement* contingent upon the organism emitting the correct response. To reinforce in this context means to strengthen. Reinforcement is the operation of strengthening a learned response, a strengthening of the bond between response and stimulus, which is measured in terms of the likelihood of an operant occurring (Baars, 1986; Gregory & Zangwill, 1987; Reber, 1995).

Skinner's (1986) analysis of behaviour differs from Pavlov's and Watson's insofar as it is a purely functional analysis (Skinner's discern was to establish the function of behaviour) (Baars, 1986). Skinner (1986) is not concerned with reducing behaviour to a sequence of causes and effects. His aim is to show the lawful relationships between objectively observable phenomena. As Baars (1986) describes: "A stimulus is defined by the way an organism responds to it, and a response is defined by how effective it is in gaining from the environment a reinforcing stimulus" (p. 63). Further, unlike classical conditioning which involves associated learning through pairing, operant conditioning can, at least in principle, explain new behaviour. Such behaviour, Skinner claims, has been operantly conditioned at some time "in the history of the organism" (ibid.). By referring to the history of the organism, Skinner (1986) claims that one could in principle explain all current behaviour without resorting to mental constructs such as memory.

The relevance or challenges of behaviourist thought will now be considered in the context of research for people with PMLD.

Part II

Behaviourism and people with PMLD: early research

People with developmental disabilities have been the focus of applied behavioural research since the early 1950s. Reviewers of research have described how hundreds of investigations demonstrated the successful use of behaviourist procedures to improve research participants' adaptive functioning (their ability to interact with the world), and reduce maladaptive behaviours (actions which are considered counterproductive or inappropriate for interactions with the world) (Reid et al., 1991). However, although behaviourism is said to have had a positive impact generally, historically there is one group of people with developmental disabilities for whom the impact is less clear. Specifically, the utility of behaviourist intervention for people with PMLD has been questioned (Ivancic & Bailey, 1996; Lancioni et al., 2001; Logan et al., 2001; Reid et al., 1991).

The degree to which behaviourist methodology supports learning in people with PMLD is an important consideration, as Reid et al. (1991) explain:

> [B]ecause operant-orientated behavioral programs currently represent the predominant treatment approach for attempting to teach skills to persons with very serious developmental disabilities, if these programs are not effective then questions must arise as to what should constitute appropriate treatment for these individuals. (p. 320)

Over twenty years has passed since Reid et al. (1991) voiced the above concerns, and much has changed during this time. The amount of published research literature has grown dramatically, and the topics currently under investigation include new methodologies for assessing potential reinforcers (Cannella et al., 2005; Ivancic & Bailey, 1996; Lancioni et al., 1996; Tullis et al., 2011); identification of which behaviour is best suited to conditioning—for example, when attempting to teach switch-press behaviour (Lancioni et al., 2005a); the impact of behaviour states on conditioning success (Mellstrom et al., 2005; Murphy et al., 2004); the use of behavioural approaches to improve levels of happiness (Green & Reid, 1996; Green et al., 1997), and a continued concern for reducing stereotyped behaviours (particularly those that are self-injurious) (Denis et al., 2011; Lancioni et al., 2009). Furthermore, there has been increasing recognition that people with PMLD require opportunities to develop functional skills that they can employ on a daily basis. One example of this is research to develop microswitch-pressing in people with PMLD, which in turn allows them to communicate choice and develop some level of control over their immediate environment (e.g., the presence or absence of a stimulus, or a choice between two or more stimuli) (Lancioni et al., 2001). Thus people with

PMLD are increasingly framed as people with the capacity for agency given appropriate intervention strategies. Reference to "internal" states such as alertness (Guess et al., 1993) or happiness (Dillon & Carr, 2007) has marked a shift away from pure externalism to subjective variables that mediate the stimulus-response relationship, which in turn affects the efficacy of conditioning programmes. However, some researchers have made a more radical step away from traditional behaviourism by exploring how operant conditioning can be used to foster the cognitive ability of people with PMLD, such as developing their contingency awareness (awareness of cause-effect relationships) (Saunders et al., 2007; Saunders et al., 2003b). However, behaviourist work in this field is still in its infancy and studies that bridge behaviourism and cognitivism in this way are few and far between.

This chapter explores the research described above in detail in order to illuminate the core themes and constructs at the heart of contemporary behaviourist work as it relates to people with PMLD. It begins by describing projects that utilise classical conditioning theory to train people with PMLD. However, since little work has been done using a classical approach, the majority of the chapter will focus on work undertaken that has been drawn from operant conditioning theory. With regards to operant conditioning theory, we first describe the early work (i.e., research from the 1950s to 1980s). This serves to provide context and reason for what may be dubbed as behaviourism's "crisis" at the end of the 1980s. Since the early research literature is vast and typically out of print, discussion will draw from pre-existing literature reviews of this era (Lancioni et al., 2001; Reid et al., 1991; Remington, 1996). Second, the "new wave" of behaviourist research will be discussed (i.e., from the late 1980s to the present day) in order to highlight contemporary behaviourism's key areas of concern and application. At the end of the chapter the main points will be summarised.

Classical conditioning for people with PMLD

Earlier in the chapter we described how classical condition theory conceptualises learning as the development of an association between an unconditioned stimulus and a conditioned stimulus. This association results in the conditioned stimulus eliciting the same behavioural response as the unconditioned stimulus. When the response is elicited by an unconditioned stimulus it is an unconditioned response, but when the same response is elicited by the conditioned stimulus it is known as conditioned response.

There has been very little research investigating how classical conditioning theory can be used for people with PMLD. Studies published in this area tend to describe attempts to condition eye blinking (Hogg et al., 1979; Ross, 1972). In this procedure the unconditioned stimulus is usually a puff of air to the eye which elicits a blinking response (an unconditioned response). The puff of air is preceded by a neutral stimulus, such as an auditory tone. After a number of air puff and auditory tone pairings the latter begins to elicit the same behavioural response as the former. Thus, the auditory tone becomes a conditioned stimulus (and the eye blink a conditioned response when it is caused by the auditory tone) (Remington, 1996).

Studies to condition eye blinking through classical means have reported mixed or unclear results. For example, whilst Ross (1972) reported positive results, her sample consisted of people with severe learning disabilities (SLD) and people with profound and multiple learning disabilities (PMLD). She averaged her data and did not report individual differences so there is no way of knowing how many people with PMLD demonstrated learning (if any at all) (Remington, 1996). Hogg, Remington and Foxen (1979) attempted a similar procedure for five people with PMLD and reported that they successfully conditioned blinking in two people.

The value of classical conditioning research is debatable. Remington (1996) argues that the occurrence or non-occurrence of conditioning provides direct information about the learning capacities of people with PMLD. He also notes that classical conditioning may be an option for people who fail to respond to operant conditioning. However, Reid et al. (1991) are less positive and argue that an important measure of conditioning's value (classical or operant) is its ability to support the emergence of functional or adaptive skills in people with PMLD (skills that increase independence or self-determination). This point will be revisited later in the chapter.

Since the vast majority of behaviourist research involving people with PMLD draws from operant conditioning theory rather than classical conditioning theory, the remainder of this chapter will be dedicated to summarising operant approaches. We do this by providing a historical and thematic overview.

Operant conditioning for people with PMLD

Similar to classical conditioning research described above, early operant conditioning research involving people with PMLD was primarily concerned with determining whether operant procedures provided a method for altering behaviour patterns of research participants. As Reid et al. (1991) describe:

> Researchers were not concerned necessarily with teaching a useful skill per se, but rather with demonstrating that a principle of learning—namely, positive reinforcement—could be used to change behaviour. (p. 322)

Positive reinforcement is Skinnerian (1986) in nature, insofar as it defines behaviour operantly—that is, in terms of its effect on the environment. A reinforcer is defined as an environmental object, subject, or event that increases the probability of the research participant(s) emitting particular behaviours (Baars, 1986). In a review of early literature (1949 onwards) Reid et al. (1991) describe how behaviourist researchers evaluated the potential responsiveness of research participants to reinforcement by contingently providing stimuli after the execution of very simple behaviours, with the frequency of executed behaviours being recorded. Vastly different stimuli were tested during this early period, such as food, drink, verbal praise, music, film, vibrations, lights, toys, and pictures. The stimuli were used to control different behaviours, including limb and head movements, object manipulation, smiling and vocalisation. Almost all research reported the successful control of behaviour frequency through operant methods. However, despite the reported successes, Reid et al. (1991) remain sceptical with regards to the value of such research. First, unlike the diversity of chosen stimuli, the chosen target behaviours were limited in number. Second, the target behaviours were not of a functional nature and consisted of largely arbitrary executions, such as lifting an arm. Third, the research design itself puts the findings in doubt. Experimental sessions typically lasted thirty minutes or less, with no more than three sessions being recorded. Finally, no study reported follow-up measures to evaluate durability of behaviour change, and many studies did not report on interobserver agreement. Such difficulties led the reviewers to conclude that:

> [T]he early behavioural research as a whole did not soundly demonstrate that substantial changes in simple behaviours could be controlled through behavioural procedures. (Reid et al., 1991, p. 324)

Research undertaken during the 1970s onwards is described by Reid et al. (1991) as being much more complex in design. Investigations are said to have employed adequate research designs and typically included interobserver agreement indices. Research was also typically undertaken in natural environments, such as classrooms, unlike most of the earlier research which was largely laboratory-based, and virtually all studies resulted in apparent behaviour change for some individuals, with almost half of the studies including follow-up measures to demonstrate the durability of the changes.

This later research can be grouped according to two popular research topics: the improvement of postural control, and the development of adaptive skills.

Improving postural control

Postural control research was a popular topic for behaviourist investigation during the 1970s and 1980s. The aim of such research was typically to evaluate the potential reinforcing effects of certain stimuli for increasing and/or maintaining bodily position. People with profound disabilities can have difficulty maintaining posture (e.g., holding their head in an upright position). Amongst other things, such difficulties are said to complicate development of bodily control and interactions with the environment. As such, the improvement of posture is deemed to be a useful target for behavioural change.

In their literature review on the topic, Reid et al. (1991) cite Grove et al. (1975) as a typical example of the kind of research which investigated the efficacy of positive reinforcement in improving postural control. Grove et al. (1975) evaluated the use of contingent music and social praise upon research participants raising their heads. A special collar was designed such that mercury switches were activated whenever the position of the head moved out of therapeutic range (i.e., was no longer upright). When out of range, positive reinforcement stopped. Results showed that music provided contingently on appropriate head position, and music paired with social praise, increased upright head positioning among all participants (Grove et al., 1975). Variations of this research consisted of using different reinforcing stimuli applied contingently to different bodily movements (Murphy et al., 1979; Wolf, 1980). However, as Reid et al. (1991) summarise, these projects typically suffered from variable results, with some reporting no behaviour change, whilst others reporting small and/or inconsistent changes across participants.

Further, the reviewers note that even when behaviour change was demonstrated, the change was short-term (i.e., a brief moment) and no longitudinal studies were conducted to explore any long-term change. Because of these shortcomings, the research findings are said to only tentatively indicate that a limited level of change was observed.

Developing adaptive skills

Another popular area of research in the 1970s and 1980s was developing adaptive skills in people with PMLD. Adaptive behaviours are broadly defined as behaviours that allow people to interact with the world (Reid et al., 1985; 1991). The results of such research were typically mixed. For example, with regards to development of communication skills, positive reinforcement promoted behaviours that may be deemed socially beneficial, such as smiling, head turning, extended periods of looking, and happy vocalisations (Reid & Hurlbut, 1977; Sternberg et al., 1983). However, these behaviours by themselves were not deemed to be indicative of communicative intent or symbolic awareness (e.g., smiling is indicative of happiness but is not necessarily intended to be symbolically communicative). Various projects attempted to develop leisure skills among people with PMLD and increase the amount of time such people typically spend engaging in leisure. Leisure skills here are defined as meaningful actions that allow an individual "to function similarly to non-handicapped persons in regard to use of leisure time" (Reid et al., 1991, p. 321). Investigations included measuring the amount of time students interacted with stimuli placed on wheelchair desktops or how the frequency of microswitch presses differs when various electronic stimuli (e.g., flashing lights) are attached and activated per switch use (Realon et al., 1998; Wacker et al., 1985; 1988). However, studies typically reported the failure of some people with PMLD to engage in any of these leisure activities, or failed to do so without the support and prompting of support staff (Lancioni et al., 2001; Reid et al., 1991).

Concluding comments regarding early research

The early research literature is thus a problematic and controversial body of literature. As Reid et al. (1991) summarise, whilst the teaching of skills to people with PMLD has been demonstrated, it has only done so inconsistently and on a small scale. Further, very few investigations targeted behaviours which can be said to be meaningful, and no investigation is said to have changed behaviours during a substantial portion of the research participants' lives. Finally, no investigation succeeded in teaching independent skills, since the assistance of caregivers was still necessary for those participants who demonstrated some behavioural change. These points combined led Reid et al. (1991) to conclude that:

> [T]he applied behavioral research has not been successful; the research has not demonstrated that persons with profound multiple handicaps can acquire any independent adaptive skills. ... In essence, applied behavioral investigations have not attempted to affect the lives of participants beyond brief experimental sessions. (pp. 329–330)

Such conclusions are illustrative of the 1980s crisis of doubt regarding the efficacy of behaviourism as an appropriate research and teaching methodology. In response to this crisis, researchers began to refine behaviourist methodology and improve the success of its conditioning interventions for people with PMLD. In doing so it made increasing reference to subjective or internal variables that may mediate the stimulus-response relationship, such as stimuli preference, contingency awareness, and alertness. This research is summarised below.

Part III

Behaviourism and people with PMLD: the "new wave" of research

Preferred stimuli assessment

One reason given for the lack of demonstrable learning among people with PMLD through behaviourist methodology is that research failed to identify stimuli which acted as reinforcers. Thus, one important area of research has been developing a method for identifying "preferred stimuli"—that is, stimuli which appealed to people with PMLD. A common method for identifying preferred stimuli is the "successive choice procedure" (Pace et al., 1985). The successive choice procedure can be summarised as an elaborate approach that involves presenting numerous stimuli on different occasions and measuring how many times a person with PMLD approaches or avoids each stimulus and for how long. Approach behaviour is defined as the participant making an apparent voluntary body movement toward the stimulus, maintaining contact with the stimulus for a short duration, exhibiting positive facial expressions, or making a positive vocalisation shortly after the presentation of the stimulus. Avoidance is defined as negative vocalisation, pushing the object away, or making a movement away from the stimulus. If a stimulus is approached 80% of the time or more after a series of presentations it is deemed to be a "preferred stimulus" (Green et al., 1991; Green et al., 2000; Reid et al., 1999).

Since Pace et al. (1985) published their original work there have been various modifications of the successive choice procedure as well as numerous alternative strategies designed for identifying stimuli preference. In a review of the choice and preference assessment literature for people with severe to profound disabilities, Tullis et al. (2011) identified fifty studies published between 2002 and 2010 which made use of eight different preference assessment formats. These are summarised below.

In the single stimulus (SS) format only one stimulus is presented; the paired choice (PC) format requires people with PMLD to choose between one of two stimuli; in the multiple stimulus with replacement (MSW) format and multiple stimulus without replacement (MSWO) format an array of stimuli are presented, and people with PMLD are required to choose preferred stimuli from the array. In the MSW the chosen stimulus is then replaced in the array, but in the MSWO the chosen stimulus is not replaced. In the free operant (FO) format people with PMLD can engage with as many items in an array for as long as they want. The response restriction (RR) format is similar to the FO format but once a stimulus is determined to be preferred it is no longer included in the array of items. In the concurrent operant (CO) format people with PMLD are given the opportunity to select treatment from an array and, following a treatment session, they are given the opportunity to choose what treatment/therapy they would like next. Finally, in the questionnaires (Q) format parents and/or staff are asked what they think would be preferred stimuli for people with PMLD.

There has been a considerable amount of research published into the efficacy of approaches to identifying preferred stimuli. Some reviewers of this research have been optimistic about the findings, which support the view that people with severe learning disabilities and people with profound and multiple learning disabilities (S/PMLD) are able to indicate preferences and choose between stimuli if the right methodology is in place.

For example, Lancioni et al. (1996) reviewed research between 1977 and 1995 and found that seventeen out of twenty studies were positive insofar as they suggested that people with S/PMLD could indicate which stimuli they preferred. Three studies reported problems when people with S/PMLD did not appear to express a preference or choice. Cannella et al. (2005) reviewed fifteen preference assessment studies published between 1996 and 2002 and found that eight studies reported positive results (meaning preferences were identified for all study participants), whilst seven studies reported mixed results. In this context, mixed results mean that the studies had one experiment or phase with mixed results, or the studies with multiple phases had a combination of results that were positive, negative, or mixed. Tullis et al. (2011) reviewed preference assessment literature published between 2002 and 2010 and found that fourteen out of eighteen studies reported positive results insofar as preferred stimuli could be identified for all participants. The remaining studies were mixed, meaning that the studies were successful in identifying preferred stimuli for some but not all participants.

Whilst the above reviews shed stimuli preference assessment in a promising light it is important to note that the reviewers do not differentiate between people with severe learning disabilities (SLD) and people with profound and multiple learning disabilities (PMLD). For example, the inclusion criterion for the research reviewed by Tullis et al. (2011) was that the studies "must have at least one participant with severe to profound disabilities" (p. 577). Thus, whilst many of the studies report positive findings it is not always clear which studies included people with PMLD. By contrast, reviews of literature exclusively about the efficacy of stimuli preference assessment for people with PMLD tend to exercise more caution. For example, Logan and Gast (2001) reviewed thirteen PMLD-specific studies published between 1985 and 1998. The reviewers found that there was variation in success rates of identifying preferred stimuli, with some studies reporting 100% success rate and others reporting 50% success rate. Furthermore, preferred stimuli did not always act as reinforcers, and individual preferences often changed over time demonstrating stimuli habituation. Similar difficulties have been reported elsewhere (Mechling & Bishop, 2009; Mechling, 2006; Spevack et al., 2006).

Choosing alternative responses to condition: microswitch-pressing and contingency awareness

Another reason for the apparent lack of success of early behaviourist interventions may be that researchers failed to target behavioural responses that could be easily conditioned. Lancioni et al. (2005a) reviewed research between 1986 and 2005 in order to give an overview of the types of responses people with PMLD were required to execute in relation to microswitch training programmes. Microswitches are defined as "tools of access allowing persons with profound and multiple disabilities to develop a successful interaction with the immediate world and establish a form of control over it" (Lancioni et al., 2002b, p. 151). Microswitch programmes are aimed at establishing specific responses that people with PMLD can exercise independently, which "enrich their situation with preferred events" (ibid.). These programmes typically involve placing microswitches near part of the body in the hope that the person with PMLD will accidentally or deliberately activate the switch resulting in the presentation of stimuli. It is hoped that repeated activations will support the development of contingency awareness (awareness of cause-effect relations) insofar as people with PMLD learn that the stimuli are contingent upon switch-press behaviour.

> Consider, for example, the case of a child with a limited voluntary response repertoire (infrequent lateral head movement) who displays little interaction with the object world. A microswitch is placed to the side of the child's head within the child's range of motion. This switch is attached to a toy with visual and auditory features (e.g., a musical, moving train engine). Head movements by the child that cause the switch's closure would activate the train. Increases in this head movement would increase the reinforcement, and might engender some beginning awareness on the child's part that something the child has done has caused the train to be activated. (Schweigert, 1989, p. 192)

If this awareness has been established, and if the stimuli are desired, then independent switch-press behaviour will be high in frequency/duration. Stimuli which are correlated with high frequency/duration switch-press behaviour are defined as reinforcers, insofar as they are deemed to strengthen the likelihood of switch-press behaviour (Lancioni et al., 2002b; Logan et al., 2001; Saunders et al., 2003a; Schweigert, 1989; Schweigert & Rowland, 1992).

In their review of the literature regarding the types of behaviours targeted in microswitch training programmes, Lancioni et al. (2005a) identified forty-eight studies that varied widely in terms of the number and types of response that participants were required to perform.

The variation in response and switch choice was said to stem from an increased attempt to reach a greater range of individuals, including those individuals at the "lower end of the developmental spectrum" (p. 178). The reviewers grouped the forty-eight studies into four categories based on the nature of targeted behavioural responses: (1) a single, typical response (e.g., head turn or hand push); (2) a single, non-typical response (e.g., a chin movement); (3) multiple responses (e.g., a combination of 1 and 2); (4) multiple vocal responses (e.g., a combination of vocalisations). The results of these studies showed that 151 out of 190 participants involved had a positive outcome (in the sense that there were clear increases in response frequency, suggesting that participants had learned that preferred stimuli were contingent upon particular responses). Those participants who showed inconsistent or no signs of learning (thirty-nine people) were concentrated in the first group of studies (single, typical response).

Theorising internal variables: behaviour states and alertness

The above discussion details the difficulty that behaviourist researchers experienced when trying to identify stimuli to act as reinforcers. When no reinforcers were identified, researchers typically attributed such failings to methodological inadequacy and called for more sophisticated adaptations of stimuli preference assessment methodology (Green et al., 1988; Green et al., 1991; Green et al., 2000; Ivancic & Bailey, 1996; Logan & Gast, 2001; Logan et al., 2001; Reid et al., 1999) or more appropriate selection of behavioural responses (Lancioni et al., 2005a). Guess et al. (1990; 1993) offer a different view in which the difficulty is not described as methodological but biological. People with PMLD are said to have difficulty in attending and responding to environmental stimuli because of a problem with behaviour state. Behaviour states are described by Guess et al. (1993, citing Wolff, 1959) as levels of alertness and responsiveness reflecting behavioural and physiological conditions. Extending this description, Guess et al. (1993) cite Helm and Simeonsson (1989), who define behaviour states as: "... expressions of the maturity, status, and organization of the central nervous system ... which mediate the child's ability to respond to the environment and stimulation" (p. 203). In other words, the relative success or failure of behaviourist interventions to alter behaviour patterns of people with PMLD is contingent upon the readiness or alertness of participants. From this point of view, the strength of the potential reinforcer is important only insofar as the participant is in a state to be affected by it.

The *Behavior State Observation Schedule* (BSOS) (Guess et al., 1993)—or some variation of it—has been used in studies to explore behaviour state patterns (Munde et al., 2009; Munde, 2011). The BSOS is based on the *Neonatal Behavioral Assessment Scale* (Brazelton, 1984) and originally contained eight behaviour state codes (see Table 1).

Table 1. Definitions of behaviour state, taken from Guess et al. (1993), p. 33.

Sleep states	S^1 Asleep-Inactive: Person's eyes are closed, respiration is relatively slow and regular. Exhibits little or no motor activity (startle, mouthing, brief limb/body movements).	S^2 Asleep-Active: Person's eyes are closed. Respiration is generally uneven, sporadic movements (tossing and turning, head and limb twitching) may occur but muscle tone generally low between movements. Person may exhibit rapid eye movements (REM). Other behavior may include facial expressions (smile, grimaces, frowns) and/or vocalizations (sighs, grunting, gurgling).
Indeterminate states	DR Drowsy: Person's eyes are either open and eyelids appear "heavy" or eyes are opening/closing repeatedly. Vocalizations may occur.	DA Daze: Non orientation to visual, auditory, or tactile stimuli predominates. If person's vision is intact, eyes are open and appear glassy, dull, and immobile. Motor movements (that are not orientating) may occur such as brief limb/body movements, startles). [sic] Respiration is regular.

(Continued)

Table 1. Continued.

Preferred awake states	**A^1 Awake Inactive-Alert:** Person's eyes are open and some active visual or auditory orientation, focusing or tracking is displayed (oriented/focused on stimuli, turning head, eyes toward stimuli, or following stimuli). Motor movements (that are not orienting) may occur such as brief limb/body movements, startles). [sic] Demonstrates regular respiration. Vocalizations may occur.	**A^2 Awake Active-Alert:** Person attempts to engage/interact using visual, auditory, or tactile modes. If person's vision is intact eyes are open, bridge, and shiny. Visual, auditory, or tactile interactions patterns are exhibited with distinct fine and gross motor movements (reaching, leaning towards/away, moving towards/away, eating, touching, etc.). Vocalizations may occur.
Other awake states	**A^2/S Awake-Active/Stereotypy:** Person exhibits behaviors of A^2 with movements that are self-stimulatory or stereotypical (idiosyncratic, repetitive rhythmic movements or body or body parts). Movements may include head-weaving, rocking, mouthing hand or objects, arm and finger flapping.	**C/A Crying/Agitated:** Person may exhibit intense vocalizing, crying or screaming. Self injurious behavior possible. Respiration may be irregular and eyes may be open or closed. Intensive motor activity possible.

In addition to behaviour state codes, Guess et al. (1993) defined five environmental codes: the occurrence or non-occurrence of direct interaction with others (i.e., peer or adult); the type of activity (self-help, maintenance, or play/instructional/other); the presence or absence of material; the position of the person's body (sitting, standing, prone, supine, or side-lying), and the person's location (school, community, outdoors or moving between settings) (Guess et al., 1993).

Studies which have explored the relation between behaviour state and environmental variables have found positive relationships between preferred awake states and opportunities for social interaction. For example, Guess et al. (1993) investigated the relation between behaviour state and environmental variables for sixty-six people with PMLD. Percentages were calculated regarding the amount of time each participant was observed in the eight state conditions and the correlative environmental variables. The researchers found a weak association between environmental events and state changes, insofar as 35% of observed state shifts were preceded by a changed environmental condition. However, when they did occur, most state shifts were preceded by an interaction with an adult. A different study found that ten people with PMLD were often in the awake active-alert state and less in the awake inactive-alert or awake-active stereotypy states after interactions with an adult. When there was no interaction there was a higher occurrence of people being in the awake inactive-alert, daze, awake-active stereotypy and crying/agitated behaviour states (Arthur, 2004).

Foreman et al. (2004) explored the relationship between behaviour state and learning environment (i.e., segregated classroom *vs.* inclusive classroom). The researchers observed eight matched pairs of people with PMLD for one full day each in either a segregated classroom or a mainstream school classroom. The researchers found that people with PMLD in inclusive classrooms spent more time in desired behaviour states compared to their matched peers in a special school. For example, students in the mainstream environment were observed to be awake active-alert for 63% of the time, compared to those in special schools who were in the same state for only 44% of the time. Furthermore, the researchers found that communicative interactions occurred during 49% of observations in general education classes compared with 27% in special classes, and that the instances of "no communication" were significantly lower in inclusive classes than in special classes. The communication partner in the inclusive class was usually a learning support assistant (44%) or non-disabled peer (17%). In the special—school classes, teachers were the main communicators (21%) and peers were observed engaging with each other 4% of the time.

Researchers have reported difficulties when trying to observe behaviour states in people with PMLD. Some (Arthur, 2000; Mudford et al., 1997; Mudford et al., 1999) have reported significant difficulties with interobserver agreement during the coding of both their own data and the video data provided by (Guess et al., 1998). Other researchers have experienced problems trying to find a consistent pattern for all participants involved in the research. For example, (Green et al., 1994) analysed alertness among five people with PMLD and found the alertness levels of three out of the five individuals increased with provision of skill-acquisition training programmes. Results also indicated no predictive relationship between alertness levels prior to training and subsequent responsiveness to training. Vlaskamp et al. (2003) explored whether multisensory environments (MSEs) could increase the alertness of nineteen people with PMLD. The researchers compared observations in the MSEs to observations in people's everyday living environment and did not find a higher level of alertness in the MSE. Consistent with previous research (Arthur, 2004; Foreman et al., 2004; Guess et al., 1993), Vlaskamp et al. (2003) found that people with PMLD reacted more frequently to personal stimuli, but large individual differences were observed. Lindsay et al. (1997) found that MSEs improved alertness, or "concentration" (p. 201) of eight people with PMLD. Jones et al. (2007) have reported an increase in alertness for six people attending rebound sessions (trampoline activities).

Theorising internal variables: indices of happiness

Research has also explored indices of "happiness" as a variable indicative of quality of life. As discussed above, behaviour state research is concerned with variables related to readiness to learn. Learning here is understood as the acquisition of adaptive skills. In contrast, happiness research is concerned with the consequences that emerge when adaptive skills are not acquired. When such skills are lacking, people with PMLD are said to have less access to stimuli associated with happiness because they are ineffective at communicating their stimuli preferences. Further, people with PMLD lacking in relevant skills are said to experience problems in making contact with preferred stimuli and avoiding unwanted stimuli. Thus, the quality of life of people with PMLD is said to be at risk. The goal of happiness research is to find ways of manipulating the environment in order to enhance levels of happiness and reduce levels of unhappiness (Green & Reid, 1999a).

Research concerned with enhancing the happiness levels of people with PMLD begins with Green and Reid (1996). Their foundational paper reported attempts to increase levels of happiness through the presentation of preferred stimuli, selected via a modified version of the successive choice procedure (Pace et al., 1985). Happiness was defined as any facial expression or vocalisation typically considered to be an indicator of happiness among people without disabilities, including smiling, laughing, and yelling while smiling. Unhappiness was defined as any facial expression or vocalisation typically considered to be an indicator of unhappiness among people without disabilities, such as frowning, grimacing, crying, and yelling without smiling. Green and Reid (1996) observed an increase in happiness for the five participants when presented with the most preferred stimuli. Increases in unhappiness indices were observed when they were presented with least preferred stimuli. Classroom staff subsequently increased happiness indices through presentation and contingent withdrawal of activities.

Replications and variations of Green and Reid's (1996) research are numerous, and each study has reported an increase in happiness for most or all of the PMLD research participants. For example, Green et al. (1997) increased the happiness of three participants through the presentation of preferred stimuli and reported that those stimuli chosen through the successive choice procedure (Pace et al., 1985) were more likely to increase the happiness of the participants than those items chosen by classroom staff. Ivancic et al. (1997) replicated the Green et al. (1997) study and reported that whilst the presentation of preferred stimuli increased levels of happiness or reduced levels of unhappiness, preferred stimuli could not be found for all participants. Logan et al. (1998) found that indices of happiness were stronger when preferred stimuli were present with able-bodied peers than when preferred stimuli were present with moderately to profoundly disabled peers. Green and Reid (1999b) reduced indices of unhappiness during painful therapeutic exercise routines by presenting preferred stimuli before, during, and after the routines. Using similar methods, Lancioni et al. (2002a) reported mixed results, with two participants showing strong increases in happiness, and two showing moderate or minimal increases. Davis et al. (2004) compared the differences in levels of happiness of three participants during presentation of stimuli alone, social interaction alone, and social interaction with stimuli. They found that social interaction with presentation of stimuli increased participant happiness the greatest, a finding also reported by Singh et al. (2004). And finally, Green et al. (2005) reported a reduced resistance to teaching and therapy in three individuals with PMLD when presented with preferred stimuli during teaching and therapy sessions.

The relation between microswitch behaviour and behaviour states/alertness

Attention has been given to the ways in which mediating states (behaviour states/happiness) relate to conditioning. Conditioning here is understood in operant terms, with the target behaviour typically being microswitch-pressing.

Some studies have reported positive relationships between mediating state and switch-press behaviour when stimuli were preferred by the participants with PMLD. For example, Lancioni et al. (2002b) conducted a study to assess whether the impact of a microswitch programme on indices of happiness would be comparable with that of a stimulation programme. The stimulation programme consisted of the presentation of "pleasant stimuli" (p. 150) with the aim of promoting happiness and reducing unhappiness. There were no learning expectations within the stimulation programme in the sense that presentation of stimuli was not contingent upon a behavioural response from the participant. In contrast, the microswitch programme entailed some form of action from the participant since stimuli presentation was contingent upon successful execution of switch-press behaviour. The researchers found that the microswitch programme produced increases in the research participants' happiness which are said to be comparable with those happiness frequencies of the stimulation programme.

Some studies have reported mixed results. For example, Murphy et al. (2004) explored the effects of different types and amounts of environmental stimuli on microswitch use and behaviour states of three people with PMLD. The participants' switch use and behaviour states were measured under three setting conditions: (1) natural stimuli (the participants' daily recreational setting with regular others); (2) reduced visual stimuli (the participants' daily recreational setting with others, whilst being surrounded by screens, which blocked vision); (3) reduced visual and auditory stimuli (the participants' daily recreational setting, with screens but with nobody else present except the researcher). Results indicated differential switch use in all participants with the varying environmental setting conditions. No clear relationship was observed regarding rate of microswitch usage and environment—each participant showed a consistent but idiosyncratic pattern of behaviour state scores and switch-use percentages across the three experimental setting conditions.

Similarly, Mellstrom et al. (2005) also explored the interaction of behaviour state and switch-press behaviour of three people with PMLD. Observations were conducted during a regularly scheduled leisure activity where each participant was provided with a switch that was connected to preferred stimuli. The introduction of microswitches did not cause participants to become more alert. Furthermore, high rates of switch use were only observed when the participants were in high states of alertness to begin with.

Stereotyped behaviours

Behaviourist research has also been applied to the topic of maladaptive behaviour—that is, behaviour that fails to provide adequate or appropriate adjustment to the environment (Gregory & Zangwill, 1987). One type of maladaptive behaviour said to be common for people with PMLD is stereotyped behaviour (Denis et al., 2011; Poppes et al., 2010). In a review of the literature, Murdoch (1997) discusses the criteria used to define stereotyped behaviour. Popular criteria include repetition, topographical invariance (meaning that the behaviour is performed in the same way each time), a lack of responsiveness to environmental change, and a lack of purpose or function. Such behaviours are said to disturb or alarm others, and include such things as rocking, hand-flapping, head-weaving, and light-gazing. Stereotyped behaviour can also be self-injurious and include eye-gouging, biting, and head-hitting.

A different interpretation sees stereotyped behaviour not as fixed and inflexible (Murdoch, 1997) but as contingent upon or maintained by environmental stimuli. From this perspective, stereotyped behaviour is "derive[d] from contingencies of reinforcements and particular responses made in the presence of stimulus situations" (Reber, 1995, p. 90). Stereotyped behaviours are thus said to result from "unfortunate contingencies" (ibid.) in the life of the individual, leading to the acquisition of maladaptive behaviours. Behaviourist attempts to reduce the frequency and intensity of stereotyped behaviour begin with the functional analysis of conditions maintaining the behaviour. Functional analysis involves observing behaviour in context and interpreting observed relations using concepts derived from operant conditioning theory. For example, it may be observed that the stereotyped behaviours of a student occur only in specific contexts (e.g., in a classroom rather than at home), and that such behaviour results in a particular outcome (e.g., the teacher stops working with the student). Under these circumstances it may be postulated that self-injury is an operant response, which has the consequence of the teacher terminating a task—a reinforcing consequence (Remington, 1996). Functional analysis can focus on a complex stimuli arrangement (e.g., a social milieu) or a simple stimulus (e.g., a sound). If it is unclear which stimuli are maintaining behaviour, then researchers can systematically manipulate the antecedent and consequential conditions of the behaviour in order to identify the conditions under which the individual is most likely to perform the undesired behaviour. The next stage involves the use of extinction—that is, the removal of stimuli maintaining the behaviour, leading to a weakening and eventual extinction of the relationship between stimuli and behaviour. Another approach involves introducing positive and negative reinforcement (Hanley et al., 2003). There are several types of reinforcement described in the literature, such as differential reinforcement of other behaviour (DRO) in which the reinforcer is provided as long as inappropriate behaviour does not occur, and differential reinforcement of an alternative (DRA) in which the reinforcer is given after desired or more appropriate behaviour is observed (Novak & Pelaez, 2004). Furthermore, reinforcement can be used alongside other forms of intervention to reduce stereotyped behaviour. For example, in a review of research literature about strategies for reducing hand-related stereotyped behaviour (i.e., hand-to-head body responses such as hand-mouthing, eye-poking, and face-slapping) Lancioni et al. (2009) found five main approaches: (1) mechanical restraints; for example, wrist weights sometimes combined with other intervention variables (such as reinforcement); (2) response-blocking by members of staff, sometimes in combination with other intervention variables (such reinforcement); (3) non-contingent stimulation sometimes in combination with prompting or contingent reinforcement; (4) contingency manipulations differing from those relied upon by the other strategies (e.g., the extinction of certain stimuli); (5) programmes based on microswitch clusters. The reviewers concluded that the forty-one studies reviewed were generally successful in reducing or eliminating stereotyped behaviour. However, studies that reported limited or no success used response-blocking, non-contingent stimulation, or contingency manipulations.

Chapter summary

We began this chapter by exploring the main theoretical premises of behaviourism. We described how learning is typically construed as conditioning, and that two forms of conditioning theory inform research concerning people with PMLD: classical conditioning theory and operant conditioning theory.

Classical conditioning involves the pairing of an unconditioned stimulus with a neutral stimulus resulting in the neutral stimulus becoming a conditioned stimulus. A conditioned stimulus is a stimulus that has acquired the same behaviour-eliciting powers as the unconditioned stimulus. To date, there have only been a handful of studies published that have attempted to condition the behaviour of people with PMLD using a classical approach (Hogg et al., 1979; Remington, 1996; Ross, 1975). These studies tried to condition eye blink responses by pairing a puff of air to the eye with an auditory tone. Researchers in this area have reported mixed results.

Most behaviourist research involving people with PMLD employs operant conditioning theory. Operant conditioning involves increasing the likelihood of a particular behaviour reoccurring through reinforcement. The mechanism through which operant conditioning occurs is the presentation of a reinforcer (stimulus) contingent upon the organism behaving in a particular way (Baars, 1986; Gregory & Zangwill, 1987). Early operant research programmes (i.e., those conducted between the 1950s and 1980s) have been criticised for failing to develop functional or adaptive skills in people with PMLD (Reid et al., 1991). Later research attempted to improve the efficacy of behaviourist conditioning programmes. To these ends, researchers have explored ways of assessing stimuli to act as reinforcers, such as adapting the successive choice procedure (Pace et al., 1985). Whilst literature reviews portray current techniques for identifying preferred stimuli as generally effective (e.g., Cannella et al., 2005; Lancioni et al., 1996; Tullis et al., 2011), the reviewers are not always clear about the extent to which people with PMLD were included in the research sample. Consequently, the conclusions of these reviews have to be taken tentatively. There has been one review of the literature that has focused exclusively on preference assessment for people with PMLD and the reviewers reported mixed to positive results (Ivancic & Bailey, 1996).

Another important area of operant research focuses on identifying which type of behavioural response is suited to conditioning. One review of the responses adopted for microswitch activation reported that attempts to condition a single, typical response (such as a hand push) can lead to more examples of failure compared to conditioning a non-typical response (e.g., a chin movement), multiple responses, and vocal responses (Lancioni et al., 2005a).

There is a growing interest about the way "internal" states (e.g., behaviour states/alertness) (Guess et al., 1993) mediate the success of conditioning. From the perspective of behaviour state research, the strength of the potential reinforcer is important only insofar as the participant is in a state to be affected by it. To date, research has suggested that people with PMLD achieve more desirable behaviour states (e.g., being alert active-awake) when in the presence of social stimuli such as teaching staff (Arthur, 2004) and mainstream school peers (Arthur-Kelly et al., 2008; Foreman et al., 2004). However, some researchers have reported problems with interobserver agreement when observing behaviour states (Mudford et al., 1997; Mudford et al., 1999), and others have reported mixed results when trying to find common behaviour state patterns (Green et al., 1994). Several studies have explored the relationship between behaviour state and microswitch behaviour. Whilst some have associated alertness with an increase in switch-press behaviour (Lancioni et al., 2005b; Mellstrom et al., 2005), others have struggled to identify generalisable variables that are conducive to increase alertness in the first place (Murphy et al., 2004).

Another area of research that conceptualises internal states is happiness research. Behaviour state research is increasingly concerned with variables related to learning. In contrast, most research into happiness is concerned with the consequences that emerge when adaptive skills are not acquired. When such skills are lacking, people with PMLD are said to have less access to stimuli associated with happiness because they are ineffective at communicating their stimuli preferences. The goal of happiness research is to find ways of identifying and presenting stimuli that enhances levels of happiness whilst reducing levels of unhappiness. In general, research has reported that presentation of preferred stimuli increases happiness (Green & Reid, 1996; Green et al., 1997; Ivancic et al., 1997).

Finally, behaviourist research has also been applied to the topic of stereotyped behaviour (including self-injurious behaviour). Stereotyped behaviours are thus said to result from "unfortunate contingencies" (p. 90) in the life of the individual, leading to the acquisition of maladaptive behaviours. A recent review of literature to reduce hand-related stereotyped behaviour reported generally positive results using reinforcement (Lancioni et al., 2009).

As this summary shows, contemporary behaviourist research relating to people with PMLD has moved away from purely externalist and mechanistic notions of behaviour, towards an increasing recognition that people with PMLD require opportunities to develop functional or adaptive skills, such as microswitch-pressing. Thus people with PMLD are increasingly described as people with the capacity for agency, given appropriate intervention strategies. Reference to "internal" states such as alertness or happiness has introduced subjective variables to behaviourism. However, some researchers have made a more radical step away from traditional behaviourism by exploring how operant conditioning can be used to foster contingency awareness (Saunders et al., 2007; Saunders et al., 2003b). Having said this, behaviourist work in this field is still in its infancy and studies which bridge behaviourism and cognitivism in this way are few and far between.

In the next chapter we review the cognitivism literature as it relates to children with PMLD.

CHAPTER THREE

Cognitivism

In Chapter One we reviewed behaviourism as one of the dominant approaches that guides research and practice for people with PMLD. The behaviourist literature primarily consists of research papers describing attempts to operantly condition the behaviours of people with PMLD. In this chapter we describe the alternative approach found in the PMLD literature—cognitive psychology, or cognitivism. The cognitivist literature describes ways of assessing the level of cognitive functioning of people with PMLD. It also outlines intervention strategies that practitioners such as teachers can use to support cognitive development.

In this chapter we first describe what cognitivism is, then discuss the work of several cognitive psychologists (Bates et al., 1975; Schaffer, 1971a; Trevarthen & Aitken, 2001) who have influenced assessment and intervention for people with PMLD. Specifically, we will focus on the ways cognitivism has shaped the early communication assessment (Coupe O'Kane & Goldbart, 1998); Intensive Interaction (Nind & Hewett, 1988; 1994; 2001); and responsive environments (Ware, 1994; 2003). Through this description we will illuminate several key ideas salient to all three approaches. In Chapters Five and Six we will revisit these key ideas and apply them as a framework to understand empirical data.

In the previous chapter we talked about "people" with PMLD because the behaviourist research we described included both children and adults in its sample. In this chapter we also use the term "people" when referring to individuals with PMLD because it is largely consistent with the literature we review. However, the cognitivist PMLD literature tends to refer to people with PMLD in classroom contexts, meaning that its sample consists of school-aged children and young people. In addition, we use the term "adult" to refer to communication partners. Invariably, the psychology research and PMLD literature we review describes communication between non-disabled infants or people with PMLD and adults (such as parents, support workers, and teachers). There is no mention of peer interaction between infants or people with PMLD.

Part I

Summary of cognitivist theory

What is cognitivism?

Cognitive psychology, or cognitivism, is a meta-theory or methodology that defines the topic of study for psychology as complex mental processes that guide action (Baars, 1986). Cognitivism emerged during the 1960s as a direct response to the growing dissatisfaction felt by academic psychologists towards behaviourist psychology. As discussed in the previous chapter, behaviourism traditionally eschewed reference to organismic determinants of behaviour in favour of explanations that stress the role of environmental stimuli in shaping behavioural response. In contrast, cognitivism hypothesises the importance of "central structures of an enduring nature ... and it is these as much as external stimuli which will determine the form, direction and frequency of behaviour" (Schaffer, 1971a, p. 21). From this perspective, an organism does not simply emit certain responses that then become linked to particular consequences through conditioning. Instead, an organism, even in its infancy, is said to take an active part in organising its own experiences and in determining those stimuli to which they are to be exposed—either by virtue of genetic endowment, or through influences representing the residue of past experience (Schaffer, 1971a).

In agreement with behaviourists, cognitivists argue the case that the data of psychology must be publically observable. However, in disagreement with behaviourists, cognitive psychologists gather this data in order to generate theories about unobservable mental processes, which can be used to predict and explain behaviour (Baars, 1986; Bolton & Hill, 1996; Gardner, 1987).

Central to cognitive psychology is the concept of "representation". Reber (1995) defines a representation as: "A thing that stands for, takes the place of, symbolizes, or represents another thing" (p. 662). Citing Fodor (1975), both Gardner (1987) and Leahey (1994) note that cognitivism seeks to understand how the mind works in terms of processes operating on such symbolic representations. Green (1996) describes the logic behind symbolic representation in the following way: "In thinking about the physical world, we do not manipulate actual bits of the world but mental entities that represent or symbolize it ... our capacity to think, feel, communicate, and act arise because of our capacity to process symbols" (pp. 7–9). From the perspective of cognitivism, this representational process intervenes between stimulus and response. A stimulus from the world is translated into a symbolic representation of the stimulus. As a result of past experience, the individual is said to acquire certain internal representations of his or her environment—a representational model—which enables him or her to compare and assess present sensory stimulation (Schaffer, 1971a).

Cognitive psychologists have investigated the progressive changes that take place in the course of infant and child development, in which cognitive structures are reorganised and elaborated. The neonate is said to have a certain structure which predetermines the way in which she/he will apprehend the external world; but, as a result of interaction with the environment, the existing cognitive structures transform, leading to new levels of awareness and responsiveness. Cognitive psychology attempts to chart this development. It presupposes that since there are a number of fundamental similarities in the structure of all individuals and of all environments, it is possible to discern a basic, universally applicable pattern of development progressing through a number of stages common to all (Dahlberg & Moss, 2005; Mac Naughton, 2005; Muir & Slater, 2003). The charting of this developmental pattern, and the identification of the processes by which such development is actualised, is achieved through microanalysis of video-taped interactions between mothers and their preverbal infants (e.g., Beebe et al., 2005; Meltzoff, 1999; Trevarthen & Aitken, 2001).

The findings of these different studies have led to various points of agreement, such as the view that at around nine months after birth infants begin to engage in joint attention—that is, they are capable of sharing experience of objects by signalling to another person and alerting them to the same object. Trevarthen and Aitken (2001) refer to this stage of development as "secondary intersubjectivity" (p. 5) (to be discussed below), whilst Bates et al. (1975) refer to the actions of joint attention as either "proto-imperative" or "proto-declarative" behaviours. Despite points of agreement, there are also points of disagreement. Disagreement tends to emerge during discussions of the abilities of neonates. Some have argued the case that infants are born with an innate capacity for intersubjective awareness (i.e., awareness of other as subject rather than object) (e.g., Legerstee, 2005; Meltzoff, 1999; Trevarthen & Aitken 2001). Others interpret early behaviours as reflexive (i.e., void of volition) and view intersubjective awareness as an acquired ability that emerges during the same time as joint attention (i.e., around nine to twelve months after birth) (e.g., Piaget, 1952; Schaffer, 1971a; 1971b; 1984).

The following discussion will explore two opposing theories of infantile development that highlight the acquired *vs.* innate intersubjectivity distinction (i.e., Schaffer, 1971a; Trevarthen & Aitken, 2001). The purpose of the distinction is twofold. First, it serves to highlight the fact that the PMLD literature that draws conceptual resources from the cognitivism overlooks the preverbal intersubjectivity debate. The PMLD literature sometimes synthesises literature during its theory-building without drawing attention to the tensions that exist between the texts cited in the synthesis. As such, the PMLD literature presents facts about the developing infant, but it needs to be recognised that these facts are contingent upon the way the literature has been interpreted. The second purpose for discussing this distinction is to map out core ideas at the heart of the PMLD literature, which will inform analysis of empirical data in Chapter Five, in order to assess the explanatory power of these ideas.

Schaffer: acquired intersubjectivity through social imprinting

For Schaffer (1971a), newborn infants are "asocial being[s]" (p. 13) and do not differentiate self from not-self, inner from outer, or self-produced from other-produced. Consequently, the infant does not differentiate self from other, nor one person from another, and does not recognise his or her parents. When infants cry, parents attend, but the crying is not intended to confer meaning, it is not a signal that newborn infants intentionally use to control the (social) environment. Instead, crying is a simple reflex. As infants mature, they become increasingly attracted to people, who become "fascinating things to watch and feel and listen to" (ibid.). However, people do not constitute "a class of stimuli distinct from the inanimate world" (ibid.). It is not until the end of the first year that this changes, and with such change infants are said to have "joined the human race" (ibid.). By the end of the first year infants are said to have learned to distinguish familiar people from strangers and have developed a repertoire of signalling abilities that can be used discriminatively in relation to particular situations and individuals. At this stage, infants are on the verge of acquiring key social skills, such as imitation and language: "In short, the first and most fundamental steps in the child's socializing process have been taken" (p. 13).

The acquired representational capacities are said to be brought about by an environment that provides opportunities to learn that other human beings are different from other objects in the world. Other people are said to have a special significance for developing infants. However, this significance begins when infants learn to objectify the other over time. Infantile behaviour in the earliest ontogenetic stages is described by Schaffer (1971a) as being more "stimulus-directed" than "object directed" (p. 32) [italics omitted]. Differential responsiveness to stimuli emerges early in development, but this is said to initially be elicited by stimulus properties of a wider, "more primitive" (ibid.) form than specific parental characteristics: "the human baby is attracted by certain features of his surroundings that are by no means exclusive to people" (ibid.).

At the core of Schaffer's (1971a) theory is the idea that sociability is based on perceptual interaction. Sociability is rooted in infants' perceptual encounters with their environment. From birth, infants are said to be equipped with a species-specific cognitive structure, which ensures that they can be selectively attuned to certain types of environmental stimuli. Such stimuli are said to represent aspects of infants' surroundings essential to survival and, among these, parental characteristics are particularly prominent. Treated as stimulus objects, human beings are said to have a number of features that make them prone to become objects of an infant's attentiveness. For example, they are said to be in almost constant movement, appeal to a number of different sense modalities simultaneously, and are responsive to infants' behaviours so that a continuous and reciprocal sequence may be initiated. In short, other people as stimulus objects have a much higher perceptual impact value than other objects in the environment based on "inherently attention-worthy characteristics" (p. 48). Thus, from the beginning, other people exercise an attention-compelling influence on the young. In addition, other people are similarly attracted to infants, and prolonged and frequent encounters are likely to take place.

For Schaffer (1971a), infants progressively develop from the early stages in which inborn signalling patterns are elicited purely automatically (i.e., in a reflexive manner), to purposive volitional signalling. At birth infants are said to be in a state of "undisputed motor helplessness" (p. 60). Development is said to be contingent on non-motor competences. For example, infants are said to be perceptually drawn towards certain kinds of stimuli, which typically (though not exclusively) emanate from "social objects" (ibid.). However, the growth of parent–infant relationships is not exclusively based on perceptual orientation, but also on compelling stimuli that infants offer parents. Such stimuli include smiles and eye contact, and are said to act as signals to parents for engagement. However, this is not the case. These signals are, in fact, "pre-communicative reflexes" (p. 65). As discussed above, whilst crying is expressive, it is an automatic response. However, it functions as a signal to parents, who attempt to comfort crying infants. Infants gradually learn that parents appear each time she/he cries, and begin to intentionally cry for attention.

According to Schaffer (1971a), by four months of age infants are able to recognise parents and distinguish parents from other people. This recognition implies the ability to learn and retain information about the parents' appearances; to match sensory input with stored impressions on subsequent encounters; and to appreciate that parents remain the same people despite the perceptual transformations that they undergo almost continuously. Such representational constancy is said to be the product of perceptual learning. Perceptual learning is described as the registration by infants of their environments, something said to occur in the course of repeated exposure to stimuli. This learning through exposure enables infants to progress towards stimuli differentiation, as manifested in the ability to respond to variables not previously responded to. Perceptual learning may be thought of in terms of central processes and, in particular, in the building up of inner structures referred to as central representations, cognitive maps, schemata or models.

Schaffer (1971a) describes the acquisition of central representations of the environment at the level of neural processing, where it is assumed that the environment is symbolically coded as a map in the brain via the sustained, patterned organisation of neurons. A neuronal model is developed through repeated encounters with the same stimulus, each encounter further strengthening and elaborating the model. The model enables infants to recognise stimuli. In the course of development, a considerable repertoire of central representations is said to be built up, and exposure to any stimulus situation will then inevitably result in an immediate search operation in order to ascertain whether the present sensory experience can be matched with any part of the memory store.

Very young infants are said to lack capacity to store and carry forward information from one experience to another, and as a result respond to each repetition of a stimulus "as though it were a completely new event" (Schaffer, 1971a, p. 94). However, by the age of four months infants begin to retain input encountered in the past and begin to recognise previously experienced stimuli; "[f]amiliarity *per se* is what the infant desires at this stage and the pleasure of recognition is indicated by the smile evoked in encounters with familiar objects and people" (p. 96).

Perceptual learning is said to be the guiding mechanism by which infants learn about "social object[s]" (p. 48), and differentiate between alternative social objects. Social differentiation depends on the same neural processes as those that enable infants to distinguish inanimate stimuli in terms of their past experiences of them. Schaffer (1971a) explains that a period of perceptual exposure to parents must take place before parents can be recognised as different from other people. When central representations of parents are established, infants come to perceive parents "as something more than a bundle of external sensations" (p. 97).

The relevance of perceptual learning to early social development is also dubbed "imprinting" (p. 34). This form of learning is not motor but perceptual. Schaffer (1971a) explains that imprinting was initially thought of as learning to follow, so that the whole phenomenon was regarded virtually synonymous with the establishment of a particular motor response. However, Schaffer (1971a) believes that imprinting can take place without the following responses ever occurring. Imprinting is not learning to follow, but learning the characteristics of parents or objects. For Schaffer (1971a), the "main problem is not why a particular response comes to be linked to a particular object, but rather how an [infant] familiarises itself with the various features of its environment" (p. 102).

To summarise, Schaffer (1971a) holds that infants exhibit automatic, reflexive behaviour to environmental stimuli. The mind is a representational entity that maps the external world. On the basis of these maps, infants interact with the world. The mapping occurs from "imprinting", which is a neurological phenomenon in which the world is symbolically encoded in the organisation of neurons. Such representational imprinting is not dependent on action. Thus, learning is a process of passively simulating experience which later allows infants to perceive a world in which to act.

Trevarthen and Aitken: innate primary and emergent secondary intersubjectivity

Trevarthen and Aitken (2001) offer a radically alternative model to Schaffer (1971a) regarding the nature and emergence of social cognition in infants. In contrast to Schaffer (1971a), who conceptualises neonates as "asocial beings" (p. 13) lacking social awareness and communicative intent, Trevarthen and Aitken (2001) argue that neonates possess a rudimentary form of intersubjectivity and an implicit ability to communicate.

> [N]ewborn infants, with their very immature though elaborate brains, limited cognitions, and weak bodies, are specifically motivated, beyond instinctive behaviours that attract parental care for immediate biological needs, to communicate intricately with the expressive forms and rhythms of interest and feeling displayed by other humans. This evidence of purposeful intersubjectivity, or an initial psychosocial state, must be fundamental for our understanding of human mental development. (p. 3)

Whilst it is possible to conceptualise cognitive development in terms of assimilating perceptual information about physical objects in the environment—including what Schaffer (1971a) refers to as "social object[s]" (p. 48)—Trevarthen and Aitken (2001) state that it is a "logical category error" (p. 4) to assume that increasingly sophisticated object awareness is prerequisite for early social meanings.

> We believe that the prevailing logic needs to be reversed; that object cognition and rational intelligence in infants, and their perceptual preferences, should be viewed as the outcomes of a process that seeks guidance by person-perception and through communication with equivalent processes, of cognition-with-intention-and-emotion, in other persons. (ibid.)

The framework of intersubjectivity that Trevarthen and Aitken (2001) propose involves three different but interrelated concepts: subjectivity, primary intersubjectivity, and secondary intersubjectivity.

- Subjectivity

In his early work, Trevarthen (1979) described how subjectivity refers to an individual's ability to exhibit conscious awareness, recognised by others, through acts of volition. This overt manifestation of agency is said to be prerequisite for communication to take place between infants and other people.

> For infants to share mental control with other persons they must have two skills. First, they must be able to exhibit to others at least the rudiments of individual consciousness and intentionality. This attribute of acting agents I call subjectivity. ... By subjectivity I mean the ability to show by coordinated acts that purposes are being consciously regulated. Subjectivity implies that infants master the difficulties of relating objects and situations to themselves and predict consequences, not merely in hidden cognitive processes but in manifest, intelligible actions. (cited in Trevarthen & Aitken, 2001, p. 5)

In addition to possessing subjectivity, for infants to communicate they must also be able to "adapt or fit this subjective control to the subjectivity of others" (ibid.). In other words, they must be intersubjectively aware. Trevarthen and Aitken (2001) describe two forms of intersubjectivity: primary and secondary.

- Primary intersubjectivity

Primary intersubjectivity refers to the ability of neonates to engage in rudimentary forms of "active 'self-other' awareness" (p. 3). The theory of innate or primary intersubjectivity was proposed in order to account for the intricate nature of social interactions between parents and infants. These early interactions are labelled "proto-conversations" (Bateson, 1971, in Trevarthen & Aitken, 2001, p. 4). Infants are naturally social and can engage with the "interest, purposes, and feelings of parents" (ibid.) and this in turn is said to motivate "companionship, or cooperative awareness, leading the infant towards 'confidence, confiding and acts of meaning', and eventually to language" (ibid.). Parents and infants look at and listen to each other whilst regulating (controlling or maintaining) each other's interests and emotions through rhythmic patterns of expressive multimodal signals.

> Mothers and fathers were behaving in an intensely sympathetic and highly expressive way that absorbed the attention of the infants and led to intricate, mutually regulated interchanges with turns of displaying and attending. The infant was thus proved to possess an active and immediately responsive conscious appreciation of the adult's communicative intentions. This is what was called primary intersubjectivity. (p. 5)

For Trevarthen and Aitken (2001), the most compelling evidence for an "innate protoconversational readiness" (p. 7) comes from observation of the deliberate imitation and provocation of neonates engaged in intimate reciprocal interaction with parents. Infants are able to share protoconversational motives with interactive partners through mimicking the actions of others, including facial expressions, vocalisations, and hand gestures. This creates mutual pleasure which motivates and sustains interaction.

> Infants only a few hours old are capable of expressing communicative capacities adapted for psychological self-other representation. … The infants act assertively or apprehensively in appropriate coordination with the assertive phases or watchful apprehensive states of a sympathetic partner (Trevarthen et al., 1999). This active involvement in communication of rudimentary intentions and feelings confirms that the human mind is, from the start, motivated

not only to elicit, guide, and learn from maternal physical care to benefit regulation of the infant's internal biological states, but also for cooperatively psychological learning—the mastery of socially or interpersonally contrived meaning specified in intelligent reciprocal social engagements. (Trevarthen & Aitken, 2001, p. 7)

Trevarthen and Aitken (2001) describe the development of motives that drive early communication in the following way. The infant begins with "gentle, intimate, affectionate, and rhythmically regulated playful exchanges of protoconversation" (p. 6), looking at the eyes and mouth of the other whilst listening to their voice. The infant moves in predictable response cycles to the patterns of adult behaviour. During these sequences the infant moves his or her face and vocalises to modified patterns of adult vocalisation. The infant's hand movements are said to be "communicatively active" (ibid.) insofar as they make expressive movements in rhythmic coordination to the speech of the interactive partner. Because of this, Trevarthen and Aitken (2001) conclude that infants have "a coherent psychoneura organisation that specifies the timing and form of body movements" (ibid.). This organisation reacts with the dynamic changes in the expression of other people, thus matching their interactive patterns. The infant and adult are able to closely sympathise with one another's motive states "using similar melodic or prosodic forms of utterance and similar rhythms of gesture" (ibid.). This results in adults entering an "affectionate intuitive parenting mode" through which they begin to mimic the infant and engage in emotionally loaded vocal musicality, with "animated but sympathetic and joyful facial expressions and dance like postural, gestural movements that match vocal expressions, and affectionate and playful touching and moving of the infant's hands, face, or body" (ibid.).

- Secondary intersubjectivity

Secondary intersubjectivity refers to a more advanced social awareness involving an infant and parent jointly attending their environment. Secondary intersubjectivity is said to emerge just before the end of the infant's first year of life. Prior to this, infants display an increasing interest in objects and physical events (evidenced through tracking, reaching, grasping, and manipulating). The subjective motives that guide action lead infants to "experience, for themselves, the sensations and affordances of their own bodies and of things" (p. 5). At the same time infants' intersubjective motives are said to draw them into interpersonal games and self-other regulation in which infants "react alertly to the expressions of purpose and emotion in their partners" (ibid.). Before the infant's first birthday there is a sudden development of joint interest "triggered by the infant's emerging curiosity about the timing and direction and focus of attentions and intentions of the mother" (ibid.). The intersubjective capacity of the infant begins to include awareness that the self and other are jointly attending to the world. The subjective and intersubjective motives no longer operate in parallel but merge, thus guiding infants to engage with parents on a different level.

> It was confirmed that differing motives for these two kinds of objective—for object-awareness or doing with things, and for person-awareness and communicating with persons (Trevarthen, 1998 …)—where indeed, undergoing divergent and periodically competing development during the first year, leading, at around 9 months after the infant's birth, to integration in the new form of cooperative intersubjectivity (person–person–object awareness), which was named secondary intersubjectivity. (Trevarthen & Hubley, 1978, cited in Trevarthen & Aitken, 2001, p. 5)

One-year olds attend to and mimic vocalisations and gestures, and orient to/handle objects that other people use, and imitate the object-actions of others. "Motivation to regulate fluent 'person–person–object' awareness, joint attention, and mutually adjusted intentionality, all at once, is coming to the fore at this age" (p. 6).

To summarise, Trevarthen and Aitken (2001) hold that infants possess a basic form of intersubjective awareness known as primary intersubjectivity. Primary intersubjective awareness presupposes that infants are able to exhibit behaviour that portrays them as agents to others. This is what Trevarthen and Aitken (2001) refer to as subjectivity. Primary subjectivity unfolds through intricate, mutually satisfying patterns of protoconversation that are emotionally expressive and involve attending to and replying to each other's behaviours. Protoconversations include facial expressions, vocalisation, hand gestures, and mimicking. Secondary subjectivity involves joint attention. Infants engage with others using objects and develop interest in the objects that adults attend to. Secondary intersubjectivity is a higher form of subjectivity and emerges around nine to twelve months after birth.

Bates, Camaioni, and Volterra: the acquisition of performatives prior to speech

Whilst Trevarthen and Aitken (2001) and Schaffer (1971a) are concerned with identifying infant awareness of others as subjects rather than objects (i.e., infantile intersubjectivity), Bates et al. (1975) offer descriptors of early symbolic communication in typically developing infants—the emergence of proto-imperative and proto-declarative behaviours. These behaviours involve joint attention with an object and so presuppose what Trevarthen and Aitken (2001) term secondary intersubjectivity, or what Schaffer (1971a) would consider to be social imprinting. The work of Bates et al. (1975) heavily influenced the development of Coupe O'Kane and Goldbart's (1998) early communication assessment for people with severe to profound and multiple learning disabilities (discussed below). The work has also been cited by Schaffer (1984) as evidence of communicative intentionality in infants. As such, it is worth outlining Bates et al. (1975) theory of intentional communication.

In their paper, *The acquisition of performatives prior to speech*, Bates et al. (1975) examined the onset of communicative intent before the development of speech. Their framework for researching such intent drew from the philosophy of language and linguistic semantics, such as Austin's speech act theory (Austin, 1962). In speech act theory, language is more than a means of conveying information. It is a mode of action. Whereas traditional analyses of language have been concerned with propositions and whether or not they were true (constative utterances) (Van Oort, 1997), Austin (1962) argued that some sentences are not descriptions of events "but events in themselves—acts that are carried out when a sentence is used (e.g., a promise is made, a marriage is performed)" (Bates et al., 1975, p. 205) (performative utterances) (Van Oort, 1997). For Austin (1962), each time a sentence is uttered there are three kinds of speech acts being carried out: locutions, illocutions, and perlocutions. Henderson and Brown (1997) offer succinct descriptions of these acts:

> [A] locutionary act has meaning; it produces an understandable utterance. An illocutionary act has force; it is informed with a certain tone, attitude, feeling, motive, or intention. A perlocutionary act has consequence; it has an effect upon the addressee. By describing an imminently dangerous situation (locutionary component) in a

tone that is designed to have the force of a warning (illocutionary component), the addresser may actually frighten the addressee into moving (perlocutionary component). (Henderson & Brown, 1997, para. 3)

In their study of the development of performatives (illocutions) during infants' first year of life, Bates et al. (1975) applied Austin's (1962) speech act framework and proposed that the development of communicative intent in infants emerges through three stages.

First, there is the perlocutionary stage in which infants have an effect on listeners without intending to cause such an effect. According to Bates et al. (1975), when infants are first born they only engage in perlocutionary communication. Infants "react innately to certain internal physiological states by producing certain behaviours (e.g., smiling, crying) which predictably result in the satisfaction of material needs (e.g., the cry)" (p. 212). In other words, parents interpret infant responses as meaningful, intentional or illocutionary (the child is crying because she/he is hungry) and respond appropriately (by feeding the child). However, at this stage Bates et al. (1975) argue that infants are not aware that their behaviours act as signals for their parents.

Second, there is the illocutionary stage during which infants' intentionally use non-verbal means to convey requests and direct the attention of others to objects and events. Infants recognise that certain behaviours direct the attention and actions of others. Bates et al. (1975) claim that the most general illocutionary acts observed during studies of preverbal development are proto-imperatives and proto-declaratives. (In this context, "proto-"implies that meaning is conveyed prior to the development of formal speech.) Proto-imperatives are defined as "the use of the adult as the means to a desired object" (p. 209). Proto-declaratives are defined as "the use of an object (through pointing, showing, giving, etc.) as the means to obtaining adult attention" (ibid.). These behaviours are said to emerge when infants are ten-months old and may be considered the earliest examples of intentional communication.

Bates et al. (1975) give examples of such illocutions with reference to Carlotta, an infant who participated in their study of intentional communication during her first year of life. The following passage describes Carlotta using an object to gain the attention of another person (proto-declarative behaviour):

> [W]e observed the first instance in which Carlotta extends her arm forward to show an object to the adult. She is playing with a toy already in her hand; suddenly, she looks toward the observer and extends her arm forward holding the toy. In the next two to three weeks, this behavior increases and stabilizes until we observe Carlotta looking around for objects not already in her grasp, and immediately presenting them while awaiting adult response. (p. 216)

In the above example, Carlotta showed the adult the objects but had no intention to give the objects to the adult. Bates et al. (1975) note that when the adult tried to take the object, Carlotta refused to let go and pulled her hand away. Carlotta's intention in showing the object was to direct the adult's regard or attention, hence it was defined as proto-declarative.

At around twelve to thirteen months, Carlotta began using a pointing gesture in her communicative sequences. For example, she would orient towards an interesting object or event, point while uttering "ha", turn and point at the adult, look back at the object and point towards it again. This series of steps eventually developed into a smoother and shorter expression, whereby Carlotta simultaneously pointed to the object while turning to the adult for confirmation that she/he was observing the same object. Thus, the gesture towards the object was the vehicle for directing the attention of the adult.

At the same time that the pointing gestures began to appear in Carlotta's proto-declarative sequences, Bates et al. (1975) observed that Carlotta began to point during proto-imperative communication:

> C [Carlotta] is seated in a corridor in front of the kitchen door. She looks toward her mother [M] and calls with an acute sound "ha." M comes over to her, and C looks toward the kitchen, twisting her body and upper shoulders to do so. M carries her into the kitchen and C points toward the sink. M gives her a glass of water, and C drinks it eagerly. (p. 217)

Here, Carlotta used the adult to carry her as the means to achieve a desired objective, in this case drinking from a glass of water. The completion of the communicative sequence ended with the infant being satisfied with the outcome (she drunk the water eagerly).

In the framework of Bates et al. (1975) the final stage is the locutionary stage (spoken language). Utterances accompany or replace gestures such as pointing. Bates et al. (1975) describe the onset of speech in the following way:

> [W]ords as symbolic vehicles with corresponding referents emerged gradually out of the action schemes of sensorimotor communication. Within the same pointing, giving, reaching, vocalization sequences for ... Carlotta ..., we found a gradual passage from vocalization, to vocalization as signal, to word as signal, to word as a proposition with a referential value. (p. 220)

Since we are concerned primarily with the behaviours of people with PMLD who are deemed to be preverbal, we will not delve any further into Bates et al. (1975).

To summarise, Bates et al. (1975) offer a model regarding the emergence of intentional communication based on Austin's (1962) speech act theory. At the perlocutionary stage infant reflexes (such as crying) are said to be interpreted as meaningful (the infant is hungry) and result in responses from others to satisfy the infant's needs (e.g., the infant is given milk). At this stage infants are not aware that their behaviours act as signals. At the illocutionary stage the infant intentionally uses non-verbal means to convey requests and direct the attention of others. Two of the most common illocutionary acts during this stage are proto-imperative and proto-declarative behaviours. In the former the infant directs the adult to obtain a desired object. In the latter an object is used as the means to obtain the adult's attention. At the locutionary stage utterances are used alongside gestures, and eventually formal words emerge.

In the next section we demonstrate how the work of Schaffer (1971a), Trevarthen and Aitken (2001), and Bates et al. (1975) have been used to inspire and shape assessment tools and intervention strategies for people with PMLD.

Part II

The influence of cognitivism on intervention/ assessment of people with PMLD

As discussed at the beginning of this chapter, cognitivism has influenced assessment and intervention for people with PMLD, and the work of the above psychologists has shaped three popular approaches: early communication assessment (Coupe O'Kane & Goldbart, 1998); Intensive Interaction (Nind & Hewett, 1988; 1994; 2001) and responsive environments (Ware, 2003). The work of Trevarthen has been cited by academics in texts about each of these approaches, but they never explicitly discuss intersubjectivity or identify points of contention between Trevarthen's work and the work of Schaffer (1971a). We will revisit the innate-acquired intersubjectivity debate in Chapter Six, when we will test concepts by applying them to empirical data in order to explore their explanatory power.

The remainder of this chapter will outline the core approaches in the PMLD field and demonstrate how they were influenced by the cognitivist psychologists discussed above.

Early communication assessment

The early communication assessment is a tool for monitoring the development of communicative functioning in people with PMLD. It was developed by Coupe O'Kane and Goldbart (1998) and is based partly on the authors' personal experiences of the communicative abilities of people with PMLD, and partly on a review of literature describing the development of early communication. Whilst Coupe O'Kane and Goldbart (1998) cite a range of cognitive psychologists in their literature review, including Schaffer (1971b), and Trevarthen and Hubley (1978), the authors acknowledge that the work of Bates et al. (1975) was particularly influential in shaping the early communication assessment. This is because such work offers a model for identifying the earliest examples of intentional communication. Goldbart (1994) differentiates between pre-intentional communication and intentional communication in the following way. Pre-intentional communication "is the information that caregivers, teachers, and others can decode from the behaviour of people not yet intentionally communicating" (p. 16). In contrast, intentional communication involves an infant "deliberately [using] particular signals with the intention of having a predetermined effect on another person" (p. 17). It is the transition between the two that the early communication assessment is designed to assess.

This section will describe the basic structure of the early communication assessment. In doing so it will offer fuller descriptions of the pre-intentional and intentional levels of communication, and where

Bates et al. (1975) fit in the early communication assessment structure. Discussion will then ensue regarding the key aspects of Bates et al. (1975) that Coupe O'Kane and Goldbart (1998) draw from.

The early communication assessment consists of descriptions of six levels of communicative development. The first three levels concern pre-intentional communication, whilst level four concerns early intentional communication. Levels five and six concern increasingly sophisticated forms of verbalisation, including speech. Coupe O'Kane and Goldbart (1998) have reservations about whether or not people with PMLD will ever reach stage four of the early communication assessment. They support the valuing of pre-intentional communication but state:

> [O]ur own experience suggests that it is over-optimistic to anticipate the development of initiations for joint attention once initiations for social interaction have been established in individuals with profound and multiple learning disabilities. (p. 7)

In this context, initiation for social interaction involves ways of attracting the attention of somebody else in order to interact with them. Initiations for joint attention are described by Coupe O'Kane and Goldbart (1998) as acts used to direct the attention of another person with the goal of sharing an experience of an object or event, or what Bates et al. (1975) refer to as proto-declarative behaviours. For Coupe O'Kane and Goldbart (1998), initiations for joint attention require that the infant sees the other person as somebody whose interest can be engaged and directed, and this is said to be an illocutionary act, which is the first measure of communicative intent.

This section will briefly summarise the first four levels of communication development. Since people with PMLD are not deemed to reach level four, we will not spend time summarising levels five and six, but refer readers to Coupe O'Kane and Goldbart's (1998) *Communication Before Speech* for further information.

Coupe O'Kane and Goldbart (1998) identify three levels of pre-intentional communication: reflexive communication (reactive communication, and proactive communication) and one level of intentional communication (primitive communication). At the pre-intentional levels adults interpret the different behaviours of people with PMLD as intentional communication (when, in fact, such behaviours are not intended to act as signals to others). The three levels of pre-intentional communication and the first level of intentional communication are as follows.

- Level 1: pre-intentional: reflexive level

People operating at the first pre-intentional level have social significance assigned by an adult to a small repertoire of immature behaviours such as reflex responses and sounds, which are elicited by a limited range of internal (bodily) and external (environmental) stimuli. Assuming there is no sensory impairment, people may experience and orient to input to different sensory channels (such as sound, touch, and sight). At this stage adults respond instinctively to the behaviours of others and attend to the relationship through intense periods of interaction (such as face-to-face contact). The person orients to events under the control of others.

- Level 2: pre-intentional: reactive level

People operating at the second level of pre-intentional communication still have communicative significance assigned to their behaviours by an adult. The person starts reacting to a wider array of stimuli, including events and people in the environment, and the adult assigns social significance to these new reactions. Adults focus more on caregiving activity and are said to place value on vocalisations more than physical behaviours. They also expect the person to fill a turn during turn-taking interaction by vocalisation and movement. The adult follows the visual regards of the person, and the person responds to familiar, non-verbal communication by the adult. The person also follows the adult's line of regard and responds to the adult's affect (indicated through tone of voice or facial expression).

- Level 3: pre-intentional: proactive level

At the third and final stage of pre-intentional communication, adults become increasingly selective about which behaviours they respond to. Although they still respond to vocalisations, they begin to respond to newer behaviours such as where the person is looking and reaching. The adults interpret the behaviour of the person in terms of the person's intention to carry out some form of action. They also begin to interpret behaviours as the person trying to find out about something. The adult references objects, people, or events in close proximity. The person attempts to explore and act on the immediate, physical environment and they reach toward desired objects. The person now abstracts meaning from the adult's intonation pattern, voice, and facial expressions.

- Level 4: intentional: primitive level

At this level the person begins to communicate with intent. They either use an adult to obtain an object or make an event happen (i.e., proto-imperative behaviour), or use an object or event to gain the attention from the adult (proto-declarative behaviour). The intent is signalled by gestures such as pointing. The communication relates to the immediate context. Adults may still need to interpret the behaviours in some way because the person may have communication skills idiosyncratic to them. There may be an increasing level of vocalisation to people, objects, pictures, or even to themselves (perhaps after looking in a mirror). These vocalisations vary in stress, volume, pitch, and intonation. The person also responds more to adults' non-verbal communication (such as hold a hand that is offered to them). The person will respond to commands that involve gestures or situational cues.

Having just described the first four stages of the early communication assessment we will now describe how these stages have been shaped by the work of Bates et al. (1975).

In the first part of this chapter we described the communication framework of Bates et al. (1975), which was influenced by Austin's (1962) speech act theory. Speech act theory contends that communication can be broken down into perlocutionary, illocutionary, and locutionary acts. According to this framework, when infants are first born they operate at the perlocutionary stage and exhibit reflexive behaviours (such as crying) that act as signals to parents that something must be done (such as feeding the infant). However, infants are not aware that their behaviours act as signals and thus cannot be said to be communicating with intent. The perlocutionary stage corresponds to Coupe O'Kane and Goldbart's (1998) three stages of pre-intentional communication (described above). Bates et al. (1975) describe illocutionary acts as infants' intentionally using non-verbal means such as gestures to direct the attention of others. These acts belong to the fourth level of the early communication assessment. Bates et al. (1975) identify proto-imperative and proto-declarative behaviours as the most primitive form of intentional communication. Proto-imperatives involve infants using a parent as a means to obtain a desired object. Proto-declaratives involve infants using an object as a means to direct the parent's attention (so infant and parent jointly attend to the same thing). Coupe O'Kane and Goldbart (1998) use Bruner's (1975) example to highlight the differences between these two performatives. According to Bruner (1975), an infant develops a "reach-for-real" behaviour by four or five months of age. Reach-for-real involves reaching for something in order to grasp it. This act of reaching belongs to level three of Coupe O'Kane and Goldbart's (1998) early communication assessment and is thus not an intentional form of communication. By the age of ten months infants start to use the reach-for-real as a "reach-for-signal"—that is, reaching for something that is out of reach. During reach-for-signal the infant looks from the desired object to the parent and back again, and in doing so is said to communicate to the parent that she/he wants the object being reached for and knows that the parent can obtain it for him/her. This is proto-imperative behaviour. The infant may also reach for the object simply to direct the parent's attention towards it in order to share the experience of the object of interest. This is proto-declarative behaviour.

The final stage of the framework (Bates et al., 1975) is the locutionary stage involving the emergence of speech. The locutionary stage corresponds to the final levels of the early communication assessment, which were not described here (because people with PMLD are often defined as preverbal). However, Coupe O'Kane and Goldbart (1998) give examples of how early utterances can be attached to proto-imperative and proto-declarative acts, which further illuminates the nature of these performatives. In a proto-imperative act, an infant may reach with an open hand towards a banana on the table, then look from the banana to the parent and repeatedly utter, "Uh! Uh! Uh!" until the parent gives the infant a banana. In a proto-declarative act, the infant reaches or points to a cat that has jumped on the table. The infant says, "dah!", whilst looking back and forth from the cat to the parent until the parent looks at the cat and acknowledges what the infant is telling her to see (e.g., by saying "Naughty cat!"). Coupe O'Kane and Goldbart (1998) state that "Once this development has been achieved, babies are more active, directive and clearly intentional partners in interactions, being able to direct others' attention to things about which they want to communicate" (p. 8).

Coupe O'Kane and Goldbart (1998) note that when practitioners identify which level of communicative intent a person with PMLD is operating at they become better suited to intervening in order to improve the communication skills of the person with PMLD. They suggest that interventions such as Intensive Interaction (Nind & Hewett, 1994) and contingency sensitive environments (Ware, 1996) are particularly useful in encouraging people with PMLD to pass through the pre-verbal stages of development. Each of these will be discussed in turn, and their work related to the psychologists discussed in the first part of the chapter.

Intensive Interaction

> Intensive Interaction is a practical approach to working with people with very severe learning difficulties and just spending time with them, which helps them to relate and communicate better with the people around them. It is a good way of going about this because it is based on how communication ordinarily develops—on ways we know are effective—and in ways we know can be enjoyable for all involved. (Nind & Hewett, 2001, p. 4)

Intensive Interaction was developed in the 1980s by Nind and Hewett, who taught at a long-stay hospital school for young adults with severe to profound and multiple learning disabilities. Nind and Hewett (1994) explain that the approach emerged after teaching staff felt dissatisfaction with the teaching methodologies of that era. They were working at a time when behaviourism was particularly influential in shaping the educational experiences of young people in special education. Core areas of development were subdivided into components such as motor development, social skills, self-help skills, language, cognition, and play. Each of these components had a list of behaviours that were targeted using aspects of conditioning theory, such as reinforcement. In practice, the school day usually consisted of a mixture of unstructured activity, highly structured, small-step teaching of self-help skills, and negative reinforcement (such as the use of time out) to combat problem behaviour. There was a growing discomfort with this approach because of regular failures for the teacher and the student, as well as the inflexibility of the curriculum, which gave little room for following up student interests and individual strengths. Furthermore, Nind and

Hewett began to recognise that the aggressive behaviours of students were a response to situations that students did not understand, and that the students were demonstrating communication difficulties rather than behavioural difficulties:

> We came to the conclusion that these needs were almost always within the realm of communication and sociability and that the existing curriculum rarely even touched upon addressing such needs. We felt that if we could begin to establish a relationship with the students, and if we could establish a basis for communication, then all other spheres of teaching and learning would become easier and more meaningful. (Nind & Hewett, 1994, p. 6)

It was in cognitivism that Nind and Hewett discovered the foundations for an alternative approach to behaviourism. Inspired by Ephraim's (1979) ideas on using "mothering", Nind and Hewett began reading cognitivist literature on caregiver-infant interactions (e.g., Schaffer, 1971a; Trevarthen, 1979). What they found was a model for understanding how communication and sociability developed from birth via interactive play with caregivers. Intensive Interaction thus emerged as an approach that simulates the intricate caregiver-infant interactive sequences as described in the literature. The idea is that if communication partners (e.g., parents, teaching staff, support workers) organise their interactions with people with PMLD in ways that closely resemble typical caregiver-infant interactions, then people with PMLD may progress through the preverbal stages of development and gain increasingly sophisticated cognitive representations of the world (e.g., object permanence and knowledge about cause and effect), as well as social awareness and communication skills (e.g., intersubjectivity, joint attention, and communicative intent) (Nind & Hewett, 2001). Interaction between caregivers and infants is said to form an "implicit pedagogy" (Carlson & Bricker, 1982, cited in Nind & Thomas, 2005, p. 98), meaning that the social interaction develops the abilities of infants without such development being the intended outcome: "It became evident that usually these fundamental abilities are learned in the first year of life without being consciously taught" (Nind & Hewett, 1994, p. 6). Intensive Interaction transforms this implicit pedagogy into an explicit interactive style that can be adopted by those attempting to communicate with people with PMLD.

Interactive style

Descriptions of mother–infant engagement have identified characteristics or "interpersonal behaviours" (Nind & Hewett, 1994, p. 20) said to be salient in typical social interactions. These characteristics inform what Nind and Hewett term an "interactive style" (p. 28), which Intensive Interaction aims to replicate.

Some have described Intensive Interaction as a method of communication (Firth, 2006; Moore, 2008). However, there is no one way to undertake Intensive Interaction, since the nature of the interaction is contingent upon the abilities of the person with learning difficulties (e.g., sensory abilities, mobility abilities, cognitive abilities, etc.). Thus, Intensive Interaction cannot be described in a simple, formulaic way. It is perhaps more accurate to describe it as a style of social interaction in which communication partners are engaged in critically reflective thought during their interactions with people with learning difficulties. Or, to use the words of Nind and Thomas (2005), Intensive Interaction is: "a subtle transactional process in which the [communication partner] … continuously uses her abilities to observe, reflect and act with judgement, based on a set of guiding principles" (Nind & Thomas, 2005, p. 98). Intensive Interaction is a name given to this style of reflective communication. Such reflection is supported through a range of educational resources that inform communication partners of the principles of communication (BILD, 2004; Hewett, 1996; Nind & Hewett, 1994; 2001). These resources work by making explicit what is implicit—that is, by foregrounding the intuitive principles of communication, which are presupposed during social interaction. Such foregrounding breaks naturalistic interactive processes (which are normally unified wholes) into constituent components. This in turn provides communication partners with a range of components that they can identify as either missing or broken. Whilst a "missing" component is a component not present during interaction (e.g., no turn-taking), a "broken" component is a component that is not functioning as it should be (e.g., pauses intended to signal an appropriate turn taking place may be too short, which in turn fails to afford the person with learning difficulties opportunity to respond). The foregrounding of these components provides communication partners with a framework for critical reflection.

The following section will demonstrate how descriptions of this interactive style of Intensive Interaction have been informed by the prominent psychologists described in the first part of the chapter, and also illuminate how this in turn has shaped how Intensive Interaction literature guides communication partners to engage with people who have PMLD. The aim is not to provide a complete and accessible overview of Intensive Interaction (for this we refer readers to Nind and Hewett's (2001) *A Practical Guide to Intensive Interaction*). Rather, we are interested in demonstrating how psychological lenses have informed the development of the Intensive Interaction methodology—which we ourselves apply to social interaction research data in Chapter Six.

Intentionality

> To the parent the behaviour of even the youngest baby has communicative force: a cry, a smile, a shift in posture, a gaze in a particular direction—each may provide the mother with some information as to the infant's state and condition and cause her to react in some appropriate way. Whether the infant's response should indeed be labelled "communicative" is a matter of definition, but there are those who consider the term appropriate only when the sender is behaving in a clearly intentional manner, and this hardly applies to the infant's behaviour in the early months of life. (Schaffer, 1984, p. 118)

For Schaffer (1984), the first signs of intentional communication emerge near the end of the first year of life. Early interactions between caregivers and infants are only thought to be sustained because the caregiver responds to infants' immature reflexes as if they had communicative significance (Schaffer, 1977a). These caregiver responses are labelled by Nind and Hewett (1994) as "intentionality" (p. 21). Infants learn to be social when caregivers assume that infant behaviour is intended to convey meaning and they respond in kind: "intentionality helps infants to learn that dialogues are two-sided and that they themselves have a role to play" (p. 22). Thus, an important part of Intensive Interaction is responding to behaviours of people with PMLD as if they were intentional, as Nind and Hewett (2001) suggest: "Respond deliberately to something the person does which isn't intentionally a communication, as if it was a communication. By doing this regularly, you help them to realise that they can have an effect and cause you to respond" (p. 46). Intentionality is a core component of Intensive Interaction and is something practitioners are encouraged to replicate (i.e., by behaving towards people with PMLD as if their pre-intentional behaviours were intentionally communicative):

> [I]ntentionality is one of the principles which should quickly be generalised to the wider environment around the student/client. Thus staff can be causally, incidentally responsive to things which the learner does, at any stage of the day. Sometimes this may cause an interaction sequence to get going and lift off. For the learner, there will be the rewarding experience of having initiated an incidental sequence by producing a behaviour which brought about a meaningful response, and then further interaction. (p. 120)

Even if this does not happen, Nind and Hewett (1994) explain that the Intensive Interaction practitioner "can arrive at a happy situation" (p. 121) where the practitioner and person with PMLD engage with one another through an exchange of noises—even if the noises produced by the person with PMLD were not intended to convey meaning.

Imitation

According to Schaffer (1984), there is little evidence that infants imitate others before they reach nine months of age. The first step in the development of infant imitation is the caregiver imitating the infant: "from birth on mothers [and other caregivers] reflect back to their infants' gestures and vocalizations which occur spontaneously in the baby's behaviour, selecting those which they can endow with some communicative significance" (p. 122). Thus, imitation can be part of intentionality as a strategy for developing deliberate communication in the developing infant. Schaffer, (1977b) emphasises the dialogue-like nature of imitative interactions: "early interaction sequences generally begin with the infant's own spontaneous behaviour ... the mother then chimes in to support, repeat, comment upon and elaborate his [or her] response (p. 12). Nind and Hewett (1994) explain that imitation offers a good way of celebrating episodes of another person's behaviour. Nind and Hewett (1994) illuminate the role of imitation in Intensive Interaction by describing an interactive exchange between Marion (somebody with severe to profound and multiple learning disabilities") and Lin (her communication partner):

> [T]he imitation Lin uses of Marion's side-to-side head movement is a familiar routine for both of them. In the early stages it was a core part of the interactions for them, one of Marion's visible behaviours which the staff could celebrate and join in with. Through this early focus on using imitation or modified reflecting ... Marion was able to start learning more about effective communication and social activities. This initial activity enabled Lin and several other members of staff to be increasingly tuned in and available to her. At this later stage, things have moved on and there is a far wider repertoire of activities in the sequences. The use of that early imitation activity is still there, but no longer forms the main focus of an interaction. Rather, it is something which happens almost in passing or else is happening as well as several other things. (p. 126)

The role of touch and interactional flows

Nind and Hewett (1994) also take from Schaffer the need for physical contact in communication (Schaffer & Emerson, 1964) and the back-and-forth rhythm or flow of social interaction (Schaffer, 1977a). Physical contact in Intensive Interaction has been described as "inevitable" when interacting with people with limited understanding (Nind & Hewett, 1994, p. 129), assuming consent has been sought. It is "an enjoyable, natural, irreplaceable aspect of communication with a person who does not use language" (p. 130).

> During Intensive Interaction sequences, physical contact of all sorts may be the central focus for what is happening. It may also be a way of commenting on something else which is happening as the central focus. It may be just one of the incidental things which happen throughout the activity. Physical contact also makes good punctuation—'holding' a pause for instance, literally by means of a gentle hold. A sudden touch can be a way of providing new stimulus during a pause. (p. 133)

With regards to the interactional flows, Nind and Hewett (1994) note the importance of the timing within interactions: "The activity of the caregivers and infant is often synchronised, sharing a common rhythm" (p. 27). Summarising Schaffer (1977a), Nind and Hewett (1994) describe how the caregiver is involved in "elaborately interweaving her behavioural flow with that of her infant, allowing herself to be paced by the infant, watching and waiting and holding herself ready in an 'exquisite sense of timing'" (p. 23). Again, replication of this timing is something aimed at during Intensive Interaction.

Mutual pleasure

From Trevarthen (1979), Nind and Hewett (1994) take the idea that infant-caregiver interaction involves mutual pleasure: "Intrinsic and crucial to caregiver-infant interactions is the element of mutual pleasure. This is effectively what the interactions are all about" (p. 23). Some of this pleasure revolves around interpersonal games such as "pat-a-cake" and "peek-a-boo", which provide the infant with a pleasurable way of learning about the conversational rules, for example that both parties are referring to the same topic of conversation (joint reference) and taking turns (turn taking). Mutual enjoyment helps the developing infant and the person with PMLD feel relaxed and secure, whilst enabling the content and activity of the interaction to be interesting and motivating. This means that people will want to come back for more.

Responsive environments

Response environments (Ware, 2003)—referred to previously as contingency sensitive environments (Ware, 1994)—are contexts such as classrooms that provide responses to the actions of people with PMLD. Ware (2003) explains that "There are two ways in which people receive responses to their actions: from other people, and from seeing things happen as a result of what they do" (p. 1). Like Coupe O'Kane and Goldbart (1998), and Nind and Hewett (1994, 2001), Ware (2003) draws from research into how intentional communication emerges during sustained interactions between parents and their infants (Murray & Trevarthen, 1986; Schaffer & Liddell, 1984). Ware (2003) notes that infants learn to communicate by being treated as if their actions had meaning—that is, when adults respond to them "as if they had something important to say" (p. 3). Infants who experience this type of responsiveness from parents are said to engage in more social interaction, make faster cognitive gains, and become "social beings" (p. 3) more quickly. As described above, Nind and Hewett (1994; 2001) identified the interactive style of parents and infants, and developed literature to support adults working with people with PMLD to replicate aspects of this style. Whilst Ware (2003) shares Nind and Hewett's (1994; 2001) interest in parents' interactive style, she differentiates between her approach and Intensive Interaction in the following way:

> Where our work differs from that of other investigators who appear to have been thinking along very similar lines at the same time [e.g., Nind & Hewett, 1988] is that we have been concerned not with providing specific sessions of one-to-one 'interaction' [Intensive Interaction], but with all the interactions which go on in the normal course of a classroom day (during physiotherapy, drinks, and so on). We have therefore concentrated our efforts on the structure of interaction and not the content. Our contention is that pupils can be given time to respond regardless of the content of the interaction ... (Ware, 1994, p. 130)

The essential point here is that environments for people with PMLD should be consistently responsive throughout the day. Responsive environments for people with PMLD can be broken down into three types of response: (1) the person with PMLD receives responses from the environment that are contingent upon his or her actions; (2) the person with PMLD is given opportunities to respond to the actions of others; (3) the person with PMLD is given opportunities to take the lead in interaction.

Each of these response types will be briefly described.

Responding to people's behaviour

The first principle of Ware's (2003) responsive environment involves consistent and contingent responding to behaviours considered pre-intentional communication and possibly non-volitional or reflexive. The aim here is to support the emergence of contingency awareness (i.e., awareness of cause-effect relations, including the recognition by the person with PMLD that his /her actions have an effect on the world).

Ware (2003) explains how, in the absence of meaningful behaviours, an adult can take any behaviour that the person with PMLD produces and attribute meaning to it. The behaviour may be treated as a response to something the adult has said or done, or as a new initiation on the part of the person with PMLD. Once the person with PMLD develops a range of voluntary behaviours aimed at him or herself or at the environment, some way of selecting those that provide the most useful focus for development is required. In this context, the following "rules of thumb" are said to be useful. Ware (2003) recommends responding to target behaviours that can easily be developed into conventional communication, such as vocalisations that might develop into speech, or arm and hand movements that could develop into signs. These behaviours should be easy to observe, so they are more likely to attract a high rate of responses in busy situations. Further, they should be behaviours that occur regularly so there are plenty of opportunities for responding to them.

Starting a conversation, giving the person a chance to reply

The second principle of Ware's (2003) responsive environment involves ways of starting an interaction with a person with PMLD, and affording him/her opportunities to respond to what the adult does. This principle presupposes the development of intentional behaviour and contingency awareness. Central to the initiation of social interaction is the person's readiness to interact. Ware (2003) explains that people with PMLD have a significantly limited capacity for attention owing to the fact that they "function at an extremely early developmental level" (p. 56). She suggests that people with PMLD may only spend ten minutes each hour in a state of alertness, and suggests that adults learn to identify idiosyncratic signs that the person with PMLD is in optimal states of alertness. These behaviours range from simply being awake to unique listening postures and orienting to stimuli. Difficulty in gaining attention is said to be exacerbated by sensory impairments (which make efforts to attract the attention of people with PMLD less obvious) and self-stimulatory behaviours. Once behaviours/postures indicative of attentive state have been identified, the next stage is to attract this attention. Everyday strategies (such as a polite cough) are said to be ineffective for people with PMLD, since such strategies contain elements of social learning. Where no such learning has taken place, Ware (2003) suggests strategies that are used by parents during interactions with infants. Such strategies include exaggerated facial expression, calling the name of the person with PMLD, touching the person being addressing (e.g., squeezing his/her hand or stroking an arm), and making eye contact. Once attention has been gained, the next stage is to hold on to it. Ware (2003) explains that holding attention is especially problematic if the adult lacks sensitivity to the communication needs of the person with PMLD:

> [T]he exceptional slowness with which a person with PMLD may respond, and the likelihood that they will not respond as consistently as someone without difficulties, leads to an expectation that they are unlikely to respond. The other participant in the conversation may then start to behave as if they are not expecting a response and to assume a more and more dominant role in the interaction. As a consequence, fewer and fewer opportunities are provided for the person with PMLD to respond. (p. 61)

Ware (2003) discusses ways of breaking this "vicious circle" (ibid.) which involves the adult altering his or her behaviour in order to give the person with PMLD more opportunities to respond. Most examples involve the use of pause (after an adults says or does something), which is said to act as a signal for the person with PMLD that it is his/her turn to respond. Ware (2003) recommends using prolonged pauses in case it takes longer than average for the person to respond. Additionally, pauses are said to be best when accompanied by other acts, such as eye contact, vocal cadence cue, and smiles. Knowing how the person responds is also important.

Having the opportunity to take the lead in interaction

The third and final principle of developing a sensitive environment is for an adult to formulate ways of sharing control in social interactions with the person with PMLD—that is, by allowing him/her to take the lead in interactions.

Drawing from the cognitivist literature, Ware (2003) explains that parents attribute meaning to all sorts of behaviours that are not intended to be communicative. These behaviours as accepted as the infant's contributions to social interaction. Additionally, parents are said to structure their own conversational turn so that it is both a response to what the infant has just done and an invitation to the infant to make another response. Responsive environments attempt to simulate this structure. Ware (2003) refers to such simulations as "turnabouts" (p. 70). If an adult receives no response from the person with PMLD, she/he proceeds to pretend that the person has taken a turn by filling in the turn for them. Turnabouts can be used to continue the social interaction, not only after the person has responded to the adult's initiation, but also in response to any behaviour from the person that can be interpreted by the adult as an initiation. Anything a person does can be taken as a response, from waving his or her arms to yawning. This should lead to a response from the adult. By following the person's behavioural repertoire, the adult gives the person control of the interaction.

Responsive environments and the cognitivist tradition

Ware (2003) makes less reference to the cognitivist literature compared to Coupe O'Kane and Goldbart (1998) and Nind and Hewett (1994). However, there are clear parallels between the theoretical underpinnings of responsive environments and the theories that inform the early communication assessment and Intensive Interaction. For example, Ware (2003) draws comparison between people with PMLD and infants insofar as she describes people with PMLD as being developmentally delayed to the extent that they have not passed through the preverbal stages of development. Infants and people with PMLD are said to pass through these stages when adults respond to non-communicative behaviours as if they were forms of intentional communication. This way of responding has been described throughout this chapter and has been labelled in different ways. For example, Bates et al. (1975) labelled such responsiveness as "perlocutionary communication" (p. 212), Coupe O'Kane and Goldbart (1998) use the term "pre-intentional communication" (p. 11), and Nind and Hewett (1994; 2001) follow Schaffer (1984), who labels it "intentionality" (p. 118). When adults respond to infants and people with PMLD in this manner, they are said to contribute to infants' achievement of developmental milestones leading up to the development of communicative intent. Ware (2003) identifies a sequence of behaviours leading up to communication: (1) The infant develops control over their own movements and acts voluntarily, though these actions are not directed towards anything in the environment; (2) the infant begins to respond to the environment, such as looking out of the window or smiling at people walking past; (3) the infant engages in purposeful, goal-directed behaviour, such as playing with a toy; (4) the infant engages in intentional communication—that is, by reaching out to others in order to attract their attention. This sequence resembles Coupe O'Kane and Goldbart's (1998) early communication assessment (which describes steps from pre-intentional to intentional communication). However, there is one important difference. Coupe O'Kane and Goldbart (1998) use proto-imperatives and proto-declaratives as examples of the earliest form of intentional communication (Bate et al., 1975). Whilst Ware (2003) includes these performatives as early examples of communicative intent, she also adds that "Much communication is not of this type, but is participated in for its own sake" (p. 18). On one level this implies that infants can respond to the social environment by smiling at people walking past and making eye contact. On another level it implies that infants develop the ability to initiate social interaction, perhaps by crawling toward an adult, climbing onto his or her lap and engaging in playful interactions involving the kind of skills that Nind and Hewett (1994; 2001) hope to instil in people learning Intensive Interaction. Thus, there are important parallels between the early communication assessment, Intensive Interaction and sensitive environments, and these parallels have been influenced by findings in the cognitivist literature.

Chapter summary

In this chapter we explored how cognitivism—as the alternative to behaviourism—guides research and practice for people with PMLD. We used the term "people" with PMLD because it is consistent with the literature we reviewed. However, when researchers informed by cognitivism refer to people with PMLD they typically mean children and young people in classroom contexts. We began by describing how cognitivism observes behaviour in order to theorise how the world is symbolically represented in the mind. Infants are born with structures that enable basic representation of the world, and these structures become increasingly sophisticated during infants' interaction with the world. We noted that debates exist in psychology regarding the abilities of infants to represent other people as subjects rather than objects (intersubjectivity).

We described the work of different psychologists to illuminate different perspectives on the nature of infant development. We explored how Schaffer (1971a) conceptualises infants as "asocial being[s]" (p. 13) until they learn to discriminate between people and objects through perceptual learning. Perceptual learning, or imprinting, involves repeated exposure to objects in the world, which are eventually coded in the brain as reoccurring neuronal patterns. This patterning allows infants to recognise people as familiar. For Schaffer (1971a), this process of imprinting leads infants to develop intersubjective awareness about nine to twelve months after birth.

By contrast, Trevarthen and Aitken (2001) conceptualise infants as having an innate intersubjective awareness and ability to communicate. This innate intersubjectivity is labelled primary subjectivity and involves infants becoming aware of others through sustained "proto-conversations" (p. 6). These protoconversations involve infants moving in predictable response cycles to the behaviour of adults. The response cycles include vocalisation, expressive hand movements, facial looking, and mimicking. Through the response cycles, infants are said to share control of the interaction, experience emotional mutuality, and anticipate responses. Around nine to twelvemonths after birth infants are said to develop secondary intersubjectivity or joint attention. They engage with other people using objects and share their regard.

Bates et al. (1975) describe different stages involved in the emergence of symbolic communication. Infants begin at the perlocutionary stage, meaning that their behaviours (such as crying) cause an effect on the environment (parents respond to crying as a signal to feed) even though the infant did not intend to cause such an effect. Next there is the illocutionary stage during which infants intentionally use non-verbal means to direct the attention of others. At this stage infants commonly use proto-imperative and proto-declarative behaviours. Proto-imperatives involve infants using adults as the means to a desired object (e.g., pointing to the cookie jar in order to obtain a cookie from the adult). Proto-imperative behaviours involve infants using objects to direct the attention of adults (e.g., pointing to a bird in the garden to share the experience of the bird with the adult). Finally, there is the locutionary stage, which involves spoken language. Utterances replace pointing gestures.

After describing the work of Schaffer (1971a), Trevarthen and Aitken (2001), and Bates et al. (1975), we illuminated how such work (as well as other publications from the same psychologists) has shaped assessment and intervention strategies for people with PMLD. Specifically, we looked at how the early communication assessment (Coupe O'Kane & Goldbart, 1998), Intensive Interaction (Nind & Hewett, 1988; 1994; 2001) and responsive environments (Ware, 2003) were influenced by the concepts derived from the above psychologists. What unfolds through this description is the realisation that these assessment and intervention strategies adopt a particular perspective regarding the nature of people with PMLD. Whilst the researchers cite the works of cognitive psychologists on each side of the debate regarding the intersubjective awareness and communicative abilities of infants, the researchers lean towards Schaffer (1971a) and Bates et al. (1975) and presuppose that people with PMLD—conceptualised as experiencing profound developmental delay and thus having the same representational capacity as infants—exist in a pre-intersubjective, pre-symbolic and hence pre-intentional state.

In Chapter Six we will revisit these concepts by applying them to data in order to test their explanatory power. However, before this takes place we will introduce an alternative approach to thinking about the nature of consciousness, cognition and behaviour (as they relate to children with PMLD) in the form of Merleau-Ponty's (1963; 2002) phenomenology. To date, no researcher has applied phenomenology as a lens for thinking about people with PMLD. As such, the discussion about to be presented is the first of its kind. Since the focus of this book is specifically about *children* with PMLD we will use the term "children" instead of "people" in the remaining chapters. We will revisit the themes discussed in the behaviourist and cognitivist chapters but our concern will be with how these themes relate to children in classroom contexts.

CHAPTER FOUR

Phenomenology

Part I

Summary of phenomenological theory

What is phenomenology?

Phenomenology is part of the basis for what has become known as continental philosophy, where "continental" means the European continent (Gallagher & Zahavi, 2008). Phenomenology is the descriptive study of the structures of consciousness as experienced from the first-person point of view, along with the relevant contents and conditions of that experience (Woodruff Smith, 2008). Translated literally, phenomenology means the "science of phenomena" (Moran, 2002, p. 4, italics omitted), "phenomena" here meaning: "the appearance of things, or things as they appear in our experience, or the ways we experience things, thus the meanings things have in our experience" (Woodruff Smith, 2008, p. 1). Phenomenology does not focus on what appears but on how it appears (Lewis & Staehler, 2010); it is concerned with studying the structure of appearing (Moran, 2002).

The natural attitude

Moran (2000) explains how the founding father of phenomenology, Edmund Husserl (1859–1938), believed that the examination or inspection of the structure and contents of our conscious experience was deeply distorted by the normal manner of our engagement with experience in ordinary life. Husserl believed that our folk assumptions and scientific knowledge limited a pure analysis of experience as it is given to us. The combination of factors that contributed to this limitation led to what Husserl referred to as "the natural attitude" (Moran & Mooney, 2002, p. 5). It is said that the natural attitude conceals the manner in which the normal world is constituted. To prevent the natural attitude from clouding analysis of the structures of our own conscious awareness, Husserl proposed that we "bracket" (Moran, 2000, p. 11), "suspend" (Gallagher & Zahavi, 2008, p. 6), put out of play, or detach ourselves from all scientific, philosophical, cultural and everyday assumptions so as to allow access to the central features of phenomena under question. Husserl's (1964) maxim for phenomenology was: "Back to things themselves!" (Husserl, 1964, in Gallagher & Zahavi, 2008, p. 6). By this, Husserl (1964) meant that phenomenology should base its analysis on the way things are experienced, rather than on theoretical concerns, which are said to obscure and distort what is understood (Gallagher & Zahavi, 2008). Hence, phenomenology attempts to be "presuppositionless" (Moran, 2000, p. 6, italics omitted). As Moran and Mooney (2002) summarise:

> Phenomenology is usually characterised as a way of seeing rather than a set of doctrines. ... This approach involves the practice of taking a fresh *unprejudiced* look—i.e. untainted by scientific, metaphysical, religious or cultural presuppositions or attitudes—at the fundamental and essential features of human experience in and of the world. (p. 1)

The act of becoming presuppositionless, of suspending or bracketing the natural attitude, was said to allow for the examination of a pregiven world, what Husserl referred to as the "life-world" (*Lebenswelt*).

The life-world

Description of the life-world is often the starting point of phenomenology (Matthews, 2006). The concept of the life-world was introduced by Husserl (1970) to elucidate what he described as a crisis afflicting the natural sciences. This crisis was caused by science forgetting the life-world as the basis for all scientific activity (Lewis & Staehler, 2010). As Merleau-Ponty (2002) noted:

> The whole universe of science is built upon the world as directly experienced, and if we want to subject science itself to rigorous scrutiny and arrive at a precise assessment of its meaning and scope, we must begin by reawakening the basic experience of the world of which science is the second-order expression. (p. ix)

- The life-world in the narrow sense

The concept of the life-world is somewhat elusive because Husserl (1970) offered several different descriptions of what it could be. One useful way of thinking about this is to see the different concepts evolving out of each other, thus reflecting different stages of Husserl's (1970) reflections on science (Zelic, 2008). With this in mind, Lewis and Staehler (2010) offer a preliminary or "narrow" definition of the life-world as "the pre- and non-scientific world as it is encountered in simple sensuous intuition" (p. 34). In this context, intuition refers to "a direct, non-conceptual access to things, one which receives them purely, without any interpretation. It is a direct contact with the thing itself" (ibid, p. 6). The life-world defined in this way is our raw experience of the world without such experience being filtered through a scientific lens (Cerbone, 2006; Langdridge, 2007).

The world of science that Husserl (1970) contrasts to the life-world is one of abstraction. Sokolowski (2000) describes this abstraction as a product of the mathematisation of science stemming from the work of Galileo (1564–1642), Descartes (1596–1650), and Newton (1642–1727). This form of science led people to think that the world of everyday experience consisted of secondary qualities, and that the real world was that described by science. "What looks like a table is really a conglomerate of atoms, fields of force, and empty spaces" (p. 146). Merleau-Ponty (1963) identifies how this abstraction is found in the science of behaviour and perception.

> The scientific analysis of behavior was defined first in opposition to the givens of naive consciousness. If I am in a dark room and a

luminous spot appears on the wall and moves along it, I would say that it has "attracted" my attention, that I have turned my eyes "toward" it and that in all its movements it "pulls" my regard along with it. ... Science seems to demand that we reject these characteristics as appearances under which a reality of another kind must be discovered. It will be said that seen light is "only in us." It covers a vibratory movement, which movement is never given to consciousness. Let us call the qualitative appearance, "phenomenal light"; the vibratory movement, "real light." Since the real is never perceived, it could not present itself as a goal toward which my behavior is directed. (p. 7)

For Sokolowski (2000), the concept of the life-world emerged as a response to modern science. Before the advent of modern science people thought that the world they experienced and lived in was the only world there was. Hence, premodern science tried to describe the familiar world and did not claim to find a substitute for it. "The problem of how we should interpret the world in which we live—whether we should take it as valid and trustworthy, or purely subjective and unscientific—comes to the fore in response to modern science" (p. 147). Phenomenology tackles the objective description of the world (its atoms, fields of forces, and empty spaces) by showing that science takes its origin from the life-world. Thus, Husserl (1970) accords the life-world the place of perceptual primacy.

- The life-world in the broad sense

Husserl's (1970) mature concept of the life-world went beyond simple, sensible intuition toward a dynamic and culturally situated concept of experience. As Lewis and Staehler (2010) explain:

> The lifeworld in the wide sense is much more than a mere pre- and non-scientific world; as the all-encompassing, concrete world of our life or our universal horizon, it includes the sciences as well. The lifeworld in the encompassing and genuine sense is the historical world which contains nature as well as culture. (p. 40)

Thompson (2007) explains that nature described by science cannot be experienced directly because it is an abstraction or idealisation. At the same time, scientific items such as propositions, models, logical constructs and techniques are experienceable in a different sense for "they are human accomplishments that have experiential validity for members of the scientific community, and their effects flow into the everyday world and become tangibly experienced in the form of technology and social practice" (p. 34). Hence, for Thompson (2007), whilst science emerges from the life-world insofar as our everyday experience provides the "sensuous, material contents from which and with which science must work" (ibid.), science also feeds into the life-world and shapes our immediate experiences and meanings of such sensuous material. The same is said of art, philosophy, and religion—these second-order expressions turn back upon the life-world and become part of it (Varela et al., 1991).

Romdenh-Romluc's (2011) example of cultural shifts in perceptual significance highlights this circulation between culture and experience. A key theme in phenomenology (which will be discussed in more depth later in the chapter) is that perception is immediately loaded with significance, insofar as the presentation of a situation is intertwined with meaning. Romdehn-Romluc (2011) explains that "If I see someone kicking a dog, I literally perceive this act as morally reprehensible. I do not judge the act as wrong; I experience its wrongness. Similarly, a rotting carcass literally looks disgusting. A sunset literally appears beautiful" (p. 13). We do not have to think about whether or not something is wrong, disgusting, or beautiful—it just appears that way. Furthermore, this significance is said to be culture-relative insofar as different societies have different conceptions of what beauty is or what is morally acceptable, and these are bound up with the way the world appears to them. "The woman whom Renaissance people would have seen as beautiful and sexually alluring appears overweight and unattractive to people living in modern Western society" (p. 14). This is one example of the historically and culturally situated sense of the life-world, but it can be argued that there are different meanings that exist not across cultures but also within them. Thus, beauty can be relative to the perceiver, even to members in modern Western society.

Exploration of the life-world in this chapter

In this book we are interested in the double meaning of the life-world described above (the narrow and broad conceptions). First, we are interested in how phenomenology affords an alternative way of thinking about the experiences and agency of children with PMLD. To these ends we explore Merleau-Ponty's (2002) take on how the life-world is shaped by the nature of human embodiment. Morris (2012) equates Merleau-Ponty's (2002) notion of "phenomenal field" (p. 60) with the life-world. The phenomenal field is "what we discover by going beyond the prejudice of the objective world" (p. 67). This discovery entails the realisation that experience is immediately loaded with motor intentionality or "practical significances" (Morris, 2012, p. 41) that play beneath any overt sense of cognition. In this chapter we explore Merleau-Ponty's (2002) key concepts that relate the role of the body to the formation of the phenomenal field. In particular, we explore Merleau-Ponty's (2002) core notions of "pre-objective" experience (p. 281), "being-in-the-world" (p. 90), "corporeal schema" (p. 164), "body at this moment" (p. 95), and the "habit-body" (ibid.). This leads us to an understanding of the life-world in the narrow sense insofar as it is articulates a pre-theoretical and culture-free notion. In Chapter Six we apply these concepts as a framework to empirical data pertaining to the educational inclusion of a young boy with PMLD (Sam). We do this in order to "test" the extent to which a phenomenological lens leads to new reading of Sam's actions.

In the final chapter we explore the life-world in the broader sense to explicate the relationship between the methodology described in Chapter Five and the data reported in Chapter Six. Whilst the methodology was not "phenomenological" we can still use phenomenology to help us theorise how intimate ways of working with children with PMLD over time can lead to "tacit" understandings, which resist and make ambiguous the concepts we take for granted derived from psychology (the abstract scientific schematisations, such as models of behaviour, cognition, and communication described in Chapters Two and Three). Phenomenology helps us theorise this process even though it was not the original guiding principle—working intimately with children with PMLD can be thought of in phenomenological terms to sensitise us to how this process works.

Why phenomenology?

Phenomenology provides a counter-paradigm to the dominant positions used to understand children with PMLD: behaviourism and cognitivism. It is radically opposed to behaviourism (e.g., Skinner, 1986;

Watson, 1913), which privileges observable behaviour at the expense of descriptions of experience. Phenomenology is also critical of cognitivist accounts of the mind, which theorise knowledge in terms of an inner mental representation, or a copy of what exists outside the mind (e.g., Schaffer, 1971a). Phenomenology attempts to pay close attention to the nature of experience as it is actually experienced, not as it is understood by psychological descriptions of the mind or further scientific abstractions. Thus, where cognitivism is informed by specific theories of mind, phenomenology rejects such theoretical starting points and "seeks to be critical and non-dogmatic, shunning metaphysical and theoretical prejudices as much as possible" (Gallagher & Zahavi, 2008, p. 10). Phenomenology seeks to be guided by experience itself, as opposed to what we expect to find in experience given our theoretical commitments: "It asks us not to let preconceived theories form our experience, but to let our experience inform and guide our theories" (ibid.). By going back from the objective towards the pre-objective, by bracketing our theoretical commitments in a radical attempt to articulate and describe the pre-theoretical life-world, phenomenology can offer an account of conscious experience that understands objectivity as emergent from subjectivity. By shunning theoretical commitments and situating our thoughts within phenomenological description of experience, we are offered an alternative way of thinking about consciousness in children with PMLD. In doing so, it has the potential to offer a frame of reference and description that goes beneath the objective accounts of subjectivity offered by psychology by describing the pre-objective dimension of experience, which stems from the integration of the subject in the world. This pre-objective dimension is a new concept to the PMLD literature. This chapter explores the meaning of this dimension in more depth to illuminate the ways in which it can offer alternative ways of thinking about children with PMLD.

Why Merleau-Ponty's phenomenology?

Merleau-Ponty (2002) has contributed the most to developing understandings about the way in which our embodiment is the condition of our relation to the world, which in turn shapes the structure of our conscious experience (Carman, 2008; Dillon, 1997; Moran, 2000; Smith, 2007a). As such, it is Merleau-Ponty's (2002) work that lends itself to reconceptualising the actions of children with PMLD. For Merleau-Ponty

(2002), perception is essentially a bodily phenomenon. It is argued that perception is not a private mental state, nor is the body just another material object set alongside other objects. As Carman (2008) notes: "We lose sight of perception itself when we place it on either side of a sharp distinction between inner subjective experiences and external objective facts" (p. 78). Perception is said to manifest itself as an aspect of our bodily being-in-the-world. Merleau-Ponty (2002) thus cuts across the traditional philosophical dichotomies of interior-exterior, mind-body and subjective-objective by arguing that perception is intentional *and* bodily as well as sensory *and* motor. Moreover, not only does Merleau-Ponty (2002) describe how the mind and body relate, he situates the embodied mind in the world as a necessary and irreducible precondition of conscious awareness, and in doing so suggests an ecological account of embodied cognition:

> Insofar as, when I reflect on the essence of subjectivity, I find it bound up with that of the body and that of the world, this is because my existence as subjectivity is merely one with my existence as a body and with the existence of the world, and because the subject that I am, when taken concretely, is inseparable from this body and this world. (Merleau-Ponty, 2002, p. 475)

Merleau-Ponty's (2002) method of articulating his "bodily point of view" (Carman, 2008, p. 93) consists of comparing and contrasting his view to the dominant understandings of the mind and body at the time of writing, approaches often referred to as "mechanistic physiology" (Merleau-Ponty, 2002, p. 84) and representationalist or "classical psychology" (ibid., p. 103). These approaches resemble those used to understand children with PMLD (discussed in the previous chapters)—that is, behaviourism (which conceives the body as mechanistic object) and cognitivism (which conceives the mind as that which represents objects in the world, such as the body). By providing a detailed reading of how Merleau-Ponty (2002) negotiates his alternative view in relation to mechanistic and representational approaches, this chapter will demonstrate how Merleau-Ponty's (2002) bodily point of view affords alternative ways of thinking about children with PMLD.

To these ends, this chapter is divided into three parts. The first part explicates the way in which Merleau-Ponty's (2002) notions of mechanistic body and representational mind resemble the behaviourist and cognitivist perspectives in the PMLD literature. The first part also discusses some of the challenges to these paradigms. The second part summarises a range of key terms and core concepts that Merleau-Ponty (2002) uses to construct his alternative to the two positions. The third part discusses these terms and concepts in relation to some of Merleau-Ponty's (2002) examples (specifically, examples related to the act of limb substitution in insects, and phantom limb experiences in human beings). Further discussion highlights how these examples point toward a new way of conceptualising the body and explain how such conceptualisation has the power to reconfigure our understandings of children with PMLD.

Part II

Critique of the mechanistic body and representational mind

The body as object

Mechanistic physiology conceptualises the body as an object in the world under the causal influence of environmental stimuli. Merleau-Ponty (2002) describes the body-object in the following way:

> The definition of the object is ... that it exists *partes extra partes*, and that consequently it acknowledges between its parts, or between itself and other objects only external and mechanical relationships, whether in the narrow sense of motion received and transmitted, or in the wider sense of the relation of function to variable. Where it was desired to insert the organism in the universe of objects and thereby close off that universe, it was necessary to translate the functioning of the body into the language of the *in-itself* and discover, beneath behaviour, the linear dependence of stimulus and receptor ... (p. 84)

For Merleau-Ponty (2002), the body as object is an extended or material body. It is also a composite, made up of various constituent parts or elements that can be considered objects in their own right. Where these parts are juxtaposed there is only independent or external existence in which parts exist side by side (*"partes extra partes"*), related to one another deterministically—that is, through sequential surface-to-surface causal contact, a system of matter in motion. The body as a composite of such parts is a machine: "A free-standing physical system whose behavior as a whole is a function of the workings of its individual parts ..." (Carman, 2008, p. 83). Machines, as the sum of their parts, can be analysed in terms of mechanical subsystems. As such, global behaviours can be explained from the bottom up: "as macroscopic systems supervening deterministically on their underlying microstructures" (ibid.). Merleau-Ponty (2002) explains that such understandings reduce the body to an *"in-itself"*, an object that simply "is", an object lacking in consciousness (a *"for-itself"*). The body conceived as an object in-itself situated within a causally closed universe is a body understood as lacking in agency. Behaviour is not volitional (willed action) but a product of forces external to, and outside the control of, the body in-itself. For disciplines that privilege this view of the body, the objective is to discover the "linear dependence" or causal contiguities between stimulus, stimulus-receptor, and behavioural response.

Merleau-Ponty's (2002) explication of the body as object is congruent with the behaviourist view of the body. As discussed in previous chapters, behaviourism is an approach in psychology concerned with the scientific study of observable behaviour. Behaviourism defines behaviour as a non-volitional, reflexive response to environmental stimuli. To quote Gregory and Zangwill (1987) once more, from the perspective of behaviourism: "Our behaviour is the product of our conditioning. We are biological machines and do not consciously act; rather we react to stimuli" (p. 71). The behaviourist research programme is concerned with discovering the lawful linkages between stimulus and response in order to predict and regulate behaviour. Concepts related to mind (e.g., thought or experience) are rejected outright (Baars, 1986; Brennan, 2003; Leahey, 1991; Skinner, 1986; Watson, 1913).

It may be said that researchers who adopt a behaviourist perspective either *wholly* or *largely* objectify children with PMLD. Children with PMLD are *wholly* objectified when no reference to mind is made whatsoever in favour of purely objective descriptions of behaviour and correlative stimuli (Tang et al., 2003). Children with PMLD are *largely* objectified when they are conceptualised as those who lack the ability to comprehend themselves and the world around them, leading to a lack of agency or free will. Where this is the case, the actions of children with PMLD are said to be caused in some way by environmental stimuli. To quote Logan et al. (2001), children with PMLD are said to have:

[L]ittle or no control over their own movements with highly variable response patterns combined with reflexive movements, limited interaction with their environment, inconsistent responses to stimuli, sensory impairments, limited progress in learning new skills, lack of symbolic communication, and total dependence on caregivers for all aspects of daily living. (p. 98)

Behaviourist research typically consists of manipulating environmental variables in order to condition the behaviours of children with PMLD so as to increase indices of desirable behaviours, such as switch-press responses (Lancioni et al., 2005a), or orientation to stimuli conceptualised as reinforcers (Logan & Gast, 2001; Logan et al., 2001). Researchers also attempt to reduce undesired behaviours such as hand-related stereotypies (Lancioni et al., 2009). Internal states are also theorised, and research aims to monitor and invoke desired behaviour states (Guess et al., 1990; Guess et al., 1993) to result in optimal states for conditioning (Mellstrom et al., 2005; Murphy et al., 2004). Finally, behaviourist methodology has also been used to increase happiness and reduce unhappiness (Dillon & Carr, 2007; Green et al., 1997). To relate the underpinnings of these objectives to Merleau-Ponty's (2002) passage cited above, behaviourists assume that the body as object ("for-itself", as opposed to "in-itself", *"partes extra partes"*) stands in simple causal relation ("external and mechanical linear dependence") to other objects in the world ("the universe of objects").

Rejecting the mechanistic model of behaviour central to the body-object

Merleau-Ponty (1963; 2002) challenges the notion of constancy between an environmental stimulus and a reflex response found in mechanistic accounts of behaviour. He does this by calling into question the interrelated concepts of externalism and linear causality presupposed by such accounts.

- The stimulus

For Merleau-Ponty (1963), a stimulus cannot properly be defined as something independent of an organism; "it is not a physical reality, it is a physiological and biological reality" (p. 31). Merleau-Ponty (1963) does not deny the existence of objects in the world (physical reality) but makes the point that it is through the being of the organism that an object comes to exist as a *stimulus* for the organism (physiological and biological reality): "The notion of stimulus refers back to the original activity by which the organism takes in excitations" (ibid.). Merleau-Ponty's (1963) reference to an organism's "original activity" has a double meaning. First, for something to count as a stimulus an organism must be "attuned" to it (Merleau-Ponty, 2002, p. 86). This does not simply mean that organisms are passively receptive to pregiven features of the objective world. Rather, a perceived world is constituted through the embodiment of the organism in the world.

> [T]he form of the excitant is created by the organism itself, by its proper manner of offering itself to actions from the outside. Doubtless, in order to be able to subsist, it must encounter a certain number of physical and chemical agents in its surroundings. But it is the organism itself—according to the proper nature of its receptors, the thresholds of its nerve centers and the movements of the organs—which chooses the stimuli in the physical world to which it will be sensitive. (Merleau-Ponty, 1963, p. 13)

Colour perception provides a good example of an organism's "manner of offering itself". Colour is not an objective quality of the world that exists outside an organism. It is a qualitative experience based on the structure and nature of an organism's visual apparatus integrated with the world. Consequently, different species are said to have different colour experiences.

> Other species ... have evolved different perceived worlds of color on the basis of different cooperative neuronal operations. Indeed, it is fair to say that the neuronal processes underlying human color perception are rather peculiar to the primate group. Most vertebrates (fishes, amphibians, and birds) have quite different and intricate color vision mechanisms. Insects have evolved radically different constitutions associated with their compound eyes. (Varela et al., 1991, p. 181)

Thus, colour is an example of the way the organism and world "gear" in to each other (Merleau-Ponty, 2002, p. 293), and together create a "form" (Merleau-Ponty, 1963, p. 15) or "structural coupling" (Varela et al., 1991, p. 151) through which a world is not simply perceived, but enacted or brought forth. This way of thinking moves away from linear notions of causality (a stimulus causes a response) towards a model of circular causality, whereby a stimulus is constituted rather than pressed upon an organism, and this constitution leads to a personal environment for the organism.

> "The environment (*Umwelt*) emerges from the world through the actualization or the being of the organism—[granted that] an organism can exist only if it succeeds in finding in the world an adequate environment." This would be a keyboard which moves itself in such a way as to offer—and according to variable rhythms—such or such of its keys to the in-itself monotonous action of an external hammer. (Merleau-Ponty, 1963, p. 13)

The second meaning of Merleau-Ponty's (1963) "original activity" referenced above concerns how we conceptualise the observable behaviour of the organism. It can be argued that a stimulus is selected by the organism insofar as its preceding movements expose the organism's sensory organs to the world. For Merleau-Ponty (1963), this requires not empirical proof but a change in how we conceive the stimulus-response relationship.

> When the eye and ear follow an animal in flight, it is impossible to say "which started first" in the exchange of stimuli and responses. Since all the movements of the organism are always conditioned by external influences, one can, if one wishes, readily treat behavior as an effect of the milieu. But in the same way, since all the stimulations which the organism receives have in turn been possible only by its preceding movements which have culminated in exposing the receptor organ to the external influences, one could also say that the behavior is the first cause of all the stimulations. (ibid.)

The above passage draws attention to the way mechanistic accounts of behaviour presuppose linear causality whereby a stimulus causes a response. However, this is a choice—a way of thinking about the relation between two constructs conceptualised as external to each other. Merleau-Ponty (1963) invites us to think differently about the stimulus-response relationship and embeds the idea of a stimulus in the sensorimotor activity of the organism. The *Umwelt*—as a meaningful stimuli "constellation" (Merleau-Ponty, 2002, p. 10)—is brought forth through the actions and agency of the organism. This is an important theme that will be revisited later in the chapter when we describe the meaning of perception with regards to motility. However, before this occurs we will explore Merleau-Ponty's (1963) challenge to the mechanistic idea of a reflex (below), as well as further challenges to traditional understandings of perception.

- The reflex response

Merleau-Ponty (1963) makes problematic the notion of the reflex by challenging the classical notion of the reflex arc (or what is commonly known today as the reflex circuit). The reflex arc is a neural circuit that links a sensory receptor to an effector. An effector is an organ or cell that acts in response to a stimulus. Reflex arcs produce fast responses to specific stimuli. For example, if we put our hand on a hot surface or cut our finger on something sharp we experience a withdrawal reflex, meaning that we quickly move our hand away from the stimulus. In these examples, sensory cells activate the flexor muscles whilst inhibiting neurons to the extensor muscles causing the hand to be withdrawn.

Merleau-Ponty's (1963) critique of the reflex arc revolves around its decontextualised description in classical reflex theory. This decontextualisation results in proponents of the theory overlooking how behaviour is also mediated by a range of processes and conditions inside the body. For Merleau-Ponty (1963), these intraorganic states have just as much causal power as the stimulus itself.

> All reflexes demand the concurrence of a multitude of conditions in the organism external to the reflex arc which have as much right as the "stimulus" to be called causes of the reaction. ... If one forgets to mention, among the antecedents of the reflex, those which are internal to the organism, it is because they are most frequently conjoined at the critical moment. (p. 17)

Merleau-Ponty (1963) draws from diverse studies of animal and human biology to argue that the reflex arc is under the influence of "chemical, secretory and vegetative conditions" (ibid.), which are said to exercise enough power to cancel and even reverse the expected reaction to a certain stimulus. Under different conditions, one stimulus can elicit different reflexes whilst the same reflex can be elicited by different stimuli.

The same stimulation on the arm of a starfish evokes a movement toward the stimulated side if the arm is extended on a horizontal plane and, in contrast, a uniform movement toward the tautest side if the arm is hanging down. In man, a blow under the kneecap provokes a reaction of extension if the leg involved is crossed over the other, a reaction of flexion if it is passively extended. The extract of the pituitary evokes inverse reactions of the uterus depending on whether a woman is pregnant or not. The excitation of the vagus nerve has opposite effects depending on whether the cardia is contracted or dilated at the moment considered. (pp. 22–23)

Merleau-Ponty (1963) offers other examples too. The muscular contractions required to reach an itchy spot on the body can be very different depending on where the hand is originally positioned and what it is doing (e.g., on whether the hand is extended to the right or left). It may be that we are unable to reach a spot on our back so we try different manoeuvres or perhaps find an object to scratch with. Similarly, "It has been shown that a baby holding a pencil in its hand puts it back in its mouth six times successively even if it was pushed away in a different direction each time" (p. 36).

The above examples concern the immediate adaptation of a reflex with regards to space occupied by the body. Merleau-Ponty (1963) also offers an example where the reflex is adapted to external space. A blindfolded person asked to walk backwards can also travel across the traversed space by walking forwards or even sideways. The steps taken can be small or large. The movements across the space are described as "incommensurable" (p. 29), since both the direction of walking and the steps are modified. And yet, the same space is traversed without the stimulus-response constancy. It may be tempting to say intelligence intervenes, but Merleau-Ponty (1963) rejects this notion. If somebody points to an object with their right hand then is blindfolded and asked to point to the same object with their left hand, or indicate its position with head gesture, the person can do so immediately without an act of judgement.

> [I]intelligence, if it intervened, would in this case have to accomplish an extremely long task, and one which I do not even suspect before having reflected on it. It would be necessary to determine the position of my right arm in relation to a system of coordinates and

to calculate the position that my left arm should occupy in relation to the same system in order to designate the direction of the same object. In fact, I possess the conclusions without the premises being given anywhere. (pp. 29–30)

The examples given above are executed without reflection on the tasks at hand; they appear to be performed without knowledge. This is because, as Merleau-Ponty (1963) notes, "There is something *general* in our reflex responses which precisely permits these effector substitutions" (p. 30). Thus, when the blindfolded subject walks backwards it is not simply a question of there being an imprint of the muscle contractions performed. Instead, the movement is registered in the nervous system as a "global form" (ibid.) of traversed space, which is then instantly translatable into steps of a different size and direction.

Thus, for Merleau-Ponty (1963) a reflex response cannot be defined as something under the control of external environmental stimuli. The stimuli is created by the integration of the organism in the world and the action is not caused in the sense that one stimulus results in one response. Instead, there is functional flexibility. Merleau-Ponty's (2002) account of behaviour is interwoven with his account of meaningful perception. As such, we will describe Merleau-Ponty's challenge to the notion of "sensation", which is said to be caused by a stimulus impacting upon the mind. This challenges the cognitivist approach found in research literature about children with PMLD. This in turn will lead to more critical discussion of Merleau-Ponty's (1963; 2002) ideas as they relate to new ways of thinking about children with PMLD.

The representationalist mind

The notion of linear dependence between stimulus and response finds its way into descriptions of the mechanics of perception. The realist or "empiricist" (Merleau-Ponty, 2002, p. 27) view of perception takes perception to be a process of becoming aware of a pre-given, independent reality or an objective world by assembling constituent elements in experience. The world is said to produce in consciousness the corresponding presentations by way of causal interaction with the subject (Macann, 1993).

Central to the empiricist account of perception is the notion of "sensation" as the most basic unit of experience (Merleau-Ponty, 2002, p. 3). Carman (2008) notes that Merleau-Ponty's (2002) rejection of the "sensation" as the most basic unit of experience is not the rejection of our everyday understanding of sensation, which means "feeling". Instead, Merleau-Ponty (2002) rejects the technical use of the term derived from atomistic philosophy. Atomism is the view that complex wholes can be reduced to distinct, separable and independent components, or "atoms". The opposite of atomism is holism, a position that views certain wholes as being greater than their sum of anatomical parts (Brennan, 2004; Leahey, 1991; Robinson, 1981). Applied to psychology, atomism is the view that consciousness itself is an assemblage of associated, constituent elements. The basic element of consciousness is said to be a pure sensation described as "an undifferentiated, instantaneous, dot like impact" (Merleau-Ponty, 2002, p. 3). It is claimed that such sensational elements are stable in their form insofar as they cannot be reduced any further and do not present differentially under varying contextual conditions. In this sense they are the building blocks of conscious experience. Traditionally it was assumed that conscious experience consists primarily in vast quantities of individual sensations rapidly impacting upon the mind and leaving a temporary impression or representation. More recently, sensations have been conceptualised as physical stimuli that enter the sensory organs (e.g., eyes) or as neural signals received from the sense organs that lead to the "data of perception" (Gregory & Zangwill, 1986, p. 700). Merleau-Ponty (2002) refers to the notion that there is a strict correlation between stimulus and sensation as the "constancy hypothesis" (p. 9). The constancy hypothesis stipulates that for each atom of environmental stimulus received by the senses there is a corresponding atom of sensation, or mental impression. Environmental stimuli cause sensations, and the stimulus-sensation pair relate through a one-to-one mapping:

> [P]hysiology of perception begins by recognizing an anatomical path leading from a *receive* through to a definite *transmitter* to a recording station, equally specialized. The objective world being given, it is assumed that it passes onto the sense-organs messages which must be registered, then deciphered in such a way as to reproduce us in the original text. Hence we have in principle a point-by-point correspondence and constant connection between the stimulus and the elementary perception. (Merleau-Ponty, 2002, p. 8)

The PMLD literature that draws conceptual resources from cognitivism conceptualises the developing child as a pre-representational infant.

The guiding assumption of the PMLD literature is that children with PMLD, as a result of some sort of neurological impairment, lack the ability to accurately represent the objective world and thus cannot act in the world. There are two levels of representation at work in the PMLD literature. The first level refers simply to the child's ability to represent the objective world in the sense of having a coherent picture or image in the mind, and not simply "a bundle of external sensations", as Schaffer (1971a, p. 97) puts it. This view is pronounced in the work of Ouvry (1987) who describes children with PMLD as "confused and overwhelmed by the impressions they receive and their inability to filter and organise the information" (p. 117). Ouvry (1987) warns against the "bombardment" of stimuli, which will "only create confusion and inhibit learning" (p. 118). Children with PMLD are said to require "a reduced amount of information" and prolonged periods of time "to assimilate the new information and integrate it thoroughly into their understandings of the world about them before any complexity is introduced" (ibid.). The second notion of "representation" relates more to a cognitive capacity, i.e., the ability of children with PMLD to comprehend particular relations in the objective world, such as object-permanence (understanding that objects still exist even if they are not seen) (Nind & Hewett, 2001); and cause-effect relations (contingency awareness) (Coupe O'Kane & Goldbart, 1998; Ware, 2003).

The rejection of the mechanistic model of perception

Merleau-Ponty (2002) rejects the simple isomorphic relation between organism and world. He argues that the atomistic notion of "sensation" is a problematic unit of analysis because it lacks phenomenological value: the concept of sensation "corresponds to nothing in our experience" (pp. 3–4). Nowhere in our perceptual awareness do we come across discrete, qualitative bits of experience: "The pure impression is, therefore, not only undiscoverable, but also imperceptible and so inconceivable as a moment of perception" (p. 4). Merleau-Ponty (2002) contrasts the atomistic minimal unit of experience to that which gestalt theory describes. For gestalt theorists, the most basic unit of experience is that of an object on a horizon. If analysis seeks to reduce this fundamental complex into something simpler, it can only arrive at imperceptible constructs (Dillon, 1997). As Merleau-Ponty (2002) describes:

> Gestalt theory informs us that a figure on a background is the simplest sense-given available to us, ... it is not a contingent characteristic of factual perception ... It is the very definition of the phenomenon of perception, that without which a phenomenon cannot be said to be perception at all. The perceptual 'something' is always in the middle of something else, it always forms a 'field'. A really homogenous area offering *nothing to be* cannot be given to *any perception*. (p. 4)

For Merleau-Ponty (2002), this figure-ground relationship is an essential structure of experience. The relationship is not an object perceived, but a condition of perception. Objects are said to stand out against a background to which the objects belong. When focusing on an object, the surrounding is put in abeyance in order to see the object better. Objects are said to "form a system in which one cannot show itself without concealing the others" (p. 78). Neighbouring objects thus recede into the periphery and become dormant but still present. They become a horizon when an object is focused upon. This object-horizon structure is our perspective on the world. It is not an "obstacle" (p. 79) in the way of perception, but instead constitutes the means by which objects are disclosed. To perceive "is to enter a universe of beings which display themselves, and they would not do this if they could not be hidden behind each other or behind me" (ibid.).

Psychologists who rely on the notion of atomistic sensation do so after committing what Merleau-Ponty calls the "experience error" (p. 6), in which a quality of an object is mistaken as an element of experience. However, the structure of our lived experience and the structure of the object perceived are two different, but related, levels of experience. We can look through a microscope and see that objects are compounds of atoms, but the atoms that we perceive are figures upon a blurry background of the microscope slide. We do not perceive the atoms without the figure-ground structure, for it is the ground that allows the atoms (as figures) to stand out for us. We do not perceive individual sensations, but perceptual wholes. Qualities of objects are never immediately experienced in isolation.

Another error occurs when it is supposed that objects are given to us in perception "fully developed and determinate" (ibid.). This second error, like the first, "springs from our prejudice about the world" (ibid.) held by science. The constancy hypothesis stipulates a strict correlation between stimulus and sensation. For each atom of environmental stimulus received by the senses there is a corresponding atom of sensation. Environmental stimuli cause sensations, and the stimulus-sensation pair relate through a one-to-one mapping. Merleau-Ponty (2002) challenges this view by describing how perception is never completely clear but is, by its very nature, indeterminate and ambiguous: "The region surrounding my visual field is not easy to describe, but what is certain is that it is neither black nor grey. There occurs here an *indeterminate vision, a vision of something or other*" (ibid.). The edges of the visual field are said to be nothing like the edges of a canvas or television screen since they are not objects I can look at, but the horizon of my looking. Moreover, it is not as if things that fall just outside the visual field simply lapse into perceptual oblivion. Instead, "what is behind my back is not without some element of visual presence" (ibid.), for it still has a kind of perceptual availability as something there to be seen when I turn to look at it. The perceptual field thus cannot be equated with the range of objects directly affecting my sense organs at a given time (Carman, 2008).

To further challenge the assumed isomorphic relation between world and representation, Merleau-Ponty (2002) discusses several optical illusions. One of these is the Müller-Lyer illusion (see Figure 1 below). Objective thought maintains that the two lines are of equal length and simply appear to be unequal. For Merleau-Ponty (2002), the lines are neither equal nor unequal in length. The visual field is a "strange zone" in which "contradictory notions jostle each other" (pp. 6–7), and are

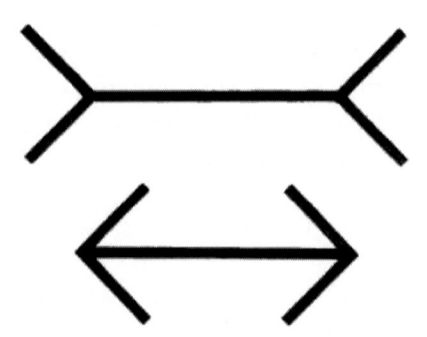

Figure 1. Müller-Lyer optical illusion.

thus ambiguous. This ambiguity is overlooked by objective thought, which takes the world and everything in it to be determinate and clear.

Merleau-Ponty (2002) describes other ambiguities to serve as counter examples to the constancy hypothesis of stimulus-sensation correlation. When red and green, presented together, give the result grey, it has to be conceded that the central combination of stimuli can immediately give rise to a different sensation from what the objective stimuli would lead us to expect. When the apparent size of an object varies with its apparent distance, or its apparent colour with recollections of the object, it is recognised that the sensory processes are not immune to central (mediating) influences. "In this case, therefore, the 'sensible' cannot be defined as the immediate effect of an external stimulus" (p. 9). Since this is so, "The law of constancy cannot avail itself, against the testimony of consciousness" (ibid.). Turning back to the phenomena reveals to us that the apprehension of an object's quality, such as size, is "bound up with a whole perceptual context, and that the stimuli no longer furnish us with the indirect means we are seeking of isolating, a layer of immediate impressions" (pp. 9–10).

Summary

So far we have equated the body-object as it is conceptualised by mechanistic physiology with the reflexive body of behaviourism. We have also equated classical psychology's notion of mind built from sensational atoms with the concept of mind found in cognitivism. We explored Merleau-Ponty's (1963) critique of stimuli and illuminated how the original activity of the organism in the world results in the constitution of stimuli for the organism. The traditional notion of the reflex was made problematic by exploring those cases where one stimulus resulted in different behavioural responses depending on circumstances, and how several stimuli could result in the same behavioural response. Similarly, the notion of a perceptual response was made problematic by exploring how there was no experiential equivalent to environmental stimuli (i.e., no sensational atom that matched an atom in the objective world), and how ambiguity was an essential feature of perception.

The account given above about Merleau-Ponty's (1963; 2002) critique of mechanistic physiology and classical psychology hints at alternative ways of conceptualising the agency and experiences of children with PMLD. With regards to agency, the introduction of concepts such as the

Umwelt and functional flexibility suggests a way of being that cannot be reduced to simple stimulus-response contiguity, nor be explained in terms of overtly intelligent action. What Merleau-Ponty (1963; 2002) is articulating here is the idea that the world can be experienced as immediately meaningful and thus acted upon without prior reflection or contemplation. We will explore the origin and enactment of this meaning during the rest of the chapter—for example, by differentiating the "habit-body" from the "body at this moment" (Merleau-Ponty, 2002, p. 95).

With regards to experience, the above account makes problematic published descriptions of the perceptual capacity of children with PMLD. It challenges the view that children with PMLD live in a world of confusion in which "sensational" units fail to integrate into a perceptual whole (Ouvry, 1987). For Merleau-Ponty (2002), there are no such things as sensational atoms and perception is always holistic rather than atomistic. This notion challenges classroom practice aimed at reducing sensory stimulation in order to support the emergence of simple mental representations. It also challenges practices aimed at developing objective perception. If perception is never completely determinate, in the sense that ambiguity is essential to perception (the perception of size varies with distance, the perception of colour varies with recollection, etc.), then there is a need to consider not the ways in which children with PMLD lack clear and concise representations of the objective world because of neurological impairments (the constancy hypothesis), but how human beings ordinarily live in a world perceived as ambiguous and varied. If ambiguity is a condition of being perceptual, regardless of neurological differences, then we need to learn how children negotiate their activities in a world perceived as dynamic and shifting.

We will explore these ideas further in the next sections during discussion of Merleau-Ponty's (2002) philosophy of embodiment.

Part III

*Concepts central to Merleau-Ponty's account
of the pre-objective body*

The experience of the body

Discussion so far has considered Merleau-Ponty's (2002) formulation of the role of the body in structuring perception of the world (exteroception). What has been absent from this discussion is Merleau-Ponty's (2002) account of the way in which the body itself is tacitly experienced in perception, and the significance of this experience. For Merleau-Ponty (2002), the tacit experience we have of our bodies expresses a layer of existence, more primordial than, and prerequisite for, the contemplative "I":

> My personal existence must be the resumption of a prepersonal tradition. There is, therefore, another subject beneath me, for whom a world exists before I am here, and who marks out my place in it. This captive or natural spirit is my body, not that momentary body which is the instrument of my personal choices and which fastens upon this or that world ... (Merleau-Ponty, 2002, p. 296)

Through analysis of this tacit layer of bodily existence, Merleau-Ponty (2002) develops his conception of what he terms the *"pre-objective view"* (p. 92) of the body, or "being-in-the-world" (ibid.) through the "corporeal schema" (p. 164). This dimension of bodily being is Merleau-Ponty's (2002) original way of accounting for the relation between the mind and body, it is his "third term between the psychic and the physiological" (p. 140, fn. 55). Discussion of the pre-objective corporeal or body schema begins by contrasting it to the experience of the "body image" (p. 114).

The body image vs. the body schema

Merleau-Ponty's (2002) position is one that understands the body as neither an object in-itself, nor something to be abstractly represented by a reflective consciousness, a for-itself. The third position is one that understands the body as playing an active role in shaping experience, and in this experience the body itself features as an immediate, pre-objective dimension of experience—that is, an awareness of the body in which the body is not posited as an object for the mind to contemplate. This pre-reflective, bodily self-consciousness is not the body image. The body image is a term given to a consciousness of the body-object. Smith (2007a) draws from Gallagher (1986) to illuminate Merleau-Ponty's (2002) differentiation of body image and body schema. According to Gallagher (1986), the body image is the representation of the body as an object. However, consciousness of the body is not limited to the body image, nor is such an image the most fundamental form of bodily consciousness. In our everyday experiences of our bodies, the body is experienced in an implicit, tacit, and pre-reflective way. Thompson (2007) describes how this pre-reflective bodily self-consciousness is evident in touch:

> [N]ot only do we feel the things we touch, but we feel ourselves touching them and touched by them. When I pick up a cup of hot tea, I feel the hot, smooth surface of the porcelain and the heat penetrating my fingers, and these sensations linger for a time after I have put the cup back down on the table. (p. 250)

Such bodily awareness is said to offer the experience of physical events that relate one's subjectively lived body to itself. In these experiences, the body does not sense itself explicitly. In picking up the teacup, we live through the heat in our fingers, but the perceptual object is the teacup and our body is experienced as perceiving and acting rather perceived.

The body schema is also said to play an active role in monitoring and governing posture and movement. The body schema plays this role independently of our contemplative conscious awareness. As Smith (2007a) describes:

> Not only do we commonly act, and act 'voluntarily', without our mind being on what we are doing; not only are there aspects to any bodily performance that, even when we are consciously intent upon our performance, escape our conscious attention or monitoring; it is also the case that consciously attending to the details of a bodily performance typically exhibits the smooth execution of it. (p. 13)

Best grip/proprioception

This immediate bodily awareness is labelled by Carman (2008) as "proprioception" (p. 68), and by Smith (2007a) as "kinaesthesis" (p. 9). What both these terms have in common is the notion that there is a direct sensorimotor awareness of the body. The awareness of being hot or cold, the awareness of body positions and movements, and the awareness of whether and which parts of the body are being touched all occur without explicit self-observation in which our gaze is consciously directed towards our bodies. Further, this bodily awareness is different from, but related to, what Merleau-Ponty (2002) refers to as "exteroceptivity" (p. 87) (sensitivity to the world outside the body): "External perception and the perception of one's own body vary together because they are two sides of one and the same act" (p. 237). He continues: "Every external perception is immediately synonymous with a certain perception of my body, just as every perception of my body makes itself explicit in the language of external perception" (p. 239). We experience ourselves in relation to the world, and this experience is loaded with a tacit motor meaning. Carman (2008) notes that a common thread in Merleau-Ponty's (2002) work that expresses this trail of thought is his relation of perception, motility and the world through the notion of "grip" (p. 295). The movements of the body are said to be invested with a perceptual significance that leads to a modification of position in the world in order to obtain optimal perception:

> [M]y body is geared onto the world when my perception offers me a spectacle as varied and as clearly articulated as possible, and when my motor intensions, as they unfold, receive the responses they expect from the world. This maximum sharpness of perception and action points clearly to a perceptual *ground*, a basis of my life, a general setting in which my body can co-exist with the world. (p. 292)

The body schema is that which mediates perception of the world. It provides our sense of equilibrium in the world and determines which postures and positions allow us to perceive the world optimally. To draw once again from Carman's (2008) reading of Merleau-Ponty's (2002) work, it is the body schema "which gives us a normatively rich but precognitive grip on our environment" (pp. 109–110), a pre-reflective sense of what is and is not optimally perceptible—it informs us of "the right distance and angle from which to see something, a preferred posture in which to listen or concentrate, or to achieve poise and balance" (p. 110). Our bodies are said to be constantly, though unconsciously, adjusting themselves to secure and integrate our experience and maintain our "grip" on the environment. The felt dispositions of the body schema are said to establish a "normative dimension" (ibid.) that gives meaning to a sensorimotor intentionality—that is, a natural orientation of organisms towards the world guided by a felt rightness or wrongness of the perceptual situation: "We have a *feel* for the kinds of balance and posture that afford us a correct and proper view of the world, and that feel is neither the buzz and hum of sensation nor the rationality of deliberate thought" (Carman, 2008, pp. 110–111).

The body is existentially poised

Whilst Carman (2008) understands Merleau-Ponty's (2002) notion of "grasping" as something that relates to optimal perception of objects, for Smith (2007a) such grasping is of an existential nature insofar as it relates not just to best percept, but to a mode of existing toward, and acting upon, objects in the world. The "here" of the whole body is its "situation in face of its tasks" (Merleau-Ponty, 2002, p. 115) in which objects offer themselves as "poles of action" (p. 122). The body "surges" towards objects to be grasped (p. 121). Our environment is described in terms of "manipulanda" (p. 120)—objects known in terms of how they can be acted upon, or with. The world is "a collection of possible points upon which ... bodily interaction may operate" (p. 121). Thus, central to the Merleau-Ponty's (2002) phenomenology of perception is the notion of existence, or being-in-the-world, conceived in terms of motility towards objects in the world (Smith, 2007a), "Already motility, in its pure state, possesses the basic power of giving a meaning (*Sinngebung*)" (Merleau-Ponty, 2002, p. 164). This is essentially what Merleau-Ponty refers to as "motor intentionality" (p. 127): "Consciousness is in the first place not a matter of 'I think that' but of 'I can'" (p. 159).

It is in action that the experience of the body is brought to life, and such experience is holistic in nature. In action, the position of the body is sensed without the need for reflection:

> If I stand in front of my desk and lean on it with both hands, only my hands are stressed, and the whole of my body trails behind them like the tail of a comet. It is not that I am unaware of the whereabouts of my shoulders or back, but these are simply swallowed up in the position of my hands, and my whole posture can be read, so to speak, in the pressure they exert on the table. (p. 115)

Furthermore, the body in its entirety lends itself to action. Whilst somebody may move with intent, this intent is not something that consciously contemplates every muscle action in the body.

> If I am sitting at my table and I want to reach the telephone, the movement of my hand towards it, the straightening of the upper part of the body, the tautening of the leg muscles are superimposed on each other. I desire a certain result and the relevant tasks are spontaneously distributed amongst the appropriate segments. (p. 172)

This notion of the body having a life of its own, or an anonymous, pre-personal level of existence, cuts across the Cartesian mind-body divide, as well as the behaviourist-cognitivist divide. For Merleau-Ponty (2002), theories that attempt to exhaustively classify body movements into either "simple" reflexes, or voluntary actions (in which the former lacks conscious agency, whilst the latter has an agent in control) overlook the coordinated and global or holistic role of the body in action. Behaviour is never purely reflexive or purely volitional. The pre-objective body cuts across such distinctions by making volitional behaviour contingent upon the pre-objective, whilst making reflex behaviours meaningful. Smith (2007a) offers an example to supplement Merleau-Ponty's (2002) examples:

> [W]hen we reach to grasp an object, as soon as our arm begins to move our fingers take up a posture that is adapted to the final act of grasping (see Jeannerod, 1986). In such cases we are typically wholly unaware of this incipient movement of our fingers; no 'intention' or 'pro-attitude' is directed towards it. And yet it is not a 'mere' physical movement. (pp. 12–13)

Smith (2007a) notes that in such cases Merleau-Ponty (2002) describes the bodily movement as "magically at its completion" (p. 119).

Summary

We have just explored Merleau-Ponty's (2002) notion of the pre-objective body, or the body schema, which we first described as our immediate, tacit experience of our body in relation to the world. The body schema relates the subjectively lived body to itself, and also plays an active role in movement through proprioception/kinaesthesia. For example, we are aware of the position of our body and whether or not we are being touched. We then explored Merleau-Ponty's (2002) account of how the perceived world is understood through the body by describing how experience is made meaningful through motor intentionality. For example, we feel whether we are in an optimal perceptual state and our bodies adjust accordingly, and we also experience the world in terms of affordances insofar as the world is perceived in relation to how we can act. Hence, our being-in-the-world is our existence in a world of motor signification. We also presuppose bodily skills in relation to this signification since we can act without thematic reflection about goal-directed behaviour.

These ideas have significant implications for how we think about children with PMLD. If there are different ways of being a body, or rather, different ways of being embodied, then there are different ways of thinking about action. Cognitivists in the PMLD field take a neuro-reductionist approach: children with PMLD are conceptualised as having extensive neurological impairments that delay or deny the capacity for explicit cognition. Because children with PMLD are thought to lack comprehension of the world around them they are deemed to require segregated and carefully controlled environments that foster the emergence of environmental awareness (described in terms of object permanence, contingency awareness, etc.). By contrast, for Merleau-Ponty (2002) first meaning is not found in abstract reasoning, but in our bodily actions and how we relate to a world signified in terms of motility. If perception is a form of enactment that brings forth a world in which an organism perceives itself, then we are led to consider how opportunities for varied interactions may lead to the enactment of a fuller or richer world for children with PMLD to learn about themselves, other people, and the surrounding milieu.

We explore these concepts further in the next section.

Part IV

Examples of Merleau-Ponty's pre-objective body at work

Limb substitution as an expression of pre-objective being-in-the-world

Now that a range of key terms and concepts related to the pre-objective body have been introduced, examples can be given which pull together the disparate theoretical components discussed above. This serves to give context to Merleau-Ponty's (2002) phenomenological description

PHENOMENOLOGY 115

of the pre-objective body. It also paves the way for further discussion about the ways in which Merleau-Ponty's (2002) phenomenology offers an alternative approach to thinking about children with PMLD.

The first example to be given is that of the act of limb substitution in insects. It is common for Merleau-Ponty (2002) to articulate his view of pre-objective being-in-the-world through non-human animal examples since this notion of being is said to be universal to all living species. The rationale for making use of the following example is not to compare children with PMLD to insects, but simply to drive home the way in which pre-objective being plays beneath, and is presupposed by, thematic awareness. Given that the following example introduces one of the central insights of the text, and given that its importance to the PMLD literature is such that it affords the first genuine break from traditional understandings of the (PMLD) body, it is worth quoting it at some length before discussion ensues:

> When the insect, in the performance of an instinctive act, substitutes a sound leg for one cut off, it is not, as we saw, that a stand-by device, set up in advance, is automatically put into operation and substituted for the circuit which is one of action But neither is it the case that the creature is aware of an aim to be achieved, using its limbs as various means, for in that case the substitution ought to occur every time the act is prevented, and we know that it does not occur if the leg it merely tied. The insect simply continues to belong to the same world and move in it with all its powers. The tied limb is not replaced by the free one, because it continues to count in the insect's scheme of things, and because the current of activity which flows towards the world still passes through it ... the insect itself projects the norms of its environment and itself lays down the terms of its vital problem; but here it is a question of an *a priori* of the species and not a personal choice. Thus what is found behind the phenomenon of substitution is the impulse of being-in-the-world, and it is now time to put this notion into more precise terms. When we say that an animal *exists*, that it *has* a world, or that it *belongs* to a world, we do not mean that it has a perception or objective consciousness of that world. The situation which unleashes instinctive operations is not entirely articulate and determinate, its total meaning is not possessed, as is adequately shown by the mistakes and the blindness of instinct. It presents only a practical significance;

it asks for only bodily recognition; it is experienced as an 'open' situation, and 'requires' the animal's movements, just as the first notes of a melody require a certain kind of resolution, without its being known in itself, and it is precisely what allows the limb to be substituted for each other, and to be of equal value before the self-evident demands of the task. (p. 90)

Merleau-Ponty (2002) is concerned with a mode of existence or being-in-the-world in which organisms have a form of bodily intentionality that plays beneath any overt sense of self, any thematic ego. This mode is not a deliberate taking up of a position, an act of reflection, or a deliberate choice, but an *a priori* of the species. Nor is this mode of existence mechanistic in nature since it endows the world with a motor significance. What Merleau-Ponty (2002) is articulating is the integration of the body in the world as a necessary *condition* for consciousness, and as such it is a presupposed state of being, forming a background of significance in which there is a perceptual world for us, as opposed to an objective world outside of us. This deep continuity is one in which the body is globally poised towards the world, but a world which is not removed from the structures of the body. Being-in-the-world implies that perception is always already "loaded" with motor significance, that the body as a whole is aimed towards its world as that which can be acted upon. The world presents itself as a "practical significance" that speaks to the body; the world as an "open situation" is ready to be interpreted by the body and transformed into a motor situation. Limb substitution reveals that it is the body as a whole that interprets the situation (not body parts): the unified body emerges as a motor value in relation to the world of perception.

Thus, when performing instinctive acts, insects use a present limb as a substitute for a missing limb. For Merleau-Ponty (2002), this substitution is not a product of a "standby circuit" that exists "just in case" a limb is severed. There are no backup circuits. Furthermore, the act of substitution does not occur after reflective thought. The use of alternative limbs is not an intentional act; the insect is not aware of an alternative limb to be used as a means by which a goal can be achieved (if this were so, the insect would use an alternative limb when one limb is tied, but this does not occur, the limb still "continues to count in the insect's scheme of things"). The organism is "anchored" (p. 78) to a certain environment, and this being-in-the-world is not at the level of thematic, explicit conscious awareness. This dimension of bodily being does not consist of knowledge or explicit representation of the body as object to be commanded. It is the condition for there being any world for the insect at all, it is the state by which the insect (and other living organisms) relate to the world and is presupposed in every act. As such it is immediate, tacit, always present, without necessarily being presented to a consciousness.

This sense of bodily being-in-the-world is absent in the PMLD literature. There is no intrinsic meaning to the situation from the perspective of behaviourism, since behaviourism is non-cognitive and is concerned primarily with the external, with that which can be objectively observed. From this perspective, there is only an objective world and an objectified body, and the research-based literature is concerned with measuring behavioural changes in relation to mechanistic circumstances, or what Merleau-Ponty (2002) refers to as "worldly causality" (p. 87). The body as reflexive object misses the *integration* of organism and world and the significance that this integration generates for the organism. There are only visible *surfaces* for behaviourism. As such, notions of global orientation are rejected explicitly. This is evident in the work of Watson (1913), who argued for a "peripheral" understanding of the organism (Baars, 1986, p. 48). As Baars (1986) notes, Watson (1913) was so distrustful of the nervous system "that he at one point proposed that the cerebral cortex was not a functioning organ" (p. 48). Watson's (1913) behaviourism was concerned with decentralised activity in which body parts were conceived as being almost segregated and independent of the body as a totality (reflexes were not centrally mediated action but the sole product of the activity of the muscles and glands—see Chapter Two). This peripheral understanding, which is only concerned with independent limbs acting reflexively to stimuli, overlooks the global orientation of the organism to its own world, and misses how the stimuli has an internal significance in the sense that (as a phenomenological description of experience reveals) the organism "confuses" (Merleau-Ponty, 2002, p. 87) the relationship of stimuli and behavioural (or perceptual) response. What counts as stimuli is mediated by the organism. Phenomenological description of such mediation reveals an intentional structure in which no simple "sensation" impinges on the organism, since the world is experienced as a whole (e.g., the figure-horizon structure), and the organism is situated and directed towards this whole world existentially—that is, in terms of action. The behaviourist-oriented PMLD literature misses this global orientation of the body to its world. By starting from the position that something "central" (i.e., the brain) is impaired, the PMLD literature overlooks the role of the holistic body and limits itself to understanding behaviour as reflexive and independent of central (of bodily) influences. The recent acknowledgement of behaviour states (Arthur, 2004; Foreman et al., 2004; Guess et al., 1993) as mediating the stimulus-response relationship has led to behaviourism conceptualising events underneath the skin once more. However, these states are considered to be states that mediate the "readiness" of the organism to respond to environmental stimuli. From the perspective of being-in-the-world, these states take on new significance. The behaviour states emerge when the body finds itself in a situation of significance. Whilst being in a segregated classroom governed by behaviourist principles of learning is said to be non-stimulating for children with PMLD (Guess et al., 1993), being around others (especially peers) is meaningful and raises bodily expectations, alertness, etc. and primes the child to engage with the environment. It works beneath representational consciousness and motivates its emergence. Australian behaviour state research (Foreman et al., 2004) indicates that children with PMLD are in optimal states when in social milieus. These milieus are understood by the body as being central to the vital and motivate or support or prime the child to engage with these environments.

The PMLD literature that draws conceptual resources from cognitivism also overlooks being-in-the-world. For this body of literature, movement is considered to be either reflexive (in the behaviourist sense), or explicitly goal directed. Goal-directed behaviour is understood as behaviour emitted after the child has represented the objective world, represented the body as something that can be controlled, represented a task to be accomplished, and then represented how the body can be steered around the world to achieve the task. Central to the notion of goal-directed behaviour is the role of an actor: a rational subject, a self or an "I" that can comprehend the world existing in a particular kind of way and as a result can act in the world. Interventions for children with PMLD try to develop forms of representation deemed prerequisite for agency. For example, goal-directed behaviour presupposes contingency (or cause-effect) awareness. Nind and Hewett (2001) define cause and effect as:

> [T]he idea that 'when I do x, y happens', this involves the person ... understanding that they can have an effect on the world, the range

of ways this can happen and the range of effects; social cause and effect involves understanding that we can cause another person to do (or feel) something. (p. v)

For Nind and Hewett (2001), there must be a self that can comprehend that what she/he ("I") does has a direct consequence in the world. There must be a rational subject that is in possession of such knowledge and understands the relation between self and world. A lack of contingency awareness stems from the lack of representational capacity on behalf of the child with PMLD. Furthermore, this "I" to which Nind and Hewett (2001) refer is said to comprehend the world through ideas—that is, the "idea" of contingency: the thinking subject must represent itself acting, and represent the consequences of those actions prior to the actions been executed. It is this mental act that is presupposed in goal-directed behaviour. The capacity for abstract thought in this way is prerequisite for communication. Although Nind and Hewett (2001) make reference to what they call "body language" (p. v), defined as unspoken "unconsciously delivered or interpreted" (ibid.) communication grounded in posture, gesture and body movement, they reserve the status of "communicative intent" (ibid.) for a more abstract activity involving the transmission of information from one subject to another. Intentional communication is defined as:

> [T]he intention to communicate; you need to be aware that you can communicate deliberately (i.e., influence another person's thoughts or feelings) to have communicative intent—this is more deliberate and active than reading another person's body language ... (ibid.)

Intentional communication is promoted to a more abstract and personal state of mind, which is not simply "sub-conscious or accidental" (ibid.), but personal or rather interpersonal, a deliberate taking up of a position that is something additional to the immediacy of understanding the other. There is an explicit awareness of the capacity of the self to convey such and such to another self.

As described above, Merleau-Ponty's (2002) notion of being-in-the-world suggests a mode of existence that cuts across the distinction between the mechanistic body and the thematic mind. In doing so, it foregrounds an alternative concept of tacit subjectivity and agency that is not contingent upon explicit conscious representation, or cognitive acts upon such representation, but instead provides a ground and structure for such thematic reasoning. This moves debate away from how to develop cognitive awareness in children with PMLD in order for them to make sense of the objective world (described by psychology), towards understanding how the pre-objective world is meaningful in the first place. We will explore this notion further by looking at how Merleau-Ponty (2002) extends his description of the pre-objective body by differentiating between the body at this moment and the habit-body.

Phantom limbs: the body at this moment and the habit-body

Merleau-Ponty (2002) discusses the experiences of hospitalised patients who have phantom limbs after amputation. Phantom limb experiences are said to reveal a deep continuity between the body and world that manifests itself temporally through the differentiation of the body at this moment and the habit-body.

The phantom limb is said to emerge when a stimulus is applied "to the path from the stump into the brain" (p. 87) resulting in the feeling of a phantom limb. From this perspective, it appears that the phantom limb is maintained by physiological conditions. This is said to be further supported by those patients who, as a result of brain injury, experience phantom limbs without amputation. However, the experience of a phantom limb is also said to emerge from "psychic determinants": "An emotion, circumstance which recalls those in which the wound was received, creates a phantom limb in subjects who had none" (ibid.). Furthermore, Merleau-Ponty (2002) notes how "the imaginary arm is enormous after the operation, but that it subsequently shrinks and is absorbed into the stump *'as the patient accepts his mutilation'*" (ibid., *my italics*). What Merleau-Ponty points (2002) towards is the fact that the same phenomenal condition (the phantom limb experience) can have both a physiological explanation in one context, and a psychological explanation in another. Psychologists refer to the phantom limb as a memory or belief. However, "no psychological condition can overlook the fact that the severance of the nerves to the brain abolishes the phantom limb" (pp. 88–89).

> What has to be understood, then, is how the psychic determining factors and the physiological conditions gear into each other: it is not clear how the imaginary limb, if dependent on physiological

conditions and therefore the result of third person causality, can in *another context* arise out of the personal history of the patient, his memories, emotions and volitions. (p. 89)

Merleau-Ponty (2002) addresses the topic of the phantom limb by refusing to situate himself within the ontological dualism of mind and matter, which informed the thought of his contemporaries. For Merleau-Ponty (2002), the binary, either/or accounts (either psychology or physiology) miss something essential. Since the condition is said to emerge out of both physiological third person causality *as well as* out of the first person, personal history of the patient, there needs to be a third way or "identical point of application" (ibid.), a sort of common ground where the mind and body meet, allowing both to support the emergence of the phantom limb experience. Merleau-Ponty (2002) explains that it is impossible to find this middle ground where the mind and body are considered to be two distinct ontological entities, the for-itself and the in-itself. As Merleau-Ponty (2002) describes, the phantom limb is not the mere outcome of objective causality, nor is it a *cogitatio*:

> It could be a mixture of the two only if we could find a means of linking the 'psychic' and the 'physiological', the 'for-itself' and the 'in-itself', to each other to form an articulate whole, and to contrive some meeting-point for them: if the third person processes and the personal acts could be integrated into a common middle term. (p. 89)

To elucidate the case of phantom limb experiences is to point towards a new way of conceptualising the body. Merleau-Ponty (2002) begins to outline an alternative conception by first appealing to the psychoanalytical notion of "repression". He states: "In order to describe the belief in the phantom limb and the unwillingness to accept mutilation, writers speak of 'a driving into the unconscious' or 'an organic repression'" (ibid.). For Merleau-Ponty (2002), such "un-Cartesian terms force us to form the idea of an organic thought which the relation of the 'psychic' to the 'physiological' becomes conceivable" (ibid.). Organic thought implies both thought and substance, allowing a conceptual unification of mind and body. The body has a role to play in cognition and consciousness—it is not simply an object existing *partes extra partes* with other objects, but has an intrinsic significance.

This notion of "organic thought" is missing from the PMLD literature and as such is an original concept to the field. The notion of organic thought appeals to a different aspect of the body, which is neither mechanistic (behaviourism) nor thematic (cognitivism) and as such is a genuinely new point of departure from the traditional PMLD concepts.

Merleau-Ponty (2002) continues his discussion of the pre-objective body with reference to the ambiguous nature of phantom limb experiences. For Merleau-Ponty (2002), this ambiguity reveals different modes of bodily existence or different ways of being a body, and consequently, different ways of being-in-the-world. The phantom limb experience is an experience of a limb that is both present and absent. On the one hand, the patient appears to be unaware of the loss of limb insofar as she/he relies on the phantom limb as if it were real, evidenced by the attempts to walk with the phantom limb without fear of falling. On the other hand, when prompted, the patient reveals knowledge that the real limb is missing. Thus, the presence of the phantom limb is not a product of false judgement: "the awareness of the amputated arm as present ... is not on the kind of 'I think that ...'" (p. 94). The experience is not a deliberate decision and does not take place "at the level of positing consciousness which takes up its position explicitly after considering various possibilities" (ibid.). But neither is the experience simply a sensation (e.g., a pain) since it has intentional content about the patient's intuitive sense of bodily being, such as its position and possibilities in relation to the world (Carman, 2008). For Merleau-Ponty (2002), this paradoxical experience emerges because the body itself is still committed to, and tends towards, its world:

> To have a phantom arm is to remain open to all the actions of which the arm alone is capable; it is to retain the practical field which one enjoyed before mutilation. The body is the vehicle of being in the world, and having a body is, for a living creature, to be intervolved in a definite environment, to identify oneself with certain projects and be continually committed to them. (p. 95)

A body intervolved with the environment is a body intertwined or coiled with the environment. The body and world shape each other through the intertwining and make a unique whole. This intervolving is translated by Merleau-Ponty (2002) in terms of actions in the world, or what he calls "projects" (p. 129). Customary behaviours are engraved on the body, leaving a long-term impression. In the case of the phantom limb experience, the impression remains despite the absence of a limb. It is this impression that is important for the notion of being-in-the-world. The impressed body is a long-term body that signifies the present, and it is a signification that remains after body modification. The phantom limb experience is indicative of a body that remains committed to a world that can no longer be acted upon in quite the same way. The world is signified for the patient in terms of projects, but this signification is a bodily aspiration that motivates action and maintains a personal zone of motility, or what Merleau-Ponty (2002) refers to as the "practical field" (p. 94). This practical field is not something posited by consciousness, but emerges as a relation between body and world through recurrent sensorimotor activity. And yet, it is this relation that structures first personal experience and leads to the emergence of the phantom limb experience:

> In the self-evidence of this complete world in which manipulatable objects still figure, in the force of their movement which still flows towards him, and in which is still present the project of writing or playing the piano, the cripple still finds the guarantee of his wholeness. But in concealing his deficiency from him, the world cannot fail simultaneously to reveal it to him: for it is true that I am conscious of my body via the world ... (p. 94)

The ambiguity of the phantom limb stems from the competition of different modes of being embodied. The personal world of the patient arouses intentions (to write a letter, to play the piano) that the patient can no longer engage in, or at least not in the same way. Objects known as that which can be utilised (the pen, the piano) present themselves as utilisable and appeal to a body part (a hand) that is no longer present: "Thus are delimited, in the totality of my body, regions of silence" (p. 95). Here, the patient is both aware and unaware. For Merleau-Ponty (2002), this paradox is not simply restricted to patients with phantom limbs. Rather:

> This paradox is that of all being in the world: when I move towards a world I bury my perceptual and practical intentions in objects which ultimately appear prior to and external to those intentions,

and which nevertheless exist for me only in so far as they arouse in me thoughts or volitions. (ibid.)

For Merleau-Ponty (2002), the body compromises two distinct layers: that of the "habit-body" and that of the "body at this moment" (ibid.). The habit-body is composed of lived through, recurrent sensorimotor patterns that have disappeared from the body at this moment. The problem of phantom limb experience is a problem of how the habit-body relates to the body at this moment. Merleau-Ponty (2002) asks: How can the amputee perceive objects as manipulatable when she/he can no longer manipulate them? The answer involves a switch from the personal to the anonymous:

> The manipulatable must have ceased to be what I am now manipulating, and become what *one* can manipulate; it must have ceased to be a thing *manipulatable for me* and become a thing *manipulatable in itself*. Correspondingly, my body must be apprehended not only in an experience which is instantaneous, peculiar to itself and complete in itself, but also in some general aspect and in the light of an impersonal being. (ibid.)

Merleau-Ponty (2002) is articulating a perspective which is absent from both behaviourism and cognitivism. He is describing the role of the body in perception, a bodily point of view (Carman, 2008) that steers between the competing accounts of mind as representational and body as reflexive. From the perspective of cognitivism, the mind is a representational entity that knows the body and world only insofar as they can be explicitly represented. The body becomes an image of the body, and the world becomes an image of the objective world. Successful representation is the ground for the autonomous, cognising agent. The other perspective is that of behaviourism, which conceptualises the body simply as a mechanistic entity responding to stimuli in the objective world. Children with PMLD who are described as lacking in representational capacity become the mechanistic organism of behaviourism, and the body is objectified. Merleau-Ponty's (2002) alternative is the bodily perspective. This bodily point of view is the first-person point of view, and yet it is not the subjective or personal point of view traditionally theorised. Not all experience centres around a self-conscious subject, an "I" thinking about itself:

Underlying that (more or less) transparent personal subject is a more primitive, one might say merely *translucent* layer of bodily experience that has a more impersonal character better captured by the French pronoun on ("one" or "we"), as in *one blinks every few seconds*, or *we breathe through our noses*. The *pre*personal bodily subject of perception is thus not my conscious, reflective self, but simply "the one" (*le "on"*). (Carman, 2008, p. 94)

It is "one" that typically perceives and acts, not "I". As Merleau-Ponty (2002) describes:

Every perception takes place in an atmosphere of generality and is presented to us anonymously. I cannot say that I see the blue of the sky in the sense in which I say I understand a book, or again in which I say I decide to devote my life to mathematics ... if I wanted to render precisely the perceptual experience, I ought to say that one perceives in me, not that I perceive. (p. 250)

Merleau-Ponty's (2002) discussion gives rise to notions of multiple embodiments that cut across the entrenched distinctions of body and mind. The PMLD literature does not differentiate between the habit-body and the body at this moment, between the anonymous and the personal self. For the PMLD literature, there is only the absence or presence of an "I". Where the "I" is present, the body is controlled by the subject. Where the "I" is absent, the body is reflexive and controlled from environmental conditions conceptualised as external stimuli. Because of the severity of their impairments, children with PMLD are said to lack a point of view. Ware (2004) is very clear about this. For Ware (2004), children with PMLD have no concept of future events, since such a concept presupposes a subject at a stage of "relatively advanced cognitive development" (p. 177). Further, for Ware (2004), to have a view about a future event requires the ability to anticipate that event, and compare the event with similar events. Being able to compare one event with another involves the ability to draw similarities and differences between events. Children with PMLD are said to lack a sense of time, and cannot draw distinctions between ongoing events or future events, "Yet it is surely precisely events of this type which are the crux of the issue when we talk about obtaining a pupil's view ..." (p. 178). For Merleau-Ponty (2002), it is the body that has a point of view, and it is the body that is temporally situated. This is not to say that children with PMLD have no points of view in Ware's (2004) sense of the term. Rather, it is to make problematic Ware's (2004) sense by questioning the extent to which a point of view is necessarily an abstract, theoretical activity. For Merleau-Ponty (2002), the habitual body involves the embodiment of recurrent sensorimotor patterns engaged in by the body at this moment. Such embodiment allows the pre-objective body to anticipate the world in the sense that the world becomes signified as that which can be acted upon. The comparison between what is familiar and what is not familiar occurs at the immediate level of the pre-objective body, allowing for a distinction between what is and is not immediately significant, at any given moment.

For Merleau-Ponty (2002), to have a self (an "I") requires a distancing between the *body at this moment* and the emergent "I". It requires a habitual body that can be presupposed, allowing a little space to accrue between the here and now and the body-subject, so thought can be reflective and distant. Cognitive structures emerge from *recurrent* sensorimotor patterns that enable action to be perceptually guided (Varela et al., 1991). Such patterns are embedded within wider cultural contexts that constrain what counts as recurrent patterns (and thus experience and cognition). For the PMLD literature, the child with PMLD lacks an explicit "I" and therefore cannot act in the world. Merleau-Ponty (2002) inverts this logic and says that an "I" requires opportunities to act.

The fact that the habitual body can act as a "guarantee" for the body at this moment implies that "one's" lived body is not static, but grows and changes in relation to its engagement with the world. Or, as Thompson (2007) puts it: "one's lived body is a developmental being thick with its own history and sedimented ways of feeling, perceiving, acting, and imagining" (p. 33). These sedimented patterns are not limited to the material space that the body lives at this moment, but "span and interweave the lived body and its environment, thereby forming a unitary circuit of lived-body-environment" (ibid.). This moves the debate to how habitual bodies can be developed through opportunities to engage in rich and diverse interactions with the world.

Analysis of Merleau-Ponty's (2002) text so far has revealed how his notion of being-in-the-world relates organisms to the world and essentially carves out a personal world for the organism that is loaded with motor significance. The nature of the organism's embodiment allows the organism to enact a world. Merleau-Ponty (2002) extends this view by adding a temporal dimension to existence: the body can be understood in terms of past and present action. The ambiguity of the phantom limb experience is a fundamental expression of our bodily being-in-the-world, and this body is understood through aspects of time.

Chapter summary

In this chapter we have described some of Merleau-Ponty's (1963; 2002) key concepts central to his account of embodied consciousness. We began by exploring Merleau-Ponty's (1963; 2002) critiques of the traditional accounts of mind and body. We equated the body-object as it is conceptualised by mechanistic physiology with the reflexive body of behaviourism. We also equated classical psychology's notion of mind built from sensational atoms with the concept of mind found in cognitivism. We explored Merleau-Ponty's (1963) critique of the stimulus and illuminated how the original activity of the organism in the world results in the constitution of stimuli for the organism. The traditional notion of the reflex was made problematic by exploring those cases where one stimulus resulted in different behavioural responses depending on circumstances, and how several stimuli could result in the same behavioural response. Similarly, the notion of a perceptual response was made problematic by exploring how there was no experiential equivalent to environmental stimuli (i.e., no sensational atom that matched an atom in the objective world). This critique paved the way to explore Merleau-Ponty's (1963; 2002) notion of the pre-objective body or body schema.

The body schema was described as the experience of the body that emerges through interaction with the world. This experience is not an explicit or thematic awareness of the body-object (the body image) but a tacit, pre-personal or anonymous awareness of embodiment. Such bodily awareness relates the subjectively lived body to itself and plays an active role in movement described as proprioception/kinaesthesis. Thus, we are immediately aware of being hot or cold, whether we are being touched or touching, and we sense the position and movement of our body. Furthermore, our experience of the world is always loaded with motor meaning. We sense whether or not our perception of the world is optimal and move accordingly, and objects in the world present themselves as things that can be acted upon in a particular manner. This is what Merleau-Ponty (2002) means when he says that the environment presents itself in terms of "*manipulanda*" (p. 120)—objects are immediately perceived in relation to motor intentionality. Our being-in-the-world is our existence in a world of personal motor signification. It is the "impulse" (p. 90) that runs through us. However, this impulse is general and flexible. In the act of limb substitution in insects we see a functional reorganisation and a new form of locomotion in the insect, which can move in novel ways to achieve the same ends (walking). Thus, being-in-the-world does not imply that specific stimuli cause specific behavioural responses. Instead, we can act in multiple ways to achieve the same ends. Finally, in the example of phantom limb experiences we discover how our embodiment relates to time. The body compromises two distinct layers: that of the habit-body and that of the body at this moment. The habit-body is composed of lived through, recurrent sensorimotor patterns that have disappeared from the body at this moment. The phantom limb experience relates the habit-body to the body at this moment. I learn to manipulate objects in a particular manner, and this manner becomes signified in perception when objects immediately appear as manipulatable. Thus, there is a shift from the thematic "I" to the pre-personal "one". The phantom limb is revealed in the presence of objects immediately experienced as manipulatable even though this manipulation can no longer take place. Thus, the phantom limb presents an experiential paradox, because the "I" recognises that she/he can no longer manipulate the object, but the pre-personal body still projects meaning—the present is signified in terms of past actions.

For the PMLD field, Merleau-Ponty's (1963; 2002) phenomenology introduces a new way of conceptualising the experiences and agency of children with PMLD that cannot be reduced to mere stimulus-response relationships, nor be explained in terms of explicit cognition. Since there are different ways of being embodied (the living body, the lived-body/body schema, the body image) there are different ways of experiencing embodiment and different ways of understanding action. Instead of presupposing that agency requires thematic representation of the world in order to engage in goal-directed behaviour, we can begin to explore the lived experiences of children with PMLD in terms of their immediately meaningful but tacit experiences of themselves in relation to the world. This moves the focus of PMLD research away from supporting the emergence of abstract reasoning towards understanding how opportunities for varied interactions may lead to the enactment of a richer lifeworld, and the impact this has on children learning about themselves, other people, and the surrounding milieu. The differentiation between the habit-body and the body at this moment provides a temporal framework for thinking about how immediate signification grows over time. Ultimately, Merleau-Ponty's (2002) phenomenology leads us to the view that children with PMLD (like all children) require diverse opportunities to explore the world and build relationships in order to flourish, and placing such children in segregated environments may restrict their potential to grow as individuals.

CHAPTER FIVE

Interpreting Sam: the search for a sensitive methodology

In the preceding chapters we explored both traditional (psychological) and non-traditional (phenomenological) approaches to thinking about children with PMLD. In this chapter and the next we present a research project concerned with the ways in which inclusive education could support growth and learning in a young boy with PMLD. Specifically, in this chapter we describe the project's research methodology and locate it in wider debates about accessing marginalised voices. In the next chapter we present the findings of the project and "test" the extent to which the three theoretical perspectives described in this book (behaviourism, cognitivism, and phenomenology) can make the data intelligible.

In this book we use the term "inclusion" to mean "mainstreaming". However, we are aware that inclusion is a contested concept with a long history of debate regarding its meaning (Armstrong et al., 2010).

Project background

The project reported in this book involved a nine-year-old boy with PMLD called Sam, who lived with his family in rural south-west England. Sam has cerebral palsy but could sit on the floor unaided and started bum-shuffling when the project began. Sam was diagnosed with partial hearing loss and was believed to experience visual impairment. He attended a special school in a nearby city four days a week and was placed in a class for children with profound and complex disabilities. Sam was described by his special school teacher as operating at a pre-intentional level of communication. Sam also spent one day a week in a mainstream class at his local primary school where he was aided by two learning support assistants (LSAs) who used to work for a special school. The LSAs were primarily responsible for delivering the curriculum and differentiating the teacher's lesson plans. They also provided personal care and organised transportation.

Our research was concerned with whether or not Sam's different schools provided different opportunities for engagement (particularly social engagement), and how this impacted upon his growth and learning. We wanted to develop a methodology sensitive enough to capture Sam's experiences in his different settings and relate this to patterns of growth. At the time, we drew conceptual resources from Trevarthen and Aitken (2001) and we were interested in whether Sam's different social milieus supported primary intersubjectivity and emergent secondary intersubjectivity (see Chapter Three). We also drew from behaviour state research (Foreman et al., 2004) and we wanted to know if Sam's levels of alertness could be linked to different social milieus (see Chapter Two). However, given the behavioural idiosyncrasies of children with PMLD (e.g., the ways in which their mobility, sensory, and cognitive differences lead to personalised forms of action), we devised a methodology based on explicit forms of interpretation. We wanted to understand the meaning of Sam's idiosyncratic actions and this involved learning from Sam and negotiating meaning with significant others (such as his LSAs and teachers). This moved us away from objective epistemology found in the post-positivism paradigm towards a constructionist epistemology found in the critical paradigm (Crotty, 2003).

In this chapter we describe the design of this methodology and relate it to other research designs discussed in contemporary PMLD literature. Our discussion is located within a perspective on childhood that foregrounds children as rights bearers with agency. This challenges the dominant psychological and medical perspectives ordinarily brought to bear on discussions of children with PMLD (and largely evidenced in Chapter One)—as to be a "rights bearer" suggests a level of autonomy, agency and control that is traditionally absent from debates regarding children with PMLD. The United Nations Convention on the Rights of the Child (UNCRC) (UN, 1990) gives children across the globe forty substantive rights that include the right to be heard on matters affecting the child (Article 12) and the right to freedom of expression in any media of the child's choice (Article 13). How these rights can be asserted by children who do not use traditional forms of communication has framed the choice of methodology and methods that underpin how Sam's interactions and intentionality were explored, to which we now turn.

Research design

Epistemology

Our assumptions about the nature of knowledge, about its possibility, scope and general basis have a profound effect on the focus of the research, the ways in which we conduct research, and how we present the research outcomes. The dominant research paradigms in education (post-positivism, interpretivism, and critical theory) each have their own very distinct epistemological assumptions resulting in contrasting research approaches.

An objective epistemology, traditionally associated with post-positivism contends that objects of study have meaning prior to, and independently of, any consciousness of them. They have truth and meaning residing in them as objects (objective truth and meaning) and that careful (i.e., "scientific", value-free, neutral, empirically verifiable) research can obtain that objective truth and meaning (Crotty, 2003). Such a position stands in stark contrast to a subjectivist epistemology. Subjectivism (located within the interpretivist paradigm) contends that human beings *impose* meanings on objects. The objects themselves contain no inherent meaning (they are "meaningless"); rather all meaning is generated from the consciousness of human beings. A subjectivist epistemology contends that no external, objective truth is waiting to be discovered, and that no meaning exists without the mind.

Neither of the above epistemological positions (objectivism/ subjectivism) was suitable for the type of enquiry pursued in this study. The aim of the research was to explore the extent to which social engagement within an inclusive environment allowed gains to be made by Sam. In order to determine levels of engagement it was important to understand the purpose of Sam's behaviour (e.g., whether or not movement or action from Sam was socially motivated). At first glance, objectivism appears to be the appropriate epistemological position for this type of enquiry, which, under post-positivistic rubric, was to "discover" the meaning lying behind the actions of the child (as the "object of study"). However, the discovery of the meanings lying behind Sam's actions is incredibly problematic given the idiosyncratic nature of children with PMLD. Children with PMLD are extremely diverse in their abilities (be that cognitive, communicative, physical, etc.) and determining the intentions lying behind the actions is very much a matter of interpretation. For example, Sam was diagnosed as having cerebral palsy—a common diagnosis amongst the PMLD population. One of the symptoms of cerebral palsy is involuntary muscle spasms (i.e., involuntary limb movement or spasms of the facial muscles resulting in unintentional facial expressions). Determining whether or not a movement of a limb was voluntary (an attempt to communicate with others) or involuntary (a symptom of cerebral palsy) was a matter of *judgement* based on an array of contextual factors (time of the day, location, behaviour leading up to the movement, etc.). If the research was undertaken with an objectivist epistemology then the aims would be to reveal objective "truth" and meaning. This type of knowledge ("absolute certainty") cannot be attained and as such an alternative epistemological position was needed.

Subjectivism was also a problematic epistemological position. Within a subjectivist epistemology the meanings lying behind Sam's actions are not found in Sam's intentions for performing the actions, but rather in the researcher who determines the meanings of the actions. Sam is essentially denied any responsibility for his actions since it is the researcher who *imposes* the meaning of such actions. Although subjectivism allows interpretation, by not making the child responsible for his or her actions, the researcher essentially denies the child as the "limiting factor" within the interpretation. The notion of "limiting factors" has its origins in Levi-Strauss' (1966) concept of a *bricoleur*—somebody who constructs or creates something from a diverse range of things used for other purposes. Levi-Strauss (1966) saw objects as pre-constrained: the qualities of the objects limit what they can be created in to (Crotty, 2003). Within the context of research, the child should be the limiting factor. If the researcher wishes to determine the meaning lying behind the actions of a child (assuming the action was intentional) there are only so many motives surrounding why a child would perform the action. However, if the researcher denies the limiting factor and does not take into account the child's intentions then the action could possibly have an endless amount of imposed meanings—which potentially could be very far from the actual intentions of the child.

In framing the research and consideration of debates within objectivist and subjectivist thinking, it became clear that there was not one epistemological or ontological commitment that could be made, as such theoretical constructions are framed within understandings of intentional, agentic and intelligible actions, behaviours and human communications, and these taken-for-granted assumptions of the social world could not be made in Sam's case. This resulted in a research design that drew on aspects of different ontological, epistemological and methodological philosophies in a unique synthesis particular to exploring and understanding the lived realities of Sam (as opposed to being imposed upon Sam as an object of study). This began with a consideration of the merits of critical theory.

Critical theory transcends the limitations of objectivism and subjectivism and sees knowledge as dependent on both the object or subject of study and the subjectivity of the researcher. Such a view sees all knowledge and meaningful reality as constructed through the interaction between human beings and their world(s). Meaning is not discovered, or imposed, but is constructed (Crotty, 2003).

Meaning-construction guided the research process located in constructionism as the *collective* construction and transmission of meaning, as opposed to constructivism as the meaning-making activity of the *individual mind* (Crotty, 2003). This difference between the individual and the collective has extremely important implications for research methodology. If the research was guided by a constructivist epistemology then knowledge construction would have been restricted to the knowledge generated during interplay between the researcher (the "individual mind") and the behaviour of Sam. The researcher's gaze is informed by their biography and dispositions yet, given the complexities and idiosyncrasies of children with PMLD, relying on this knowledge alone is not sufficient. Understanding the behaviour of a child with PMLD requires an appreciation of subtleties, since many of these children are limited in their movement and communication abilities. Knowing what to look out for and interpreting the child's movement is a difficult process and, without the involvement of significant others who know the child intimately (e.g., parents, teachers, support staff), may not be achieved within the timescale of the research. Different people construct the child in different ways based on their experiences of, and with, the child (the "interplay" of construction). Our constructed meaning of behaviour may be very different from the constructed meaning of the child's parents. Rather than ignoring the interpretation of the parents and relying solely on researcher meaning generation (constructivism), significant others played an important role and the constructed meaning was a joint, collective, agreed-upon construction (constructionism) allowing a fuller understanding to develop.

Ontology

Ontology is the study of being: "it is concerned with 'what is', with the nature of existence, with the structure of reality as such" (Crotty, 2003, p. 10). Each of the dominant research paradigms has its own ontological assumptions that complement its epistemological assumptions in guiding the research process. However, for the purpose of this research, simply adopting one of the dominant ontological positions was inadequate, and a hybrid of realism, anti-reductionism and relativism was developed, whilst notions of "naïve" realism, idealism and reductionism were rejected allowing a dynamic view of reality, which complimented the constructionist epistemology.

Objectivism and subjectivism were rejected and constructionism was embraced as the chosen epistemological stance of the research. The decision to adopt constructionism was not only based on assumptions about the nature of knowledge, but also because of assumptions about the nature of reality and "how the world is". Different people interpreted Sam's behaviour in different ways. Because of this assumption, the research was designed to take into account the multiple views of different people who knew Sam intimately in order to develop a fuller view of Sam's meaning as opposed to the single, authoritarian view of the researcher. The research also benefited from relativism since it acknowledged that Sam behaved differently in different contexts allowing the research to view Sam's world as dynamic.

Notions of intersubjectivity were used to assess preverbal development. Intentionality is central to the measurement of intersubjectivity, since determining the intentions of Sam's social behaviour in turn determined the level of intersubjective awareness Sam was capable of operating at. Once intersubjective ability was determined, the extent to which opportunities arose allowing Sam to operate at higher, secondary intersubjective states could be explored (i.e., the difference between mainstream school and special school opportunities was determined). Progress through the intersubjective stages could also be monitored. It is this link between intentionality and intersubjectivity that allowed the research to define Sam's behaviour as purposeful and, as such, located the research assumptions within an anti-reductionist ontology.

Having a constructionist epistemology does not automatically result in the research world view forfeiting a realist ontology. To say that meaningful reality is constructed is not to say that it is not real, but rather reality that is meaningful depends on the mind. From this point of view, constructionism and realism are compatible. Embracing this vision of realism as an ontological position had important consequences for the research insofar as it did not deny Sam's actions in any way. Whereas an idealist ontology contends that reality exists in the mind only, thus leading to a research process concerned solely with ideas, realism is an ontological position that acknowledges an external reality exists and thus allowed the focus of the research to be with Sam at all times, rather than purely with the "idea" of Sam.

Realism was also important for the epistemological position of the research, for it acknowledged that a physical, external world existed outside of the mind, which lent itself to notions of constructionism—the epistemological position, which sees meaning as being generated out of interplay between subjects (the internal mind) and objects (external reality). Furthermore, there was an ethical dimension to realism that allowed those involved in the research to ensure that Sam maintained a physical state of wellbeing, an issue to be discussed in more depth later in this chapter.

The above world view (incorporating a constructionist epistemology with an anti-reductionist, relativist, realist ontology) led to the development of a new and unique research methodology that allowed the exploration of meaning, engagement, intentionality, and intersubjective awareness in Sam. A review of approaches that have been taken in research with children with PMLD is presented next, before we return to consideration of what methods were employed with Sam.

Accessing "voices" and experiences in research

It has long been recognised that the majority of research in the field of PMLD has been positivistic and quantitative in nature and does not adequately capture the "voices" and lived experiences of the people with PMLD. For example, Edgerton (1993) discussed a study dating back to the early 1960s that attempted to understand the ways in which deinstitutionalisation affected the lives of people with learning difficulties:

> An outstanding void in existing sociological knowledge of the mentally retarded is a detailed description of the everyday lives of such persons outside of custodial or treatment institutions. Neither the details of their everyday conduct nor their own thoughts and emotions concerning their life circumstances have been documented. (p. 6)

In many ways the above passage resembles the current situation for children with PMLD. At present there is a distinct lack of detailed description of the everyday routines and lived experiences of children with PMLD. Research about children with PMLD is typically concerned with the efficacy of intervention strategies that aim to change behaviour (which is often conceptualised in non-volitional terms). Edgerton (1993) not only argued that adequate explanations of behaviour require understandings of subjectivity, but also that such understandings are best gleaned by developing intimate knowledge and awareness of the actor through prolonged and personal contact.

For many years disability activists and researchers have argued for inclusive methodologies that were built on principles of equity and social justice and that echoed more strongly the principles of the emergent social model of disability, whilst challenging incremental perspectives associating the extent of a person's disability and their ability to participate in research:

> Some elements of humanity are open to sociological investigation ('mild learning difficulties'), while some are left in the realms of static, irreversible, individualised biology ('severe learning difficulties'). (Goodley, 2001, p. 231)

Goodley et al. (2004) describe an ethnographic approach and recognise the importance of developing intimate knowledge of research participants through sustained engagement in their lives. Ethnographic research is said to be partly defined by this act of familiarisation. Yet ethnography with its focus on cultural understandings does not provide the space required for a concentrated examination of Sam's development and learning. This is not to say that the research made no contribution to understanding classroom culture, but rather that the methodology was designed for a different purpose (the study of an individual). Furthermore, because the research participants that Goodley et al. (2004) engaged with could speak, there is no discussion of how ethnographic research could be applied in the PMLD context.

The difficulty of giving authentic voice to research participants who communicate non-verbally has been discussed by Moore, Beazley and Maelzer (1998), Edgerton (1993) and Goodley et al. (2004), who made use of verbal interview techniques. Moore et al. (1998) expressed discontent with such techniques during data collection with the d/Deaf (sic) community:

> We felt rather despondent because if the primary form of communication used in the interviews was, after all, to be speech with the written form and some gesture used as a back-up ... this would structure the research project in ways which members of the Deaf community would find oppressive. (p. 41)

In order to support alternative forms of dialogue between the researchers and d/Deaf community the researchers devised a graphical technique that d/Deaf interviewees found liberating:

> [W]e made further effort to avoid over-reliance on spoken language during the course of interviews and planned parts to be focused around pictures we asked respondents to draw. This technique had been used by one of the researchers in a previous project where it was found that drawing pictures greatly enriched the respondents thinking around focal topics and their ability to express themselves. (p. 42)

In a methods review for the Economic and Social Research Council (ESRC) on qualitative research with people with learning, communication and other disabilities, Nind (2008) concludes that whilst it is challenging, it is achievable to access disabled voices in research and that "addressing them as human beings with something to say that is worth hearing" is of foremost importance (Nind, 2008, p. 16). Interestingly, in an earlier article Nind's view appears to be more aligned to the critique offered by Goodley (2001) that there is a continuum of the extent to which the most profoundly disabled people can be involved in research on the basis of their inability to use language (Sheehy & Nind, 2005).

Much of these debates focus on "*people* with profound and multiple disabilities" as opposed to *children* and this mirrors the debates in the childhood studies arena, which has fought to develop appropriate participatory approaches to engage all children in research (Christensen & James, 2008; Harcourt et al., 2011; Punch, 2002; Tisdall, 2012; Tisdall et al., 2008) and where children have been denied rights based on arguments that suggest "they lacked rationality, they lacked competence, they needed protection not autonomy" (Tisdall, 2012, p. 182). There are also concerns over the coercion of children's voices and the need to respect their silences as well as their voices (Lewis, 2010). This issue becomes more complex when non-communication is viewed "as reflecting a lack of communicative ability" (Lewis, 2011, p. 99).

So there remains debate about how children's voices in research can be "heard" and, in particular, the voices of children with PMLD. Some researchers argue that rights-based approaches to enable people with PMLD to express a view are unrealistic on the basis that the label of PMLD suggests someone operating at a "pre-intentional level who reacts to an event" (Ware, 2004, p. 176). Ware (2004) argued that this is about expressing a *choice* or a *preference* and not a *view* as prescribed in rights-based approaches. This arguably reflects a reductionist, postpositivist perspective that denies rights to people with PMLD, but is a prevalent perspective in respect of research agendas. Others are more optimistic for the possibilities of research with disabled children in order "to define disability in their terms to allow for the intersection of childhood and disability" (Watson, 2012, p. 199). Questions over the facilitation of "voice" for those with severe disabilities do however remain, with concerns raised about the representation of disabled children's voices through researcher-chosen quotes or observations of interactions and of the need for transparency in respect of the researcher's decisions (Abbott, 2012). This reflects the need for a constructionist stance that ensures the presence of the researcher in interpretation and data display and allows for non-verbal communications to be captured (Morris, 2003). Morris reported a methodology of "being with" young people who had no language in order to understand their experiences:

> Sometimes this took the form of straightforward observation of what was going on in a situation; other times it involved joining

in an activity, such as having a meal, or accompanying them on an outing. (p. 345)

Morris' (2003) experiences challenged parent, carer and professional perspectives of children and young people who were deemed non-communicative and incomprehensible and resulted in her assertion that:

[A]ll children and young people—whatever their communication and/or cognitive impairment—have something to communicate. It is up to us to find ways of understanding their views and experiences. (p. 346)

This raises the methodological problem that this project sought to address. Not only does Sam's story challenge the received wisdom in respect of theoretical understandings of PMLD, it also opens new possibilities in respect of methodology—to which we now turn.

The search for a methodology

As articulated earlier, the aim of the research was to explore the extent to which inclusive education could contribute towards Sam's development and learning, measured in terms of intersubjective gains. This suggested an alternative perspective was needed that acknowledged intentionality and allowed for the exploration of purposeful behaviour. Constructionism provided the methodological framework within which methods could be developed that recognised that, given the idiosyncrasies of children like Sam, identifying intentionality was very much a matter of interpretation, rather than the discovery of absolute truth. Different people could interpret Sam's unique behaviour in different ways. Rather than choosing one interpretation (i.e., that of the dominant researcher) over another equally plausible interpretation, the world view sought to benefit from multiple realities by valuing collective knowledge construction, and this draws some parallels with the approach taken by Morris (2003).

Children with PMLD lack what is understood as formal speech in that they do not speak the English language. Thus, they do not have a "voice", in the literal sense, since they do not have speech and cannot "speak for themselves". This means that their points of view must be represented and voiced by others, and this is an act of meaning construction that is not without challenges both ethically and methodologically. One of the great pillars of quality in qualitative research is that of authenticity of participants' voices and experiences and was one of the reasons for the choice of a number of data collection methods in order to enable all the people directly involved in Sam's education and care to contribute to co-constructed meaning-making.

The literature on disabled people and disabled children in research is relatively sparse and has been widely critiqued as marginalising and disempowering, suffering from the domination of researcher agendas and misrepresentation of disabled lives (Hodge, 2008). Traditional methods of inquiry have largely contributed to much of the misrepresentation and tokenistic inclusion of disabled people in research, particularly those with communication difficulties. As such, it could be argued that the research community has lacked the expertise, imagination and capability to engage the most disabled (especially children) in research processes that can genuinely capture their experiences and enable positive and emancipatory changes to result (Hodge, 2008). This chapter will present a review of methods that have been developed for researching with disabled children in particular, in order to convey the decisions underpinning the methods that were employed in the study with Sam.

With very few exceptions, research with disabled children has relied on traditional approaches of interviews, focus groups and questionnaires with creative or technological facilitation (Lewis & Porter, 2004). Increasingly, it is evident that traditional methods, particularly questionnaires and rating scales, are not appropriate for research with people who have learning disabilities and do not have the verbal skills required (Hewitt, 2000b). Interviews are usually supported with visual and arts-based methods, such as photo elicitation or "photo voice" (Boxall & Ralph, 2010; Burke, 2012); or visual communication devices such as "talking mats" (Germain, 2004), sometimes facilitated by trained speech and language therapists as opposed to researchers (Whitehurst, 2007).

Critics of talking mats identify concern that through facilitation we are effectively putting words into people's mouths (Brewster, 2004) and challenge the extent to which such facilitated approaches can truly enable severely disabled "voices" to be heard, particularly as the symbols presented to children are researcher chosen. Some researchers report encouraging children to identify additional symbols, but with little success, which suggests a framing of the conversations possible according to the symbols provided (Mitchell, 2010). Attempts at more open-ended drawing methods that gave young people greater control over what is communicated through pictorial forms have also had mixed success and are often hampered by poor fine motor control (Beresford, 2012).

In recognising the importance of longitudinal understandings, Brewster proposes an approach to "accessing views as an ongoing process" (2004, p. 169) rather than seeing it as a one-off data collection activity as may be the case with non-disabled participants. This suggests the need for relationships to be made with participants and peers/family/carers over an extensive period of time in order to truly understand the extent to which individuals are able to have their views heard through facilitated approaches (Mitchell, 2010). This is even more the case when we consider children with severe communication difficulties, who are reliant on interpretation of their views and wishes through adult intermediaries (Beresford, 2012; Lewis & Porter, 2004). The absence of long term research relationships is evident in some studies that have attempted to interview children and young people whilst relying solely on teachers' and carers' advice and guidance in establishing relationships. A study that was largely focused on obtaining questionnaire responses from parents, teachers and respite care staff on levels of distress experienced by children with learning difficulties in respite also attempted to gain the views of six children in individual interviews (Radcliffe, 2007). Not surprisingly, the interview data lacked depth, and in one case a child was visibly agitated by the process. This raises some of the critiques of tokenism that are widely applied to the inclusion of children in research (Farrell, 2005; Lewis & Porter, 2004; Mitchell, 2010). This also indicates a wider concern as to the extent to which individual accounts can be applied to a wider cohort of disabled experiences. The sociology of childhood has as a founding principle the idea that childhood is a "variable of social analysis that cannot be entirely divorced from other variables such as class, gender or ethnicity" (Jenks, 2001, p. 50), so the question arises that, with access to so few disabled children's voices in the research community, how can we "move from hearing individual children's views, to helping children to present a collective 'choir'" (Lewis & Porter, 2004, p. 196).

Visual methods of research with children who have little or no language are increasingly common and often used in combination (Brewster & Coleyshaw, 2010; Preece & Jordan, 2009), such as the use of participant-taken photographs and "talking mats" (Germain, 2004). In this study by Germain (2004), teenagers were encouraged to take photographs (with instructions in Makaton) and then used talking mat aids to communicate their feelings and emotions about the photos. These approaches mirror methods developed to engage children in research more generally, and have been adapted for children with disabilities by building on understandings of children's capabilities from developmental knowledge of children more generally; with an explicit focus on the use of different modes of communication, avoidance of direct abstract questioning, and the encouragement of children to be confident to say they do not know the answer (Lewis, 2004).

Other approaches that are documented (although less so with children) are life story approaches drawn from narrative methods of inquiry. Life story books have been used with adults, particularly to recount experiences of institutional care (Atkinson, 1997; Middleton & Hewitt, 1999), although these have tended to rely on the verbal skills of people to recount their stories and there are few incidences of storytelling for, and by, profoundly disabled people (Grove, 2012). Attempts that have been made to construct life story books with profoundly disabled adults have drawn upon family and caregiver accounts with the stories relayed back to the disabled person and "their reactions were monitored" (Hewitt, 2000, p. 93). Despite this limited ownership of the stories that were conveyed, Hewitt (2000) reported changes in caregiver attitudes and a shift in focus from "viewing them as 'subjects' or 'clients' and consider[ing] them as people with their own unique life" (p. 95). Grove (2012) suggests that stories do not need to be individual in order to give people agency and that narrative is an essential element of how we make and sustain relationships. This suggests a narrative that resides in complex networks of families and communities, not solely in individual accounts, which opens up a methodological space in respect of research with profoundly disabled people:

> This recognition of mutual dependence is of clear relevance to an ethic of social inclusion that promotes interpersonal interaction and relationships as the fundamental mechanism of achieving social inclusion. (p. 346)

A storying approach that is documented with children is the use of cue cards to enable the co-construction of interview narratives in order to achieve greater depth and coherence of story (Lewis, 2002), which could combat the lack of qualitative data achieved in some studies—although this approach was not used with children with PMLD; rather it was used with children regarded as MLD. The cards include symbols about people, talk, settings, feelings and consequences (ibid.) and are used as prompts in interview discussions to provide the contexts and links for richer accounts to emerge. However, such an approach also suggests the need for some verbal communication skills.

Debates are apparent in the literature about the extent to which the use of child-friendly and creative methods are strategically facilitative in giving the researcher access to the views of disabled children, or whether they are part of a broader project enabling the fuller participation of children with disabilities in research processes (Beresford, 2012). A study in Australia focusing on the play experiences of disabled children is one that appears to embrace the participation of children through the use of self-taken photographs (with the assistance of child "buddies") and photo-elicitation interviews that involved a number of visual tools (Burke, 2012). The data from this study is presented in photographic and narrative ways and offers detailed and rich understandings of the children's play experiences resulting in the author's claim that:

> All children, including children with impairments, are essentially social, relational beings who interact with each other and with their environments through self-selected play experiences. (Burke, 2012, p. 979)

This claim is founded on the accounts of children that read as authentic and messy, and indicate a way forward for valid research with disabled children.

Direct observation of children with PMLD is a final method reported in the literature. These approaches fall into participatory and non-participatory methods. The non-participatory have been largely rooted in medical and developmental assessments of disabled children's progress and interactions and are utilised in the Intensive Interaction methodology (Nind & Hewett, 1994), which is explored in more detail in Chapter Three. This approach was developed as a teaching programme in supporting people with severe and complex learning difficulties to learn and relate to others (Nind & Powell, 2000) and is reported to reduce stereotyped behaviours in adults (Nind & Kellett, 2002). It aims to emulate caregiver interactions with babies and focuses on the very early stages of communication development in infants and as such has been described as a naturalistic approach to instruction for severely disabled children and adults (Nind & Powell, 2000).

The efficacy of Intensive Interaction has been researched widely and predominately through the use of direct and non-participant observation methods including a range of published measures (*Pre-verbal communication schedule* and the *Cuddliness scale*) (Kellett & Nind, 2001; Kellett, 2000). The use of observation is within a structured quasi-experimental design and involves the video recording of a child's interactions in classroom situations and the systematic analysis of these recordings according to structured themes, such as attempts to initiate social contact, interactive behaviour, and responses to teacher's physical proximity (ibid.). This systematic approach yields detailed and highly nuanced data showing very small changes in behaviour over time that allow for the capture of very small developmental gains as displayed by severely disabled children (Kellett, 2000).

Criticisms that could be drawn of the observation methods employed with Intensive Interaction are that it is a form of applied behaviour analysis (Hogg, 2002), which diverts attention to certain behaviours and interactions only and does not allow for a more holistic observation to be captured, which itself has been taken to task for "failing to demonstrate that behavioural interventions influence the wider lives of the individuals involved" (ibid., p. 296). Small gains may be recorded in specific behaviours but these are arguably reductionist in approach and raise concerns about how these contribute to the overall development of communication and relationship-building with others, particularly when the extent of observer interpretation is not acknowledged (Munde et al., 2011). There are also concerns voiced about how it is possible to reconcile the acceptance of diversity within a developmental approach that aims to facilitate changes in people (Goldbart, 2002). The proponents of Intensive Interaction and the associated methods employed in defining its utility seem overly exercised by the reliability and validity of the measures chosen, without really questioning the measures themselves; so there is also an ontological challenge that goes unanswered particularly as there is poor evidence that standardised clinical assessment measurements are even appropriate for use with children with PMLD (Carnaby, 2007; Munde et al., 2011; Vlaskamp &

Cuppen-Fonteine, 2007), particularly in respect of the "idiosyncratic communicative repertoire" (Nakken & Vlaskamp, 2007, p. 86) apparent in people with PMLD.

Interestingly, Kellett (2005) herself challenges the relevance of the reduction of behaviour to observable items in the case study she presents of a profoundly disabled eleven-year-old girl, "Catherine"; who died shortly after treatment—as Kellett (2005) reports of her mother:

> She described the joy of the family in being able finally to "connect" with Catherine and wrote that those last few months were their happiest times together. The fact that Catherine died only a short time after these communicative developments made the "connection" all the more potent and it is impossible to measure this in human terms. (p. 119)

This challenges the purpose of research with children like Catherine as the focus shifted away from minute behavioural observations to the human and emotive interactions that were observed:

> The video was alive with smiles, eye contact, warm physical interaction and the sound of Catherine using her tongue in a tutting sound as part of a playful imitative game. (Kellett, 2005, p. 120)

Beyond the methodological critiques, ethical critiques have also been offered focusing on the ethical challenge posed by Nind and Kellett's (2002) explicit focus upon reducing stereotyped behaviours that are arguably of the individual's identity (Hogg, 2002) and may indeed serve a functional purpose (Harris, 2002). This is particularly critiqued by those who suggest there is little evidence that so-called "stereotyped behaviours" do negatively impact inclusion (Goldbart, 2002) as claimed by Nind and Kellett (2002).

Other studies report the use of "behavioural observation" methods (Hussein, 2010) or the keeping of observational "notes" (Stickley et al., 2011). These are largely unstructured observational studies that occur in naturalistic ways and combine observation with other methods such as interviews with professionals. The study by Hussein (2010) involved the researcher collecting "anecdotal evidence" written up in detailed notes along with photos to describe children's use of a multisensory garden. The data presented allows insights into the ways children directly interact with the built and natural environment and provide evidence that the environment offers sensory stimulation. There is however a complete lack of methodological information provided on the research design and processes, which limits the overall validity of the study and this is also the case in the Stickley et al. (2011) study.

Participant observation is less well documented in studies researching PMLD children. One study utilised participant observation with children "who do not use formally recognised methods of communication" (Cocks, 2008, p. 163) in specialist social care services. Given this description it is difficult to ascertain whether these were children with PMLD, but the paper raises some interesting ethical issues in respect of participant observation as the researcher took on the "least-adult" role and played alongside the children in ways that challenged their own, and professionals', perceptions of her identity. Cocks (2008) also identifies gaps in her understandings of children's behaviours that remain without their accounts of their motivations and intentions-this highlights the level of researcher interpretation of disabled children's voices discussed earlier. The data was recorded in naturalistic field notes and this provides insights into peer interactions with the claim that "interaction came out of the general environment rather than being exclusively initiated by the children themselves" (p. 176). This is an important observation in respect of the ways in which environmental context may influence interactional behaviour. Whilst many of the children did not use spoken language it was apparent from the field notes that they all had high levels of mobility, so it is unlikely that this participatory, interactive observational approach was conducted with children with PMLD.

This section has reviewed a number of approaches that have specifically been used in research with disabled children and adults and with a focus on capturing the "voices" of children with PMLD. What is apparent is that research about children with PMLD is the most underdeveloped in methodological terms of all social science research. Some approaches hold promise and possibilities for development; but there is a genuine gap in our methodological "tool box" for researching with children with PMLD in respectful, ethical, and authentic ways. The discussion of methods that have been previously employed in research with severely disabled children, or those specifically identified as

PMLD, suggests a number of emergent issues that were taken into the design of the project with Sam:

- the benefits of longitudinal research that allows for the researcher to know the disabled child and develop abilities to see differences in behaviour "being with" (Morris, 2003) the child;
- the need to develop methods that allow for mutual dependence and multiple voices (including peers, caregivers, family members and professionals);
- methods that capture and foreground the emotions, wishes, preferences, tendencies, intentions of children with PMLD are essential;
- that changes in interactions and behaviours may be very small and methods need to be sensitive enough to capture these;
- the importance of environmental context (and changing contexts) in observing interactions.

Methods

Drawing on the review of previous studies and Ben's experience working with Sam, it was apparent that interviewing him directly was not an option. Instead, participatory observation and non-participatory observations through the creation of "vignettes" were the primary research methods employed. Focus group meetings and regular informal discussions with significant others also provided the basis of the research. Developing methods based upon arts-based approaches may have been relevant. However, Sam strongly resisted attempts by staff to engage him in any kind of artistic endeavour and this was evidence of his expression of preferences and helped to frame the choice of methods that "sat alongside" him rather than impose additional demands on him. Why such methods were chosen and how they were used will now be discussed.

- Pre-observation focus groups

Before observation commenced it was important to first consult significant others (e.g., teachers and learning support assistants) who knew Sam intimately. The justification for these methods combined together is that conducting observations in order to determine intention would have been incredibly difficult if the views of those that knew Sam well were not sought prior to (and during) observation. These views helped guide the observations and provided Ben with an initial lens through which he could begin to interpret Sam's behaviour. In particular, discussions with significant others taught Ben to appreciate how subtle differences in Sam's behaviour could indicate different emotions and intentions. For example, during many observations Sam displayed various "unhappy" states of behaviour. Determining why Sam was unhappy would have been more difficult if it were not for others who had suggested prior to observations that they believed instant "real tears" and head-banging indicated that Sam was in pain (it was believed that he suffered from trapped wind a great deal); whilst gradual reaching out to others, moaning and increased rocking indicated boredom and frustration. Without such guidance, the discrimination of behaviour states and intentions would have been a much more difficult and slower process and perhaps unachievable within the timescale of the research if observation alone (leading to solitary construction of meaning as opposed to the co-construction that was sought) was the only method of data collection.

Thus, prior to observations, significant others including Sam's parents, staff from Sam's mainstream school and special school (i.e., teachers, LSAs) and others who knew Sam from his attendance at a previous special school participated in focus-group style discussions. The use of focus groups as the medium for early research, guided by Gadamer's (1976) philosophy of hermeneutic-phenomenology, complimented the research world view (Gadamer, 1976). Hermeneutic-phenomenology is not a *method* to be adopted to get to the "right" interpretation (i.e., it is not a method guided by an objectivist epistemology to find the one true meaning residing in objects), rather it is a set of clarifying conditions through which understanding takes place (i.e., it is an ontological position that implies that the social world is different to the natural world, and that only within certain contexts can true understanding emerge, moving hermeneutic phenomenology into an anti-reductionist and relative, context-sensitive world view) (Laverty, 2003; Odman & Kerdeman, 1999). This shift in focus from epistemology to ontology has consequences for the relationship between the researcher and the researched (Radnor, 2002) in the sense that true understanding can only occur through a "fusion of horizons" (the transcendence of two or more differing views in order to reach a higher, fuller, holistic understanding), which result after negotiations and reconstructions of meaning between two or more people. Such a fusion requires the researcher and researched to be equal, for open dialogue to occur, and a willingness to be open to new experiences and understandings (Robertson-Malt, 1999).

The focus groups were formed in order to allow such clarifying conditions to emerge, since focus groups are deemed to be sites of synergism where individuals work together and interact to construct meaning and understanding (Finch & Lewis, 2003).

In order for the focus-group meetings to benefit from the clarifying conditions of hermeneutic-phenomenology, the research design sought to create an emancipatory context in which every individual was deemed equal, and that every opinion was equally valued, regardless of differences in hierarchical role (e.g., between that of the SENCO and an LSA). Harrison et al. (2001) argue that "good data" that is thick and rich in description relies heavily on the relationship between researcher and researched, hence a need existed not only for the school staff to relinquish their hierarchical identities during the focus-group sessions, but Ben's role as dominant researcher also had to be relinquished in order to allow the right conditions for a fuller understanding to be achieved. Through self-disclosure and intimacy, focus-group sessions resembled conversations. Reciprocity was central to this process and was achieved through openness (e.g., Ben's research diary, thoughts and opinions were openly shared with the focus group and were open to scrutiny and questioning). Through the medium of the focus groups, ideas were constructed and reconstructed until a higher level of understanding was reached (i.e., a fusion of horizons) as a consequence of reciprocity (Harrison et al., 2001) and democratic participatory processes (Kemmis & McTaggart, 1998; Kemmis & Wilkinson, 1998), which resulted in an ideal speech situation for those in the group (Habermas, 1974).

The above emancipatory conditions were created to allow the focus groups to discuss Sam in a way which maximised understanding. Such conditions could not be achieved if group *interviewing* was the chosen method, as comments would have been directed by the researcher (Malin, 2003) as opposed to discussions taking place between colleagues who work with Sam. During discussions, every member of staff, regardless of rank within the school, had the "right" to speak about their interpretations and understandings of Sam, allowing the research to benefit greatly from fusions of horizons.

152   THE PMLD AMBIGUITY

Synergistic, constantly open and reciprical focus-group discussions were achieved by shifting the control and power of the group away from Ben as a dominant member due to research expertise to them as experts in Sam's life. Significant others were encouraged to consider multiple stances on Sam's behaviours and interactions and open inviting questions were used such as: "Could you tell me how Sam behaves in his mainstream school?" Ben's role in the focus group was primarily to stimulate and maintain conversations, providing prompts, suggestions and statements when the conversations dwindled. In order for staff to achieve a fusion of horizons, they were asked to discuss the idea that, if all these differing interpretations were equally plausible, then what would a theory look like that encompassed all of these views? This invoked a very imaginative discussion which led to various suggestions and meta-theories encapsulating all of the ideas into one "supratheory". For example, during discussions, staff were divided in their opinions over whether Sam was benefiting from circle time (i.e., it was explained that by being with other children, Sam learned to behave), or was left out because the lessons were beyond Sam's comprehension (i.e., Sam cannot do Key Stage 1 number bonds). The staff agreed as a collective that Sam benefited *under certain conditions*, leading to various hypothesis-styled statements ("If X then Y")—that is, "if Sam was to benefit from circle time, then the following elements had to be in place: opportunity for socialisation, group work, peer support, etc." This lead to discussions on how we may tell if Sam was engaging and/or benefiting, and possible behaviours were listed as indicators of engagement. Such a process, guided by the ontological notions from Gadamer's (1976) hermeneutic-phenomenology allowed the right conditions for fruitful discussions to take place, resulting in knowledge and understanding being constructed socially in order to transcend individual constructions and form a collective construction resulting in a fusion of horizons (Laverty, 2003). Such horizons not only provided an initial lens through which to view Sam, but also provided indications of where to conduct observations and what to look out for.

There was also room within the focus-group meetings to clarify interpretations of what was being discussed by the staff. Because of the ontological positions guiding the research, description and narration could no longer be seen as straightforward representations of reality. Language could no longer be seen as merely mirroring "what is there", as Crotty (2003) explains: "when we describe something, we are, in the normal course of events, reporting how something is seen and reacted to, and thereby meaningfully constructed, within a given community or set of communities" (p. 64). Thus, it was important to gain access to the meanings of these given communities and to make sure that Ben had understood what the staff were trying to say, rather than assuming that he had understood their meanings based on interpretation of their language. Notions of symbolic interactionism (Radnor, 2002) were addressed via the medium of hermeneutic cycles. During the focus-group discussions various themes, suggestions and quotes were recorded in the research diary. Understandings, constructed socially between the discussions of staff and interpretations of the discussions, were then communicated back to the staff, often with a statement beginning: "Did you mean …?" This process of checking interpretation allowed notions of authenticity (Appleton, 1995) to be addressed, since clarification was frequently sought.

- Participatory observations

Throughout the project Ben undertook participatory observations and was effectively a learning support assistant (LSA) for Sam once a week in his special school and once a week in his mainstream school. The purpose of participatory observation was to allow for alternative ways of "getting to know Sam" and "being with" (Morris, 2003) him beyond solely using the distant observer role as it involved data collection with Sam and the capturing of his reactions and responsiveness. By interacting with Sam and supporting his learning and development alongside other specialist LSAs, Ben was able to learn about Sam's day (i.e., his routines, his curriculum, his responses to different teaching methods, his behaviours, etc.) much more effectively than without participating. Participatory observation reduced the reactivity of the researcher and helped to develop rapport and trust from the other members of staff who worked with Sam (Wellington, 2000). This was particularly important since a good relationship was needed if joint knowledge construction was to occur (Harrison et al., 2001). An element of "real-time" construction (as opposed to construction in hindsight) benefited the research since informal, open and relaxed discussions could take place throughout the day about Sam's various behaviours in order to develop a fuller understanding of Sam's intentions. For example, the themes that emerged out of the initial focus group discussions (e.g., the difference between Sam in pain and bored Sam) were then discussed and subtleties highlighted whilst Sam was actually expressing his unhappy state and thus clarifying what the staff had said during discussions and enhancing notions of authenticity.

Participatory observation allowed Ben to construct his understandings of Sam's intentions and methods of interaction by engaging *with* him. By working with Sam, meaning was constructed between Sam's actions and our interpretations of the intentions of such actions, based on our growing knowledge of Sam in general. If the research was guided by more idealist ontologies then the research methodology may have steered away from participatory observations and interactions with Sam and relied solely on methods that allow clarifying conditions to emerge, since reality would be seen as existing only in the mind, and hence "external" reality (i.e., *actual* Sam as opposed to the idea of Sam) may not have been consulted.

- Non-participatory observation (vignettes)

Non-participatory research was also undertaken and provided the main opportunities for data generation. However, observations were not conducted in the "systematic" manner (i.e., use of observation schedules) usually undertaken in more quantitative research (Wellington, 2000). Very few observation schedules are available for research on children with PMLD, since most schedules are designed with reference to "more able" children. Children with PMLD are idiosyncratic and applying generalisations based on non-PMLD observations is inappropriate. Given such idiosyncrasies, a method was needed that easily leant itself to notions of joint knowledge construction by allowing others who observed the same phenomena, but who potentially interpreted the phenomena in different ways, to contribute towards construction of meaning and thereby transcending limited single constructions. A method was needed that went beyond descriptive, quantitative recordings and allowed meaning about intentionality to be constructed, since determining the motives of behaviour in turn allowed measurement of intersubjectivity. Systematic observations are useful for determining frequencies of behaviour states and the relationship between behaviour and context (i.e., to determine if Sam presented as more happy in mainstream school or special school), but such a method could not determine the motives of behaviour, as intentionality was a matter of interpretation and judgement, not observable scientific truth.

The above circumstances led to the need to develop a methodology based on qualitative, interpretative methods of observation whereby data collected was rich enough in detail to convey a vivid picture of how Sam was behaving at a given moment in time (as well as the events leading up to and after the behaviour), and which also could be scrutinised by significant others and thereby lend itself towards collective knowledge construction. The use of video recordings was inappropriate for both practical and paradigmatic reasons. Several parents specifically requested that their children (Sam's peers) were not to be recorded and avoiding recording particular children during observations of important group work sessions was far too problematic. Moreover, during group work Sam was at his most active and thus avoiding observations during this time was not an option. The purpose of sustained observations (both participatory and non-participatory) was to reduce reactivity by submerging in the culture of Sam's educational life. Frequent use of video-recording equipment would have increased reactivity (thereby altering the natural "flow" of the classroom activity), which in turn risked disturbing the children's education.

In order to avoid the above difficulties found in traditional observation techniques, the research methodology incorporated "vignette" creation. Vignette creation is a relatively new, qualitative research method that has not been used in PMLD research before, making this project pioneering in its methodology. The creation of vignettes involves essentially writing in great depth about small events in Sam's life. Since the focus of the research concerned social engagement, then whenever Sam was socially engaged, or was thought to be socially engaged, Ben would sit back and write extremely detailed and lucid accounts of what he was seeing during that episode. For example, during the early days the research focused on determining what Sam looked like when he was expressing particular behaviour states (i.e., angry, happy, sad, etc.). Every time Sam displayed particular moods, the aim was to write about the subtle differences in order to determine exactly how Sam looked when he was feeling "X". So, for example, Ben would write about the direction of his eyes, if he raised his eyebrows, the shape of his mouth, the direction of his head, what his arms and legs were doing, the noises he were making, and the events that led up to and after this behaviour. The following is an example of an early vignette:

> Sam is sitting on the carpet, leaning on several children, they are talking to each other and Sam appears to be listening, his mouth is open, his eyes are rolled back to the top left and his "good ear" is facing in the direction of the conversation. He appears to be concentrating. Every now and again, when the children get excited and laugh Sam twitches suddenly and his gaze moves—his eyes dart in the general direction of the noisy children and then roll back again. "Buggabuggabuggabugga!!!" Sam shouts out loud and wiggles his legs and claps his hands. He now appears excited …

Notice how the description is not only on Sam's behaviour, but also on contextual factors. Judgements were made based on how Sam behaved in relation to others around him. Previous discussions highlighted the need to differentiate between movements caused by cerebral palsy, and movement intended by Sam. Being able to differentiate between behaviour states and determine if Sam was feeling happy and was focused on other children allowed better judgement of whether or not Sam was reaching out to others.

The purpose of vignette creation was not to convey an accurate "truth", but rather offer a rich, thick, descriptive piece of writing constructed out of the interplay between Sam's interactions with his world and Ben's interpretation of it. The creation of vignettes allowed Ben to record not only Sam, but his perceptions and constructions of Sam. These constructions, in the form of descriptive chunks, were then read by other members of staff who observed the same behaviour. Joint construction of meaning occurred when we combined our individual constructions of Sam and negotiated meaning of Sam in a way that allowed a higher, joint construction of knowledge to emerge. Vignettes are instant—they can be created in "real time" and shown to other members of staff potentially straight after the event, which was crucial with busy learning support staff, who could not come out of the educational environment to review, for example, video recordings.

Dozens of vignettes were recorded each day both in Sam's mainstream school and special school settings. The quantity and richness of the vignettes allowed Ben to submerge himself in the data in order to look for common themes. Submergence or immersion is the first step of data management necessary for analysis. Researchers read and reread the data in order to get a feel for it, which then leads to the identification of general themes or concepts that the data possibly contain. These themes and ideas then become categories that are used to sort the data into possible groups (Ryan & Bernard, 1994; Silverman, 1993). Submergence was not a process that only happened at the end of the research, but was something pursued throughout. Hundreds of vignettes were created during the duration of the research. Each time Sam engaged with another person a vignette was created, either "live" or in hindsight. Over time this allowed a fuller picture to emerge of Sam's social life in both his mainstream school and special-school setting. Submergence resulted in the comparing and contrasting of vignettes in relation to particular educational and social contexts. For example, vignettes could be compared and contrasted based on setting (mainstream school *vs.* special school), and social partner (disabled special school peers *vs.* mainstream school peers, adults *vs.* peers, etc.). This allowed themes to emerge from the data, which then formed the focus for further exploration.

The vignettes were also shown to staff and the ideas and themes that emerged after submergence in the data discussed with them. Often, staff agreed with the construction of behaviour or interpreted meaning. However, when they did not agree, the discussions often resulted in Ben and members of staff reflecting and considering alternative viewpoints. For example, a very complex phenomena observed was Sam's "self-harming". Sam often hit himself and appeared to hurt himself by slapping his face, pinching the back of his neck, and hitting his arms and legs. Sam's special school teacher and most of her LSAs were certain that the self-harming was non-communicative, whereas discussions in the mainstream school had led staff to the conclusion that *all* his hitting was communicative in some way. Anti-reductionism is the view that human action is intended behaviour and this is how Ben framed his interpretations. Such a view contrasts with the postpositivist notion of reductionism, which contends that human action is not intended but rather is caused by external forces. The polemic arguments of reductionism and anti-reductionism were seen in the different educational contexts of the special school and mainstream school which had differing perceptions of Sam's behaviour. Over the space of a few weeks, the special school staff began observing Sam in a new light and attempted to see Sam's behaviour as intentional. During the same time the mainstream school staff attempted to differentiate more between the hitting for communication and hitting for attention. The special school staff eventually agreed that the hitting, which was typically described as "self-harm", was intentional communication. The special school staff's observations led them to believe that certain particular hitting motions were communicative, whilst others were purely self-stimulatory or were stereotyped behaviours. The mainstream school staff reached similar conclusions during the same time period: not all of Sam's behaviours were intentional but certainly some of them were. The creation of vignettes and the subsequent submergence in the data had led Ben to believe Sam displayed a high level of intentionality during particular contexts, which in turn led to staff from both Sam's schools reading the vignettes and offering their own constructs of Sam's behaviour. By taking the mainstream views to the special school staff, and vice-versa, a fusion of horizons occurred whereby the collective knowledge of the special school was fused with the collective knowledge of the mainstream school resulting in staff from both educational settings considering alternate views of Sam, which eventually led to knowledge construction incorporating both views. The fusion of horizons lead to an agreement that Sam displayed a greater level of intentionality than first expected in the special school and was a major outcome for the research. After the fusion, the special school staff changed their practices with Sam by altering their targets and structuring their lessons to empower Sam with new communicative methods (i.e., basic vocalisations, pointing, eye contact), which, it was believed, directly led to Sam reducing his hitting as a consequence.

In the next chapter we present a series of vignettes generated through the research to illuminate how Sam experienced and engaged with his different learning environments. We also analyse these vignettes using the theoretical perspectives explored in this book (behaviourism, cognitivism, and phenomenology) in order to assess the extent to which each perspective can make Sam's contextually located behaviours intelligible.

CHAPTER SIX

Sam's life-worlds: subjectivities and intersubjectivities

Introduction

This chapter presents eleven vignettes that were recorded by Ben as part of the non-participant observations conducted with Sam. Ben spent one day a week with Sam in his special school and one day a week in his mainstream school for an academic year. The vignettes presented here include examples drawn from the special school and the mainstream school. The vignettes are analysed using one or more of the theoretical lenses introduced in earlier chapters (behaviourism, cognitivism, and phenomenology). It is hoped that taking this postmodern turn to theorising will provide different insights on the same data and new vantage points on Sam's behaviour in the two school contexts. As such, this is not a neat and tidy presentation of qualitative data; it is to be read more as an experiment in theorising, which we hope the reader will recognise allows for novel presentations of Sam.

The chapter commences with introducing the reader to essential tools to comprehend the vignettes. These are first a discussion of the range of behaviour states observed and the presentation of a taxonomy of behaviour states that was generated on the basis of coding the observations and looking for key patterns. We also discuss the importance of switch-based activities in Sam's special school environment, as these impacted substantially on the observations that were recorded of him in that environment.

Behaviour states

The qualitative research process described in Chapter Five led to the agreement of eleven dominant behaviour states in Sam (see Table 2 below). These were co-constructed in discussion with staff in both schools and with Sam's parents and as a result of systematic analysis of the observation records. These states were used to interpret Sam's behaviour and to determine which environment Sam was socially active in, to what extent, and which subjective or intersubjective state he exhibited. It was determined that Sam's level of social engagement varied significantly depending on which school he attended and which type of communication partner was accessible to him. These findings were not static but changed over time, with changes in the quality of interaction and choice of interactive partners, particularly during the third academic term. Submersion in the rich data throughout the data-collection stage and the sharing of data with significant others has led to the collective agreement that the data conveys a strong impression that each of Sam's schools are qualitatively different and Sam engages with these settings in different ways. The states are presented in the table below and will be referred to in discussion of the vignettes presented.

As discussed in Chapter Five, when the project started we drew conceptual resources about the nature of intersubjectivity from Trevarthen and Aitken (2001) and the nature of behaviour states from Foreman et al. (2004). These concepts partly framed the initial interpretive lens, which was elaborated and enriched through interaction with Sam and regular discussions with his teaching and support staff. Our description of Sam's "behaviour states" in Table 2 present as a rough appropriation of concepts—alertness, object cognition, and social engagement (Foreman et al., 2004; Trevarthen & Aitken, 2001) but the detail relating to meaning and description of behaviour emerged over time after working with Sam and school staff.

Table 2. Behaviour descriptors.

Behaviour state	Meaning	Description	Context
Passive-unhappy	Bored or not want/not like.	Refuses to move or participate, unhappy noises (e.g., moans), unhappy facial expressions (e.g., frowns).	Mainly in special school.
Passive-distant	Unfocused, "day dreaming".	Unfocused eyes ("looking into space"), showing no interest in phenomena around him.	Both special school and mainstream school. Often when tired and hungry, before lunch and near end of day.
Passive-focused	Focused on phenomena.	Keeping still, listening (head tilted so "good ear" in direction of phenomenon), gaze at ceiling when concentrating, darting in direction of phenomena occasionally.	During lessons designed for sensory experiences in special school and on adults in general. Often on children in mainstream school.
Passive-happy	Enjoying things done to him by others (e.g., massage or physiotherapy).	Happy but not reaching out, happy noises, "smiley eyes", still, big grins, relaxed.	Adults in mainstream and special school. Children in mainstream school (leaning on them, letting them support his weight during circle time etc.).

(Continued)

Table 2. Continued.

Behaviour state	Meaning	Description	Context
Self-active-happy	Self-stimulation.	Exploring himself, happy noises, smiles, exposing and rubbing belly, arching back.	Seen in both settings, but more common in special school.
Other-active-happy	Positively engaged with others. Displaying primary intersubjectivity.	Reaching out, happy vocalisations, eye contact, putting his face close to others, head tilted when listening, very physical, tugging others, putting his legs on others' laps, etc., vocalisations: "ooohwaaah", "buggabuggabugga", giggles, initiation and maintaining social interaction.	Very rare with peers in special school, sometimes with adults. Mainstream school—frequently with children and often with adults. Behaves in this manner much more in mainstream school than special school.
Self-active-unhappy	Pain/frustration/bored.	Self-harming. Sudden high pitch scream, "real tears", frantic slapping and hitting (when in pain), progressively hitting side of head and pinching back of neck harder and faster (boredom and frustration).	Seen in both settings, but mostly in special school where behaviour is much more intense.

(*Continued*)

Table 2. Continued.

Behaviour state	Meaning	Description	Context
Other-active-unhappy	Pain/ frustration/ bored and expressing it to others.	Very rare. Hitting others, pushing them away, trying to communicate discomfort. Pulling hair and not letting go, tears, etc.	Occasionally in both settings.
Object-exploration	Exploring objects.	Exploring object with fingertips, or mouth (chewing, tasting), occasionally visually.	Both special school and mainstream school.
Object-awareness	Understanding purpose of object/ object has meaning for Sam.	Use of object for intended purpose (i.e., attempting to use door handles) or use of object in a way which is meaningful for Sam.	Both special school and mainstream school. Wider selection of items in mainstream school.
Other-object-awareness	Sharing object with other person. Secondary intersubjectivity.	Interacting with object and person at same time. Predicting/ anticipating response of individual with object. Focused gaze between object and person.	Both settings. Only really food-as-object orientation in special school. Various additional items in mainstreams school (e.g., balls, bucket and spade, toys, clothes, books).

Switch-based activities

Many of Sam's planned learning opportunities in his special school revolved around the use of microswitches. These switch-based activities resembled those described in the behaviourist-oriented PMLD literature as described in Chapter Two. A brief summary of the relevant points discussed in Chapter Two should give context to Sam's switch-based learning opportunities and aid comprehension of our analysis of the vignettes.

Behaviourism construes learning as conditioning. Conditioning has two forms: classical (Pavlovian) and operant (Skinnerian). Classical conditioning involves the pairing of an unconditioned stimulus with a neutral stimulus resulting in the neutral stimulus becoming a conditioned stimulus. A conditioned stimulus is a stimulus that has acquired the same behaviour-eliciting powers as the unconditioned stimulus. By contrast, operant conditioning involves increasing the likelihood of a particular behaviour reoccurring through reinforcement. The operation through which operant conditioning occurs is the presentation of a reinforcer (stimulus) contingent upon the organism behaving in a particular way. Both classical conditioning theory and operant conditioning theory understand behaviour as reflexive (i.e., non-volitional) and both theories rely on a notion of linear dependence or constancy between stimulus and response (Baars, 1986; Gregory & Zangwill, 1987; Reber, 1995; Skinner, 1986).

The behaviourist principles of learning are extended in the PMLD literature. Children with PMLD are still understood as a reflexive organism, but the repeated occurrence of stimulus-response constancy is said to support the growth of contingency awareness (knowledge of cause-effect relations) and is said to motivate volitional action (Saunders et al., 2003b; Saunders et al., 2007; Schweigert, 1989), whilst also being prerequisite for communicative intent (Coupe O'Kane & Goldbart, 1998). Terms such as "awareness" and "preference" in the behaviourist PMLD literature marks a genuine departure from the original behaviourist conception of the organism where consciousness was deemed epiphenomenal or irrelevant to scientific accounts of behaviour.

Behaviourist-oriented switch-based training programmes are typically operant in nature and aim to either establish new switch-press behaviour or evoke a rise in frequency of established behaviour through the presentation of preferred stimuli contingent upon switch-pressing. The switch-press behaviour can be accidental or deliberate but always results in the presentation of stimuli. It is hoped that this process of prompting will support the development of contingency awareness (knowledge of cause-effect relations) insofar people with PMLD learn that the stimuli are contingent upon switch-press behaviour. If this awareness has been established, and if the stimuli are desired, then independent switch-press behaviour will be high in frequency/ duration without the need for prompts. Stimuli that are correlated with high frequency/duration switch-press behaviour are defined as reinforcers, insofar as they are deemed to strengthen the likelihood of switch-press behaviour (Lancioni et al., 2002a; Logan et al., 2001; Saunders et al., 2003b).

Research regarding the efficacy of switch-based training programmes aimed at developing contingency awareness and/or switch-press behaviour in people with PMLD has reported mixed success rates (Ivancic & Bailey, 1996; Lancioni et al., 2001; Logan et al., 2001; Reid et al., 1991; Saunders et al., 2003b). Reasons given for mixed results include difficulties in identifying preferred stimuli to act as reinforcers (Green et al., 1991; Ivancic & Bailey, 1996; Logan et al., 2001; Pace et al., 1985; Wacker et al., 1985; Wacker et al., 1988), and problems with mediating behaviour states (Guess et al., 1993; Helm & Simeonsson, 1989; Wolff, 1959). Contemporary research has explored the relation between behaviour state, stimuli preference and microswitch usage in order to discover optimal learning conditions (Lancioni et al., 2002a; Mellstrom et al., 2005; Murphy et al., 2004). Within this research, behaviour states are understood as variables that stand between operant behaviour and contingent stimuli and mediate the probability of switch-press behaviour. Where this is the case, the identification and manipulation of environmental events that influence state conditions are of value to those wishing to alter the behaviours of people with PMLD. However, to date, behaviourist researchers have found no generalisable relationship between behaviour state, environment, and microswitch usage (Mellstrom et al., 2005; Murphy et al., 2004). Each project has found only idiosyncratic relationships between the variables that relate on an individual basis, rather than a trans-PMLD basis. The only exception to this idiosyncrasy is the novel investigation by Foreman et al. (2004), who explored the relationship between behaviour states and social milieu. All the children observed in mainstream classrooms were said to have spent more time in desirable behaviour states (awake, happy, active, alert, etc.) and participated more in some form of social interaction than their matched PMLD peers in segregated classrooms. However, no consideration was given to the extent which social milieus effect switch-press activity.

The vignette analysis below compliments and extends the conclusion made by Foreman et al. (2004) in exploring the relation between Sam's

166   THE PMLD AMBIGUITY

behaviour state, his switch-press activities, and his educational setting. The research found that Sam's range of behaviours towards switches was contingent upon the context in which his switch-based activities occurred. The following two vignettes demonstrate the way Sam usually responded to switch-based learning in his segregated setting. In the first, Sam is placed in front of a computer. The computer software is activated with a press of the switch. Sam passes from self-active-happy when by himself on the carpet (gargling saliva, shaking his head, vocalising) to passive-unhappy (his "floppy" body is a form of resistance), to self-active-unhappy (slapping himself, pinching the back of his neck, pulling his hair, etc.):

Vignette One: Sam with switch-activated computer program in his special school, adult support—passive-unhappy moving to self-active-unhappy

> Sam is sat on the carpet. His head is tilted back as if he is looking up at the ceiling, but his eyes are rolled back. He gargles and shakes his head left and right repeatedly whilst vocalising ("… aaaaah aaaaah uuuuuh aaaaah …"). An LSA [learning support assistant] walks over to him, puts her hands under his armpits, picks him up, and carries him a short distance to his wooden chair on wheels. She places him in the chair, straps him in (seatbelt around his waist, feet in the stirrups), and clips a tray to the chair. Sam is then wheeled to the computer desk. The LSA connects a switch to the computer, places the switch on Sam's tray, and loads the software. All this time Sam is passive and slouched, almost like a floppy rag-doll. The LSA tests the software to make sure the switch is working. The switch press activates a sample of loud acid house music. The beats are fast and repetitive; the synthesiser rifts are high-pitch and frantic; the vocals are shrill. Animation accompanies the music. Lights flash creating a strobe effect; silhouette figures dance; and "trippy" patterns unfold in the corners of the screen. The LSA has left me to work with Sam. He makes no attempt to press the switch and looks increasingly frustrated, moaning to himself and shaking in his chair (is he trying to get out?), looking everywhere but the screen. I encourage him to press the switch, vocally at first, and then by holding his hand and placing it on the switch. I repeat this several times. The music plays and the graphics flash. Sam becomes

aggressive towards himself. He snatches his hand away from me and slaps himself in the face, pulls his hair, pinches the side of his neck and flaps his arms. He repeats in various combinations, over and over. I pat Sam on his back and speak jovially to him, trying to calm him down. He becomes less "self-active". I ask him to press the switch again and avoid touching him. He is not looking at the screen. He shakes his head left and right, wiggles in his chair, and slaps his face occasionally. Several minutes pass. I press the switch hoping that he will look at the screen. He only briefly glances at it. He keeps raising his flapping arms and hitting the table with them. He presses the switch with his forearms (but was it accidental?). He repeats the action, but does not hit the switch. Sam is now hitting himself over and over again. His skin is becoming red. Despite holding apart his arms, I can feel him fighting me. Eventually an LSA walks over, removes Sam from the chair and places him on his favourite vibrating rug. He keeps hitting himself and it takes a lot of effort to sooth him.

From a behaviourist perspective, there is nothing here to suggest that Sam is able to engage in switch-based activities. There is one incident of switch-press behaviour—a single switch-press—but it is unclear whether or not this press was accidental. Is Sam "contingency aware"? Again, there is little in this vignette to say that he is. What counts as evidence of contingency awareness for behaviourism is data demonstrating sustained and repeated pressing (e.g., Green et al., 1988; 1991; Ivancic & Bailey, 1996; Kennedy & Haring, 1993; Logan et al., 2001), something clearly lacking in the above vignette. If switch-press behaviour is the only type of behaviour to be counted as evidence of contingency awareness then Sam is not contingency aware in this vignette.

In the behaviourist literature, explanation for the lack of switch-press behaviour includes suggestions of uneducability (Reid et al., 1991), lack of preferred stimuli to act as reinforcers (Logan et al., 2001), and problems with mediating behaviour states (Arthur, 2004; Foreman et al., 2004; Guess et al., 1993; Helm & Simeonsson, 1989; Wolff, 1959). Out of these suggestions, the first is unwarranted. Whilst the above vignette demonstrates no evidence of learning through the switch-based activity, Sam's self-directed behaviour may be considered as evidence of conditioning derived from "unfortunate contingencies" (Reber, 1995, p. 90). The second and third suggestions have some merit. It may be said that Sam is not faced with a preferred stimulus, and as such the computer program does not act as a reinforcer. With regards to the issue of behaviour states, Sam was clearly not in a state conducive to learning. His self-directed behaviours (his hitting) emerged in relation to the switch-based activity—being strapped into a chair in order to interact with a computer (first, through verbal prompting, and second, through physical encouragement) resulted in a clear decline of behaviour state (he was self-active-happy on the carpet, passive-unhappy in his chair to begin with, then self-active unhappy during intervention).

From a behaviourist perspective, Sam's behaviour would be considered stereotyped (lacking in function) and maladaptive (self-injurious). In Chapter Two, stereotyped and maladaptive behaviours were described as behaviours that fail to provide adequate or appropriate adjustment to the environment (Gregory & Zangwill, 1987). Such behaviours were described as repetitive, topographically unvaried, and lacking responsiveness to environmental change. These behaviours were also said to disturb or alarm others and include such things as rocking, hand-flapping, head-weaving, and light-gazing (Murdoch, 1997). The reduction of stereotyped behaviour was described as being motivated by three beliefs: (1) stereotypy interferes with learning, (2) benign behaviours (such as head-banging) may become self-injurious, and (3) responses to individuals with the behaviours will be typically negative (Jones et al., 1995, in Murdoch, 1997).

Whilst this single vignette does not demonstrate the topological invariance of Sam's behaviours (the next two vignettes will serve this purpose), it does show behavioural repetition and a level of unresponsiveness to environmental change (insofar as the behaviours are largely consistent throughout the switch-press activity—though varied in intensity and combination—and continue after the session; to the extent that it takes a while to sooth Sam afterwards). Although this vignette does not demonstrate it, Sam would sometimes become "locked" into his head-hitting, and would repeat the hitting throughout a lesson or therapy session. Despite varying in intensity over the course of the session, the hitting was always present over a prolonged period of time. In the above vignette being discussed, Sam's behaviour, as stereotyped and maladaptive, may be said to fit into three categories that motivate intervention to prevent the behaviours (according to Jones et al., 1995, in Murdoch, 1997): Sam does not press the switch but directs his behaviour towards himself, which may be said to be an inversion of what is required for learning to occur. His slapping, pinching, flapping, and hair-pulling are self-injurious to the extent that red marks appear on his face. Finally, Ben's response to Sam's behaviour was "negative" insofar as Ben attempted to prevent Sam's self-directed actions, at first in a non-invasive way (jovial speech, back stroking) and later in an invasive way (holding Sam's arms so he is unable to strike himself).

And yet, despite this congruence between Sam's behaviour and the behaviourist explanation, the behaviour described in the vignette contradicts behaviourism's most basic premise—that is, the notion of linear dependence or constancy between stimulus and response. Sam's "reflex responses" lack one-to-one correspondence with the presentation of the stimulus (be that the presence of the switch or the audiovisual activity of the computer). Sam's behavioural sequences are varied even though the stimulus remains the same. Behaviourism is unable to give reason to the observation that the same stimuli can provoke different responses. Whilst Sam's switch presses may be correlated with his self-directed behaviour (in the first instance, Ben places Sam's hand on the switch, in the second instance, Sam accidently hits the switch himself), this behaviour is not uniformed but dynamic and varied (despite being clustered under the headings "stereotyped" and "maladaptive").

This notion of differential responses to the same stimulus is seen in Vignette Two (below). This vignette records the daily special school greeting activity in which each child is required to press the switch during a song. The switch press results in a pre-recorded message being emitted: "Good morning!" Sam reacts adversely to the activity.

Vignette Two: Sam with switch-activated greeting in his special school, adult-support—passive-unhappy, moving to self-active-unhappy

> Sam has just been strapped to his stander (a wooden frame used to support standing and improve posture). A tray is bolted to the stander and Sam is wheeled to the centre of the classroom where the other children are "standing". The children form a circle with the teacher in the middle. Sam is looking bored. He licks his bottom lip, rolls his eyes back and shows the whites of his eyes. He shakes his head left and right repeatedly. He stops, curls up his top lip and exposes his teeth, frowns and vocalises unhappy sounds ("… uuuurgh!") whilst looking up at the ceiling. LSAs place switches on

the trays of each child. The teacher sings the "Good morning song" and calls the name of the child who is meant to press the switch at the end of each verse. The switch emits the pre-recorded phrase: "Good morning, everyone!" Sam becomes increasingly impatient. He flaps his arms like a bird. He then starts to slap the side of his face, pinches his neck, and pulls his hair. He pushes the switch off the table and it crashes to the floor. Over time his self-stimulation becomes notably self-injurious, with red marks appearing on his face and neck where he is hitting and pinching himself. An LSA restrains Sam by holding his arms apart whilst talking gently to him. It looks like Sam is fighting the LSA—his movements are centripetal and it is as if Sam is repeatedly trying to hit himself against the will of the LSA. Eventually, it is Sam's turn to say "good morning" and press his switch. The LSA gently moves both of Sam's hands over the switch and presses down. The message is played and the teacher enthusiastically wishes Sam "good morning". She makes eye contact, smiles then nods and praises Sam. The LSA lets go of Sam's hands and encourages Sam to hit the switch. Sam pauses. The adults wait in anticipation. Several seconds go by. Sam suddenly pushes the switch off the table and slaps himself in the face.

Consistent with the previous vignette (Vignette One), Sam's behaviour during this vignette (Vignette Two) is self-directed in a way that may be considered self-injurious. The same type of activity (switch-pressing) is responded to with the same cluster of behaviours directed towards Sam's own body (predominantly his head). Once again, Sam's behaviour can be described as maladaptive, a product of "unfortunate contingencies", lacking in appropriate behaviour state conducive to learning, a product of inappropriate reinforcers, etc. And once again, behaviourism is unable to give reason to the observation that the same stimulus (switch-press activity) provokes differential responses (different combinations of maladaptive behaviour: hitting, pinching, fighting the LSA, pushing the switch off the table, etc.). Now, it may be argued that Sam's stimulus in Vignette Two (the pre-recorded message) is different to the stimulus in Vignette One (a computer program), but as will be shown shortly, a pre-recorded voice was the stimulus used in his mainstream school, which resulted in the obverse of his special school reactions (Sam was active, happy, frequently pressing the switch, etc.—more on this shortly). However, even if this were not so, and the challenge that the switch-press resulted in different stimuli remained (thus negating the value of contrasting how the same stimuli could provoke differential reactions), behaviourists would still have to account for the fact that different stimuli resulted in the *same* behaviour. This is something that the behaviourists cannot do. The same argument against the behaviourist logic is present: the simple constancy between stimulus and response has broken. Behaviourism is unable to make intelligible neither the fact that the same stimulus provoked different reactions, nor that different stimuli provoked the same reaction. Sam's behaviour resists being neatly categorised in such a simple way. Inconsistency replaces constancy.

Before attempting to interpret these vignettes from the two remaining perspectives (cognitivism and phenomenology), it is worth citing one more vignette which both compliments and contrasts the previous vignettes discussed so far. In this vignette (Vignette Three), Sam is presented with a switch that has the pre-recorded message: "Good morning!" (the message is the same as that described in Vignette Two). In Vignette Three, Sam once again behaves in a way that disturbs the behaviourist stimulus-response relationship, but he does so in a "positive" way (he is happy, excited, active, and displaying awareness of switch-press behaviour).

Vignette Three: Sam with switch-activated greeting in his mainstream school, peer-support—other-active-happy, moving to other-object-awareness

> Sam is sat on his artificial grass mat on the carpet for registration. He is in the middle of a group of approximately twenty children. All the children are close to one another chatting and filling the room with hubbub. Sam groans and extends his arms and legs in front of him. He then leans back into a group of chatting girls. He giggles and lets them support his weight. The girls giggle and do not move. Although they do not attempt to talk to Sam, they do not move away either and eventually carry on chatting. The teacher calls Sam's name whilst taking register. Normally at this point Sam would be presented with a switch from his LSA. This does not happen. One of Sam's neighbours stands up, walks over to a yellow box in the corner near the teacher, pulls out his switch and returns

to the carpet. She tells Sam to press his "blue button" and smiles. Sam leans forward. The girl takes Sam's hand and places it on top of the switch. The switch is activated and emits a pre-recorded "Good morning!" message. Sam repeatedly hits the switch with both hands (he raises his hands, then suddenly slaps the switch held in front of him, lets his hands fall on his lap, and repeats several times). Sam presses the switch before the recorded message has ended, resulting in the first half of the message being played, over and over. Between each switch-press Sam flaps his arms like a bird whilst smiling and vocalises ("Ooooooh!!!"). He wiggles his legs outstretched in front of him and hits the floor with the back of his heels. He slaps his head with both hands and makes happy sounds. An LSA walks over to Sam and the girl gives the LSA the switch. The LSA crosses Sam's legs, makes him sit up straight, and walks away.

In this vignette, Sam appears happy and active around his mainstream school peers. He presents as being particularly excited during the switch-based exchange with a peer in which he strikes his "blue button" repeatedly, making "happy noises" ("Ooooooh!!!") and displaying awareness of how to behave towards switches (switches are for pressing). This behaviour contrasts starkly with his behaviour during switch-based activities in his special school (Vignettes One and Two). In his special school, Sam's switch-press behaviour was very limited, whilst being typically adult-supported and resulting in resistance and/or aggression from Sam. Sam's differential responses to the same stimulus (be that switch-presentation or a pre-recorded "Good morning!" message) extend the point made previously about the breakdown of simple linear dependence. For the behaviourist literature, a stimulus acts as a reinforcer, or it does not. There is no discussion about how the same subject can present as being contingency-aware and not-contingency aware depending on context. Sam's switch-press behaviour shifts according to where he is and who is supporting him.

This draws attention to the way switch-press behaviour is mediated by behaviour states (Guess et al., 1993; Helm & Simeonsson, 1989; Wolff, 1959) and the way the behaviour states themselves are mediated by environmental variables. As discussed in Chapter Two, behaviour state research has examined the relationship between behaviour states and environmental variables. For example, Foreman et al. (2004)

explored the relationship between behaviour states and different school environments (special school and mainstream school). The children with PMLD observed in the mainstream classrooms were said to have spent more time in desirable behaviour states and participated more in some form of social interaction than their matched PMLD peers in segregated classrooms.

Sam's behaviour states complement the findings of Arthur et al. (2004) for (as will be discussed later) Sam's behaviour state in his mainstream school was predominantly other-active-happy. Contemporary behaviourist research that explores the relation between behaviour state, stimuli preference and switch usage in the hope of discovering optimal learning conditions (e.g., Lancioni et al., 2002b; Mellstrom et al., 2005; Murphy et al., 2004) has so far overlooked the way in which mainstream classrooms affect behaviour state. For Sam, there was a clear relationship between educational context, behaviour state, and switch-press behaviour. As Vignette Three shows, in his mainstream school Sam pressed his switch freely and frequently when on the carpet with his peers. The social milieu had a positive effective on Sam's behaviour state and switch-press behaviour.

Understanding Sam's behaviour from a behaviourist perspective has so far yielded mixed results. Sam's behaviour makes problematic the notion of linear dependence between stimulus and response. His behaviour during switches-based activities is varied and complex and resists being described in terms of simple constancy between reinforcer strength and switch-press behaviour. However, consideration of behaviour states during analysis has allowed fruitful differentiation between levels of alertness in relation to activities and environments.

Behaviourism's failure to make sense of Sam's switch-press behaviour invites interpretation from a different theoretical perspective. In the PMLD literature, this alternative perspective is exclusively cognitivism. However, cognitivist psychology is equally powerless to make intelligible Sam's differential behaviours. To recap, according to the cognitivism, behaviours indicative of communicative intent must resemble descriptions of proto-imperative or proto-declarative behaviours (Bates et al., 1975). These proto-behaviours in which a subject coordinates the regard of self and other in relation to an object are described as the earliest form of meaningful communication. Without a capacity for such person–person–object engagement, the subject cannot be considered intentional. Proto-imperative behaviour involves an infant using a reach-for-real action as a reach-for-signal. Reach-for-real consists of an infant reaching for something that is within reach in order to get hold of it (Bruner, 1975). Reach-for-signal involves the infant reaching for something that is out of reach. By incorporating looking from the desired object to the adult and then back again into the reach-for-signal, the infant is said to communicate to the adult that she/he wants the object she/he is reaching for, and knows that the adult can obtain it for him/her. The infant is satisfied by the exchange when she/he obtains the desired object. Proto-declarative behaviour is a variation of proto-imperative behaviour. During proto-declarative behaviour the infant directs the attention of the adult toward something of interest in order to share the experience with the adult (as opposed to obtaining an object). During proto-declarative behaviour, an infant may point towards an object and vocalise: "Dah!", whilst shifting his/her gaze between the object and the adult. The infant is satisfied by the exchange when she/he observes the adult's gaze shift from him/her to the object, and back to him/her again. Typically, developing infants are said to engage in proto-imperative and proto-declarative behaviours around ten months after birth. Coupe O'Kane and Goldbart (1998) suggest that children with PMLD are unlikely to develop these joint attention capacities.

Vignettes One and Two describe Sam interacting (or resisting interacting) with a switch. No proto-imperative or proto-declarative behaviours are described. Thus, from the above perspective, Sam is not intentionally communicating. His behaviour would be labelled pre-intentional communication (Coupe O'Kane & Goldbart, 1998; Goldbart, 1994). Pre-intentional communication is a term given to the act of interpreting the meaning of expressive behaviours, such as crying or laughing. Such expressive behaviours occur without the expressive agent intending to communicate (she/he lacks the ability to do so). Sam's self-directed activity in both vignettes, his act of pushing switches away from his body, and his "fights" with both me (Vignette One) and his LSA (Vignette Two) are not considered forms of intentional communication. Such "negative", resistant or defiant behaviours are not considered to be sources of intended meaning. His movements are clearly expressive, but are pre-symbolic.

Trevarthen and Aitken's (2001) model of infantile intersubjective development is also unable to make sense of Sam's behaviours. As discussed in previous chapters, Trevarthen and Aitken's (2001) cognitivist model contrasts to the models espoused by the PMLD literature insofar as Trevarthen and Aitken (2001) articulate a view of primary intersubjectivity. Infants are said to be endowed with capacities for sustained social exchanges, motivated by an infant's innate ability to perceive others as subjects rather than objects. However, Trevarthen and Aitken (2001) only describe mutually satisfying social exchanges (person–person, or primary intersubjectivity) or social games involving the mutual coordination of objects (person–person–object, or secondary intersubjectivity, which is similar to the proto-imperative and proto-declarative exchanges described above). Whilst Trevarthen and Aitken's (2001) notion of primary intersubjectivity makes intelligible those behaviours that are non-triadic, primary intersubjectivity is understood solely in terms of face-to-face interaction. The nature of Sam's behaviour in Vignette One and Vignette Two is not face-to-face activity. There is no mutual satisfaction, there are no smiles, eye contact, turn-taking, giggles, etc. As such, Trevarthen and Aitken (2001) have nothing to offer. They only provide explanation of the happy (not the unhappy), and of the intimate (not the larger, more aggressive movements described in the first two vignettes). So, once again, Sam's behaviours are lost. They do not "fit" the existing frameworks. Behaviourist and cognitivist approaches cannot account for the behaviours described. They cannot make Sam intelligible.

Vignette Three describes Sam repeatedly pressing the switch that his peer offered him. During this episode, Sam was clearly happy, excited, and focused on the switch that "spoke" for him (by greeting the class "Good morning!" with each press). The description of the episode captures Sam interacting with an object that a peer is holding, and doing so with zeal. Despite the person–person–object nature of this exchange, Sam's behaviour still evades the term "intentional communication"—he does not make eye contact with his peer, point, or engage in a reach-for-signal in order to obtain an object. Trevarthen and Aitken's (2001) notion of secondary intersubjectivity may be said to offer room for theorising the interactive event. However, this room exists only because Trevarthen and Aitken (2001) fail to offer anything in the way of a description of what secondary intersubjectivity looks like. If secondary intersubjectivity is to positively afford a greater range of meaningful behaviours than the PMLD literature allows for, then there has to be an articulation of something extra. This can be found through a synthesis of Trevarthen and Aitken's (2001) notion of secondary intersubjectivity with aspects of Merleau-Ponty's (2002) phenomenological perspective of being-in-the-world.

Whilst the behaviourist and cognitivist perspectives in the PMLD literature make limited sense of the behaviours described in the above vignettes, Merleau-Ponty's (2002) phenomenological perspective allows us to foreground and theorise these behaviours in a much greater way, and does so in a way that can complement Trevarthen and Aitken's (2001) framework.

Chapter Four discussed Merleau-Ponty's (2002) phenomenology. This discussion articulated Merleau-Ponty's (2002) description of the body as that which is neither an object *in-itself* (the body-object), nor something to be abstractly represented by a reflective consciousness, a *for-itself* (the body image). This third position between subject and object is a pre-objective understanding of the body through which organisms have a form of bodily intentionality that plays beneath any thematic ego. For Merleau-Ponty (2002), the body is defined by its "projects" (p. 129) insofar as it "appears to me as an attitude directed towards certain existing or possible tasks" (p. 114). The spatiality of the body is about its "situation" whereby objects in the environment offer themselves as "poles of action" (p. 122). The body "surges" (p. 121) towards objects to be grasped; objects are understood as "manipulanda" (p. 120)—objects known in terms of how they can be acted upon, or with (p. 120). The world is "a collection of possible points upon which ... bodily interaction may operate" (p. 121). Motility, "in its pure state, possesses the basic power of giving a meaning (*Sinngebung*)" (p. 164). This is essentially what Merleau-Ponty refers to as "motor intentionality" (p. 127): "Consciousness is in the first place not a matter of 'I think that' but of 'I can'" (p. 159).

From Merleau-Ponty's (2002) phenomenological perspective, Sam's differential switch-press behaviour is a result of the way in which the different educational situations are practically signified. Different situations express different possibilities for interaction. For Sam, the stimuli contingent upon switch-press behaviour is not universally important (if it was, he would have behaved enthusiastically towards switch-based activities in each of his settings where the stimuli were consistent, which was not the case). What appears to be important for Sam was, first, his freedom. In his special school Sam was typically strapped into chairs and standers (something captured in Vignette One and Two), in his mainstream school he was typically without such constraint (captured in Vignette Three). Sam was typically aggressive towards himself during times of constraint, and as such was typically aggressive when in his special school (although self-directed aggression was observed in his mainstream school, but with much less intensity and frequency). Second, the social milieu was important for Sam. As will be discussed later, Sam was most active around his mainstream school peers. Since the social milieu was an important factor mediating Sam's switch-press behaviour, the question emerges as to what specifically Sam finds significant in these contexts—how does the social situation relate to motor significance? To reiterate a previous point, Sam's behaviour towards switches is unintelligible from the cognitivist perspective. Trevarthen and Aitken's (2001) secondary intersubjectivity (in which two people mutually engage with objects) is somewhat consistent with Coupe O'Kane and Goldbart's (1998) description of intentional communication (taken from Bates et al., 1975). Whilst Trevarthen and Aiken (2001) fail to offer any descriptors of symbolic communication related to secondary intersubjectivity, Coupe O'Kane and Goldbart (1998) offer descriptions of proto-declarative or proto-imperative competence. The vignettes above do not conform to the proto-imperative/-declarative descriptors, and as such Sam could not be considered to be an intentional communicator. And yet, Sam does engage with the switch when in the presence of peers in his mainstream school. How can we make sense of this? One explanation would be that the behaviours identified by the PMLD literature as indicative of intentional communication are too narrow. This is not to negate the value of proto-imperative/-declarative behavioural descriptors, but to call for a broader catalogue of behaviours suggestive of intersubjective awareness and communication. Another explanation may be that Sam's behaviour reveals an emergent level of awareness that is more sophisticated than Trevarthen and Aitken's (2001) primary intersubjectivity (person–person interaction) but not as sophisticated as genuine secondary intersubjectivity (person–person–object interaction as proto-imperative/-declarative). This new form of "proto-secondary-intersubjectivity" would explain why, in the presence of his peers, Sam wilfully engages with objects. There is something significant for Sam in this interactive situation, but this significance is not at the level of abstract, symbolic communication (proto-declarative/-imperative). For Merleau-Ponty (2002), being-in-the-world consists of perception and action being linked in the sense that what is perceived is immediately understood as that which can be acted upon. Experience requires or calls for movement. If this view is synthesised with that of Trevarthen and Aitken's (2001) understanding of the emergence of object cognition, then we become one step closer to theorising Sam's "proto-secondary-intersubjectivity". As discussed previously, Trevarthen and Aitken (2001) argue that infants possess an innate capacity for intersubjective awareness. Further, in contrast to the claims of the PMLD literature generally (Coupe O'Kane and Goldbart, 1998; Nind & Hewett, 1994; 2001; Ware, 1994; 2003), which leans towards the developmental models of Bates et al. (1975) and Schaffer (1971a), Trevarthen and Aitken (2001) argue that object cognition emerges through motives that drive early social exchanges, rather than vice-versa.

From the perspective of the PMLD literature, children with PMLD are pre-communicative because they are unable to comprehend the objective world (for example, they lack contingency awareness, etc.). From Trevarthen and Aitken's (2001) perspective, infants learn about the objective world through social engagement, defined in terms of primary intersubjectivity. If Trevarthen and Aitken (2001) are right, then it makes sense to say that Sam's switch-press behaviour in the presence of peers (and not adults or computer screens) emerged because it was through his peers that the switch was understood as that which can be acted upon. It was through sharing experiences with his peers that called for Sam's actions toward the switch. For Sam, the social milieu (Trevarthen & Aitken, 2001) in his mainstream school presented as a behavioural setting or *Umwelt* (Merleau-Ponty, 2002), which signified objects as that through which social engagement took place. The adults and peers in Sam's special school context did not present in this way. As will be discussed during analysis of the next group of vignettes, Sam was typically passive around others in his special school. The school was void of motor significance on the scale that was seen in his mainstream school.

Previous discussion considered the role of behaviour states (Arthur, 2004; Foreman et al., 2004; Guess et al., 1993), as mediating Sam's engagement with his environments. From the behaviourist perspective, these states are considered to intervene by disturbing the "readiness" of Sam to respond to his environmental stimuli. From Merleau-Ponty's (2002) perspective of being-in-the-world, these states take on new meaning. The behaviour states emerge when Sam finds himself in a situation of significance. Whilst being in a segregated classroom governed by behaviourist principles of learning may be non-stimulating for Sam (Vignettes One and Two), being around others (especially peers) is meaningful and raises bodily expectations, alertness, etc., and primes Sam to engage with his social milieu. The behaviour states work beneath abstract forms of representational consciousness whilst motivating switch-press behaviour. Australian behaviour state research (Foreman et al., 2004) indicates that children with PMLD are in optimal learning states when in mainstream social milieus. Observations of Sam in this study compliment the Australian research.

Stereotyped behaviours

Another point of interest for the current discussion is the way in which a particular cluster of Sam's behaviours (arm-flapping, head-hitting with closed fist, head-slapping with both hands simultaneously, slapping and pinching the back of his neck, hair-pulling, etc.) were perceived to have different meanings in different settings. In his special school context, these behaviours were deemed stereotypic, maladaptive, and self-injurious. Sam's teacher did not think that Sam's behaviours were a form of attention-seeking. As such, the classroom policy was to ignore such behaviours or to restrain Sam where these behaviours appeared to be causing him harm (e.g., when staff saw skin-reddening, bleeding, or when Sam appeared to be striking himself particularly hard). Sam's teacher explained that if the self-directed behaviours were responded to reliably, then Sam would learn to use these behaviours as signals to others, thus resulting in an increased hitting frequency (the emphasis here being that all hitting was self-harm). In contrast, Sam's mainstream school LSAs and peers deemed such behaviours to be purposeful and communicative and responded to them as such. Sam's self-directed behaviours were those behaviours through which he engaged with others (particularly peers). The purpose of this section is to explore the ways in which different positions (behaviourist, cognitivist, and phenomenological) can make Sam's self-directed behaviours intelligible.

Contrast Vignette Four to Vignette Five. Vignette Four captures Sam's "stereotyped behaviour" in the special school. Sam repeatedly hits the side of his face with his closed hand. This hitting is almost constant throughout the vignette, with only a slight pause whilst Sam appears to contemplate an object that the LSA offers him (a cardboard box within a plastic box). The hitting starts before the LSA sits with

180   THE PMLD AMBIGUITY

Sam, and continues when she walks away. Given that the hitting does not cease, and occurs before and after the social exchange, it appears in this instance that the hitting is not a social signal, but a form of stereotypic behaviour or self-stimulatory behaviour (SSB). The criteria for defining behaviour as stereotypic include repetition, topographical invariance (the behaviour is performed the same way each time), a lack of responsiveness to environmental changes, and a lack of purpose or function (Murdoch, 1997). Although this vignette does not demonstrate topographical invariance by itself (a single vignette does not show whether the behaviour is performed in the same way each time), it can be argued that the other criteria are met (repetition, unresponsiveness, non-function). From this perspective, and in agreement with the opinion of Sam's teacher, Sam's behaviour is stereotyped.

Vignette Four: Sam in his special school, sitting on the carpet, first by himself, then with an LSA—self-active-happy

> Sam is sitting alone on the carpet next to a box of toys, hitting himself repeatedly on the side of his face with a closed fist. An LSA walks over to Sam and sits beside him. Sam keeps hitting. The adult chooses the coloured slinky spring Sam usually enjoys playing with from the toy box and dangles it in front of Sam. Although Sam continues to hit himself, he reaches out for the spring, frowns, grasps it, then drops it on the floor and continues to hit himself. Sam watches the adult put a lid on a cardboard box, his attention is with the adult. She puts the cardboard box in a big yellow plastic box. Sam hits himself again, pauses, reaches for the box, looks at it and drops it on the floor and resumes hitting himself. The LSA walks away. Sam is by himself once more, hitting the side of his face repeatedly whilst looking at the ceiling. He reaches into the yellow toy box, pulls out a piece of fabric with small shiny sequins attached, and puts it in his mouth. He is still hitting himself. The class begins to sing the dinner time song ("I am hungry, I am hungry …"). All the children are placed in their chairs and wheeled to the dining hall.

In Vignette Five below, Sam's self-directed behaviour appears to serve as an attempt to communicate with Ben. It is clear that his hitting is at least correlated with Ben's presence since Sam stops hitting himself when Ben moves out of sight, and resumes hitting when he sees Ben once more. Sam's self-directed behaviours can no longer be considered as entirely stereotypic. The behaviour appears to have a function—it acts as a signal to Ben, presumably to engage with him. To the extent that this is so, the self-directed ironically becomes other-directed. Sam relates himself to the other in the act of signalling. The behaviour is responsive to Ben's presence/absence. The topological invariance of the behaviour emerges when Vignette Four is compared to Vignette Five, which in itself is a criterion of stereotyped behaviour, but what shifts is not the action itself, but the meaning. Also, whilst Vignette Four and Vignette Five demonstrate repetition, it is important to note that repetition can be understood in different ways. The hitting action has been repeated across the two vignettes, but in Vignette Five the hitting pattern changes (the shifting of presence-absence of hitting).

Vignette Five: Sam sitting in his chair in his special school—other-active

Sam is strapped into his chair. He was passive-distant or passive-happy in his chair before the straps came on (day dreaming/mumbling to himself and smiling). A wooden desktop is attached to his chair. This particular maths session is on size and shape. All the children are in their chairs which are placed in a circle. The adults are between the children and pass small, round, colourful cardboard boxes around. Each box contains a 'sensory' item (chocolate, flashing lights, etc.) and when the singing stops, the children open the box to discover what is inside. Sam gets aggravated early on (he slaps the side of his face, pulls his hair, and pinches the back of his neck). I encourage Sam to open the boxes and his hitting increases. I leave his side and go out of sight (behind him) and the hitting reduces dramatically (it becomes almost non-existent). I then sit down beside him. He sees me and starts hitting himself again, this time hitting the side of his face. I ignore Sam to see if the hitting ceases. It does not. I stand up and walk behind Sam once more so that I am out of sight, and his hitting slows down in frequency. He tilts his head back, gazes at the ceiling, and raises his arm several times as if he is about to hit himself, but for whatever reason he doesn't actually strike his face, but lowers his arm again. Once more I sit down beside Sam. He frowns, moans, curls up his top lip and slouches forward, then pinches the back of his neck and slaps himself.

The face-hitting in Vignette Six may also be interpreted as an attempt to communicate. Although the hitting occurs only once, it occurs when Sam's attempts to interact with Ben are not met with an appropriate response (i.e., Ben does not respond back). Whilst the face-hitting may be an expression of frustration not intended to act as a signal, situated amongst the rest of the communicative behaviours, and given the way Vignette Five demonstrates a "hit-for-signal", it is more likely that he intended the hit to serve as a signal. What is also of interest is the way Sam transposes his self-directed behaviours onto Ben: Sam pulls Ben's hair instead of his own, and he does so repeatedly when Ben does not respond to Sam's attempt to communicate.

Vignette Six: Sam in his special school, other-active-happy

> As I walk past Sam, he spins on his bottom 360 degrees, smiles and waits for me to sit down again. As soon as I sit down—six to seven feet from him—Sam turns to face me and shuffles on his bottom, making happy sounds ("Oooohaaaa!") and puts his feet on my crossed legs. He leans forward and looks me in the eyes, his face is very close to mine for several seconds, he hugs me, then holds my hand (very affectionate!). He touches my leg, pulls my hair gently and smiles lots (it is the happiest he has looked so far today). I am trying to write what I see but Sam won't let me, he becomes more insistent and pulls my hair (harder this time), crawls on my lap completely and puts his mouth on my clothes. This episode lasted for approximately six to seven minutes. When I fail to respond to his efforts to communicate (and not look at him directly) he begins to hit himself in the side of the face like usual and then tries to communicate with me again.

The above vignettes compliment the claims made so far regarding the limited ability of both behaviourism and cognitivism to make sense of Sam's behaviours.

Vignettes One, Two, and Three demonstrate the ways in which Sam responded differently to the same stimulus. Since behaviourism relies on a simple one-to-one relationship between stimulus and response, it was argued that behaviourism could not make intelligible those behaviours which contradicted this relationship. Vignettes Four, Five, and Six invert the logic by demonstrating that Sam could behave the same way to different stimuli. Sam's self-directed behaviours were observed in an array of contexts with an array of stimuli. The variation of behavioural response to the same stimuli, and the constancy of behavioural response to different stimuli, challenge the extent to which behaviourism alone is able understand Sam's actions in their entirety.

Furthermore, no vignette described so far can be made intelligible by the cognitivist perspective in the PMLD literature. Where the cognitivist perspective is the choice approach to understanding people with PMLD, the focus for intervention is the emergence of intentional communication. Sam's behaviours do not suggest that he coordinates objects and others in the ways described by Coupe O'Kane and Goldbart (1998) (i.e., proto-declarative and proto-imperative behaviours). In Vignette Four, Sam reaches for the objects offered to him, but promptly drops them on the floor. In Vignette Five, Sam's self-hitting is correlated with Ben's presence/absence, but there is no clear indication that this hitting expresses Sam's desire to interact with Ben using objects. And in Vignette Six, Sam's behaviour towards Ben does not include objects.

And yet, this reading of the vignettes is counter-intuitive. It "feels" wrong. Vignette Six, in particular, describes Sam in a way that strongly suggests that he wished to interact with Ben. Even at the time of writing Ben felt that this was so (note the empathic aside: "very affectionate!"). If the existing approaches in the PMLD literature are unable to account for these behaviours, then what else can? Once again we return to Trevarthen and Aitken's (2001) notion of primary intersubjectivity.

To recap, Trevarthen and Aitken (2001) differentiate between primary and secondary intersubjectivity. In Chapter Three, primary intersubjectivity was described as an immediate, innate awareness of the other as subject, something perceived when the infant recognises the behaviours of the other as contingent responding and emotionally appropriate. This perception motivates the infant to engage with the other. Subjectivity implies that the infant can predict and control the environment. During social interaction, intersubjectivity emerges when the infant and other share control of the interaction whilst predicting one another's response. Behaviours believed to be indicative of primary intersubjectivity include gentle, intimate, affectionate, rhythmically regulated and playful exchanges of protoconversation. Such protoconversations were defined in terms of the infant looking at the eyes and mouth of the adult addressing them, whilst listening to the adult's voice. Other behavioural descriptors include playful and coordinated head movements, facial expression, hand and vocal gestures and touching.

Vignette Six adheres to this description of interaction. Sam tracks Ben's movements, he moves towards Ben, he expresses himself vocally, he touches Ben with his feet, makes eye contact, wraps his arms around Ben, smiles, and attempts to grab Ben's attention when Ben does not respond (by pulling Ben's hair, mouthing Ben's clothes, sitting on Ben's lap, sharing Ben's personal space, and then by Sam hitting himself). From the perspective of Trevarthen and Aitken (2001), Sam is displaying primary intersubjective awareness. In fact, Sam's behaviours go beyond the subtle behaviours indicative of primary intersubjectivity in ways that suggest that he is becoming a symbolic communicator: Sam makes explicit gestures in his attempts to win Ben's attention and interact with him. These gestures are not of the type: person–person–object (secondary intersubjectivity), but they are nevertheless signs of Sam's desire to communicate, they are his way of initiating social interaction.

The vignette analysis so far has demonstrated that where the entry-level descriptions of communicative intent are Trevarthen's and Aitken's (2001), Sam is communicative. Where the entry-level descriptions of communicative intent are those of Coupe O'Kane and Goldbart (1998), Sam is pre-communicative. Where all of Sam's self-directed behaviours (his hair-pulling, hitting, slapping, etc.) are considered stereotypic (and thus negative), they are stripped of volition and meaning. Where his self-directed behaviours are considered in context and in relation to others, they become significant. By shifting interpretive frameworks when considering Sam's "stereotyped" behaviours we allow Sam to speak to us in new ways and foreground aspects overlooked by the dominant PMLD frameworks (and by Sam's special school staff).

Trevarthen and Aitken (2001) do not discuss stereotyped behaviour. Nor do they discuss how the same behaviour can have multiple meanings or purposes. Merleau-Ponty (2002), on the other hand, explores both of these topics.

The notion that different behaviours can serve the same purpose is explained by Merleau-Ponty (2002) in terms of global orientation, and the impulse of being-in-the-world. It is this impulse that signifies the world in such a way that it transforms a geographical environment into a behavioural one. Chapter Four discussed Merleau-Ponty's (2002) interpretation of the act of limb substitution in insects. For Merleau-Ponty (2002), this act expresses an organism's being-in-the-world as a primordial mode of existence, understood in terms of a bodily intentionality that plays beneath an explicit sense of self, a thematic *ego cogito*. This mode is not a deliberate taking up of a position, an act of reflection, or a deliberate choice, but an *a priori* of the species. Nor is this mode of existence mechanistic in nature since it endows the world with a motor significance. The world is that which speaks to the body pragmatically: the world is interpreted by the body and transformed into a motor situation. Limb substitution reveals that it is the body as a whole that interprets the situation (not body parts): the unified body emerges as a motor value in relation to the perceived world. Thus, when performing instinctive acts (i.e., acts which are not the product of reflective thought), insects use a present limb as a substitute for a missing limb. The organism is holistically "anchored" (p. 78) to a certain environment. The organism understands the motor situation and acts with all its powers in the world, its entire body aims towards a resolution of its vital problem. As such, it is not the action of a particular limb that is important, but the general process that results in an end product.

From the perspective of being-in-the-world, Sam's differential behaviours are his way of experimenting with what was available to him at that moment (a group of embodied sensorimotor patterns) in order to bring about the same outcome. In Vignette Six, Sam made various attempts to engage with Ben, not because Ben acted as a stimulus-object that caused multiple behavioural responses, but because Sam oriented towards Ben as a being-in-the-world. As such, Sam's persistence was a mark of him using his various bodily abilities to obtain the same response (a reaction from Ben). What is important here is that Sam could not know what Ben's reactions were going to be. He had no idea that Ben's intent was to ignore Sam's attempts to communicate and as such could not represent the entire interactive sequence. To do so would be to predict the future. What Sam was essentially doing during his actions towards Ben was repairing that which ran counter to Sam's being-in-the-world. Sam's attempts to initiate interaction failed, but rather than giving up he worked with what he had in order to satisfy his needs. Like the insect that relies on substitute limbs when one limb is missing, Sam still oriented towards Ben despite particular sensorimotor patterns not receiving the desired effect. Sam worked with what he had at that particular moment in order to engage with Ben (including hitting himself on the side of the head).

This notion of bodily being-in-the-world is absent in the behaviourist PMLD literature. There is no intrinsic meaning to the situation from the perspective of behaviourism, since behaviourism is non-cognitive and is concerned primarily with the external, with that which can be objectively observed. From this perspective, there is only an objective world and an objectified body, and the research-based literature is concerned with measuring behavioural changes in relation to mechanistic circumstances, or what Merleau-Ponty (2002) refers to as "worldly causality" (p. 87). The body as reflexive object misses the *integration* of organism and world and the significance that this integration generates for the organism at the level of perception.

Similarly, the notion of being-in-the-world is absent in the cognitivist PMLD literature. Central to the cognitivist approach is the role of a rational subject, a self or an "I" that can comprehend the world existing in a particular kind of way and as a result can act in the world. It is this subject (or lack of) that is the target of PMLD intervention, and, as such, descriptions of the "PMLD subject" tend to be of the kind in which the subject can or cannot understand or know something or other. Nind and Hewett (2001) describe how successful communication presupposes that a self can comprehend that what she/he ("I") does has a direct consequence in the world. There must be a rational subject that is in possession of such knowledge and understands the relation between self and world. A lack of contingency awareness stems from the lack of, or the incompetence of, a subject.

Merleau-Ponty's (2002) notion of being-in-the-world is a different mode of existence that cuts across the distinction between mechanistic, reflexive body and abstract, representational mind. In doing so, Merleau-Ponty (2002) foregrounds a positive relationship between body and world that is absent from the PMLD literature. For the core PMLD academics, children with PMLD lack an explicit sense of self, other, and the surrounding world, and as such do not engage in goal-directed activity. From the perspective of being-in-the-world, behaviour does not have to be something abstractly represented. Instead, the world is immediately signified without such deliberation. Such significance is not a product of reflective or objective thought but begins as an *a priori* of the species (though what is signified can change over time through habituation). We miss this global orientation when we construe children with PMLD as objective bodies lacking in representational capacity. For the PMLD literature, where there is a lack of personal, representational subjectivity, there is only sentience, but for Merleau-Ponty (2002), the pre-reflective, pre-thematic body is conceptualised positively in the sense that it is something that endows the world with a primitive significance that understands the world in terms of action rather than abstract representation. Thus, from this perspective, to say that Sam exists in a world, that he belongs to a world, does not mean that Sam has objective consciousness of the world. It means that the situation he is faced with is understood only in terms of practical significance—the situation is understood by the body as that which requires a particular kind of action.

The notion that Sam could use the same (stereotyped) behaviours for different purposes is understood by Merleau-Ponty (2002) in terms of Sam's ability to distance himself from, and take command of, such behaviours. Sam's stereotyped behaviours become those behaviours that he can rely upon and execute without thematic reflection. These behaviours are embodied sensorimotor patterns (innate at first, but then habituated) that aim towards a signified world. We know the world as that which we can act upon, and it is through the stereotyped behaviours that we can engage with the world. This explains why the same behaviours can be used for different purposes. Sam angrily hitting himself on the side of the face during special school switch-based activities is his way of resisting those that wish to engage Sam through switches (Vignettes One and Two), and yet those very same behaviours are executed by him in order to initiate social interaction with adults in his special school (Vignettes Five and Six). By ignoring the significance of hitting, Sam's opportunities to define himself as anything other than PMLD become unnecessarily limited. The irreducible paradox here is that Sam engages with the world through those very same behaviours that are used to define him as PMLD. Sam is denied opportunity to be not-PMLD in his special school since his *ability* to execute "PMLD behaviours" forces him into the PMLD category without him knowing it.

Sam and peers

Discussion so far has explored the ways in which Sam responded to switch-based activities, and the meaning behind certain stereotyped behaviours observed during switch-based (and other) activities. It has been argued in this chapter that the dominant approaches to understanding the behaviour of people with PMLD are unable to account for the range and complexity of Sam's behaviours. The adoption of Trevarthen and Aitken's (2001) notions of primary and secondary intersubjectivities has aided vignette analysis and pointed towards a level of communication development and intersubjective awareness that precedes that described in the PMLD literature. The shift in interpretive framework has allowed Sam's non-triadic (i.e., non-person–person–object) behaviours to be identified as meaningful and communicative. It has also allowed comparison of stereotyped behaviours across contexts in order to tease out the ways in which such behaviours can be assumed by Sam during social interaction. Merleau-Ponty's (2002) phenomenology has provided a language for understanding the shifting meaning of Sam's behaviours. Much of the discussion has revolved around Sam engaging with adults and switches in his special school. The following discussion will present the findings of the research that explored the different ways Sam engaged with his different peer groups. Since the concepts of Trevarthen and Aitken (2001) allow us to account for Sam's non-triadic communicative behaviours, and since Merleau-Ponty (2002) allows us to theorise behavioural differences across contexts, the work of these authors will continue to guide vignette analysis. Like before, the dominant approaches in the PMLD literature are unable to make intelligible the following vignettes. However, rather than repeating the points made in the previous discussion (e.g., the challenge to S-R constancy, the need for non-triadic descriptors of behaviour, etc.), reference to these dominant approaches will be kept to a minimum, allowing more room for discussion of the alternative approaches that this book propounds.

Sam's special school environment was predominantly adult-focused, the main communication partners consisting of the teacher, LSAs and therapists who supported Sam during lessons and therapy-based sessions. Previous discussions highlighted the ways in which Sam was self-aggressive in his special school during switch-based activities. Although such aggression typically manifested itself during special school activities, Sam was not always so aggressive. In his special school, Sam was largely "passive-happy" with the adult staff—things were done *to* Sam by adults (e.g., personal care, therapy-based sessions, sensory stimulation, etc.) that he enjoyed and was happy to be the recipient of. Occasionally Sam would also be "other-active-happy" (e.g., during snack-time). Sam would reach out to and engage with adults and explicitly exhibit primary intersubjectivity by mimicking particular vocalisations ("*Ooohwaa!*") and clapping every time an adult clapped, with increasing excitement. Vignette Seven captures Sam's typical passive state.

Vignette Seven: Sam and a special school LSA—passive-distant, moving to passive-focused, then passive-happy

> Sam is sitting in his chair. An LSA is kneeling in front of him with a handheld electric massager. The massager is attached to a switch, and every time the switch is pressed the massager vibrates nosily. The LSA presses the switch and the vibrations begin. The LSA does not touch Sam with the massager but the noise is loud and unusual enough to grab his attention. His gaze quickly shifts away from the open window to the massager, eyebrows raised, eyes on the device and mouth open. He is still, but focused. He reaches for the massager, the LSA laughs and says: 'No Sam, I hold this bit, you press the button'. She rubs the massager against Sam's arms and Sam chuckles, his eyes roll back and he is grinning and still. The vibrations stops and Sam does not move as if waiting in anticipation for it to start again. There is no smile on his face now. The LSA tries to encourage him to press the button. He does not. She presses it for him and the massager vibrates again, once again Sam chuckles and sits there in bliss enjoying his massage.

It was extremely rare to see Sam interacting with his special school peers. This was due to a number of factors including spatial restrictions (Sam and his peers were often in special chairs and out of reach from one another) and alternative curricular targets (the lessons and sessions were structured around domains of development such as cognitive, sensory, and physical—but no support was given for peer-peer interaction). Also, when opportunities did arise (i.e., when the children were located close to one another and were not working on curricular targets with adults), Sam simply did not attempt to initiate interaction or respond to initiations from other peers. The general opinion of the classroom staff was that Sam was unable to recognise the subtle communicative abilities of his peers and as such he was largely "passive-distant" around them.

Vignette Eight: Sam and a special school peer—passive-happy moving into passive-distant

> I put Sam near two girls who are sitting on the floor. Sam is initially facing the girls because of the way I have seated him. He soon turns to his left. Sam appears to be focusing on the actions of adults tidying up around him rather than on the girls. One girl gets up on to her knees, kisses and hugs Sam. Sam does not respond. The girl stops hugging Sam and Sam looks content, happy even. He makes a noise and flaps his lips with his finger: "Brrrbrrbrrr". The girl crawls away from Sam. Several minutes later, the other girl crawls away from Sam and the only children left are the very physically disabled who cannot crawl away from him. Sam does not try to interact with these children or move towards them. He sits there, with a vacant expression, looking around every so often and very briefly at the local activity around him.

In his mainstream school, Sam's communication partners consisted of classroom assistants and able-bodied peers, and his dominant behaviour state was "other-active-happy". Sam reached out to other children regularly and engaged *with* others, displaying primary intersubjective abilities frequently. Instances of Sam interacting with adults were recorded; however, Sam reached out to and engaged with his mainstream peers far more than he did with the adults from either schools. During the first two terms, Sam often initiated interaction by making eye contact, grabbing other children (their arms, legs, hair, etc.), leaning on them (especially during carpet time) or by simply holding on to them. Reciprocal peer-engagement was often observed, with Sam and his peers mimicking one another and waiting in anticipation. Peers often attempted to initiate interaction with Sam by talking to him, holding his hand and sharing items with him (i.e., their toys) and mimicking how the LSAs behaved with him. Sam nearly always responded back enthusiastically.

Vignette Nine: Sam engaging with a mainstream school friend—other-active-happy

> PE in the hall. The children are sat down on the cold floor with a partner. Sam is facing one of his friends. Their legs are tangled

together (Sam has his left leg under her right leg, and his right leg over her left leg). Happy sounds from Sam. He looks at her face, claps and flaps his arms and tries to wiggle his legs. Big smiles from both. Sam shouts: 'Ooooooohwaaaaaa, buggabuggabugga!', puts his hands on the floor and arches his back and groans. The girl pulls him up so he is facing her again. Sam claps and lets his hands fall on his lap. The girl copies Sam. Sam chuckles and claps again. The girl repeats. Sam exclaims once more: 'Ooooohwaaaaa' (lots of happy sounds come from him). It's time to change partners so the girl gets up, says 'bye' to Sam and leaves.

In the third term, Sam's attempts to interact with his mainstream peers became much more "socially acceptable". He was gentle (e.g., he pulled the other children's hair much less and with less force), gave children hugs (rather than grabbing and holding onto them), made much more eye contact and for more prolonged periods of time, and stroked or placed his hands on others if he wanted attention. It was agreed by Sam's mainstream school staff that this showed that Sam had learned about socially desirable communication, which was partly the result of LSAs encouraging the children to either move away or say: "No, Sam!" when they did not like what he was doing to them. The LSAs often explained to the children the reasons why Sam was behaving in a particular way (i.e., by explaining that when Sam sat beside them holding their arm it was his way of saying "hello"). By the end of the term more children were approaching Sam and those that were shy of him in the first two terms became increasingly confident and engaged with him. The LSAs provided the support, educated the children about Sam and modelled how to communicate with him. The children provided a wealth of opportunities for Sam to communicate with others and practice his communication skills—a task he embarked on enthusiastically.

There was also a marked increase in the frequency and quality of Sam's engagement with his *special school* peers in the third term. Sam exhibited some of his mainstream communication behaviours in his special school—that is, he started to crawl over to his peers and hug them. On several occasions his peers indicated their pleasure in Sam's affection by giggling, hugging him back or indicating that they wanted more in their own idiosyncratic ways. Sam sometimes recognised these cues for more and continued to show affection.

Vignette Ten: Sam and a special school peer—other-active-happy

> Sam is sitting on the carpet, one of his peers is lying on his back (he is unable to sit on his bottom because of his disabilities). The boy is twisted so he is facing Sam and his feet are touching Sam's legs. He is happy and giggling. Sam looks down at the boy, shuffles closer, hugs him gently, kisses him on his cheek and sits back up again. The boy looks surprised, but then giggles louder and raises his arm indicating 'more'. Several seconds later Sam bends down and kisses the boy again and more giggles are heard.

Despite Sam's increased social engagement in his special school, the amount and duration of mainstream interactions was much greater, with many more displays of primary intersubjectivity. Furthermore, Sam's behaviour indicated emerging *secondary intersubjectivity* in his mainstream school, with more examples of "object-awareness" and "other-object-awareness". It is important to note that secondary intersubjectivity (Trevarthen & Aitken, 2001) was not fully developed. Rather, Sam showed an increased interest in his peers' involvement with objects, often being in a "passive-focused" state when watching peers with objects. When a peer ceased using an object, Sam would often pick up the item and explore it himself (visually, orally and/or through hand tactility) and occasionally attempt to interact with the peer after his exploration of the object. Vignette Eleven is an example that captures all these qualities.

Vignette Eleven: Sam displaying emerging other-object-awareness (secondary subjectivity) in his mainstream school

> Sam and three peers are playing with a big tray of wet sand. Sam is sitting on a chair, the rest are standing. Sam picks up some sand and puts it in his mouth. He watches the girl in front of him as he tastes the sand. She is scooping sand with a spade and Sam is transfixed by her actions, staring at the spade and the sand that is being scooped. He reaches for the spade half-heartedly and then stops and smiles briefly. A peer comes over and sprinkles sand on his hands. He breaks out of his gaze, looks at the sand and sticks his hands in again. The girl is now playing with the cup Sam played with earlier. Once again Sam is focused intensely on the scooping

of the sand into the cup. She drops the cup and Sam immediately reaches for it. He tastes it, drops it, groans in a way that signals dissatisfaction and reaches for the girl.

Trevarthen and Aitken's (2001) theory of intersubjective development, combined with behaviour state descriptors (Foreman et al., 2004), has aided vignette analysis by providing a framework that has been used to understand the extent to which Sam engaged with his different social environments. This framework has allowed essential differences between Sam's social activity in his mainstream school and special school to be foregrounded. Sam's differential social activity challenges the interpretative models found in the existing PMLD literature by raising to consciousness the pre-triadic forms of intentional communication. However, there is another interesting challenge here. As the above analysis demonstrates, Sam shifts from PMLD to not-PMLD, from non-communicative to communicative depending on which communication partner is accessible to him. How can Sam be both PMLD and not-PMLD? This duality or ambiguity of intersubjectivity is an alien concept to the PMLD and cognitivist literature. For example, Schaffer's (1971a) theory of infant development is one that stresses the role of perceptual imprinting or exposure learning, in which the infant acquires a central representation of the social environment at the neuronal level, where it is assumed that the environment is symbolically coded as a map in the brain via the sustained, patterned organisation of neurons. Over time, a representation of others as subjects is said to emerge as a neuronal representation, and it is this social representation that allows infants to participate with others as subjects. The problem with this interpretation is that it cannot account for any ambiguity. Sam is either intersubjectively aware or he is not. People (peers/adults) are represented as others or they are not. Infants have a neural map or they do not. There can be no ambiguity here. There is no such thing as some peers being represented as subjects and some non-subjects. The developing infant cannot be intersubjective for half the time. There is no room for shifting levels of awareness. And yet, whilst Sam demonstrated intersubjective awareness, this awareness was almost exclusively demonstrated in his mainstream school context. Sam engaged with his mainstream peers in diverse ways, but never engaged with his special school peers until his third and final academic term (despite having many opportunities to do so). Schaffer's (1971a) model cannot make sense of Sam.

Whilst Trevarthen and Aitken (2001) offer a useful framework for thinking about early, non-triadic behaviours indicative of primary intersubjectivity, they do not articulate a theory of ecological constraint, and as such cannot make intelligible Sam's lack of social interaction in his special school (and, conversely, its emergence later in the academic year). Trevarthen and Aitken (2001) study and chart infantile development and write about observed interactions. They do not write about the significance of prolonged periods of non-interaction. It is Merleau-Ponty's (2002) phenomenology that can offer an explanation of such intersubjective discrepancy. Merleau-Ponty's (2002) differentiation of the habit-body and the body at this moment compliments and extends Trevarthen and Aitken's (2001) notion of primary intersubjectivity. It is also compatible with the behaviour state research of Foreman et al. (2004). A synthesis of these three perspectives articulates a view that contrasts the dominant approaches found in the PMLD literature and offers an alternative way of thinking about children with PMLD, including Sam.

To recap, previous analysis of Merleau-Ponty's (2002) phenomenology revealed how his notion of being-in-the-world relates organism to world through embodied structures that essentially carve out a personal world for the organism, a world loaded with motor significance. The nature of the organism's embodiment (i.e., its sensorimotor structure) is said to allow the organism to enact its world. Merleau-Ponty (2002) extends the notion of enaction by adding a temporal dimension to existence. The body is said to be composed of two distinct, but interrelated layers: the habit-body, and the body at this moment. The body at this moment is the lived through body of the here and now. The habit-body emerges as an embodiment of lived-through, recurrent sensorimotor patterns executed by the body at this moment. Such embodiment allows the pre-objective body to extend its anticipation of the world in the sense that the world becomes further signified as that which can be acted upon. Thus, the lived body is not static, but grows and changes in relation to the world. To re-quote Thompson (2007) once more: "one's lived body is a developmental being thick with its own history and sedimented ways of feeling, perceiving, acting, and imagining" (p. 33).

Merleau-Ponty's (2002) distinction between the habit-body and the body-at-this-moment, combined with Trevarthen and Aitken's (2001) description of primary intersubjectivity, builds a theory that has the power to explain Sam's intersubjective discrepancy described during vignette analysis. From Merleau-Ponty's (2002) perspective, it may be said that if the structure of perception is shaped by the way the body meets the world and where this world consists of other people, then the social world emerges through the interactive exchange between people who meet and define one another. Dreyfus (On Merleau-Ponty, Part 2/2, www.youtube.com) refers to this act in terms of "intercorporeality" (t: 09.41), understood as a pre-objective communion of bodies. This pre-objective structure to social exchanges means that intersubjectivity is predicated upon implicit bodily understanding, or "organic thought" (Merleau-Ponty, 2002, p. 89) (as opposed to explicit mental reasoning about the existence of other minds). Merleau-Ponty (2002) does not describe in detail how pre-objective bodies relate to one another, but Trevarthen and Aitken (2001) do. The notion of primary intersubjectivity is very much a notion of two bodies reading each other. Primary intersubjective awareness presupposes work already done by the body. The form and intensity of multiple micro-behaviours, which vary in pattern over split-second time frames, are too subtle and speedy for a subject to be explicitly aware of (hence the frame-by-frame analysis of video recordings in laboratories by cognitive psychologists). Trevarthen and Aitken (2001) provide an explanation of the way in which tacit bodily interactions support the perception of other as other. Through such interactions, perception becomes loaded with intersubjective significance (the other is immediately signified as subject rather than object). Primary intersubjective awareness is not a static either/or phenomenon (Schaffer, 1971a); but a perceptual unfolding or enacting with the body-at-this-moment. Such awareness is not a product, but a process. It is something embodied, lived, and in need of (re-) enactment during the immediate moments of existence. Sam initially recognised his mainstream school peers as other subjects, not because he objectively represented them, but because they enacted one another through ongoing, intimate, and affectionate playful exchanges. Over time the repeated forms of social enactment with the body-at-this-moment became habituated, the pre-objective body understood that which was familiar and began to signify the social world in perception. This allowed for an immediate perceptual awareness of other subjects without the need for constant, intimate, real-time exchanges. Vignette Ten, where Sam initiates and sustains interaction with his special school peer, can be explained through the construct of the habit-body. Sam's habit-body began to project a social significance in Sam's special school context, and in doing so Sam's special school peers became signified as subjects, without the need for either intimate enaction or a contemplative/thematic cognitive act. This view is supported by the observation of where and when desirable behaviour states (Foreman et al., 2004) emerged. Such states emerged when Sam's pre-objective body found itself in a situation of vital social significance. As the vignettes demonstrate, initially being around mainstream school peers was meaningful for Sam and raised his bodily expectations, his alertness and happiness, and "primed" him to engage with his environment. Later, desirable behaviour states emerged when Sam was interacting with his special school peers, supporting the view that such peers became significant for Sam.

The concluding chapter will revisit some of these findings and insights and draw out key messages from the data and the experience of theorising PMLD in multiple ways.

CHAPTER SEVEN

Concluding discussion: negotiating ambiguity as a means to the life-world

Identifying ambiguity

In this book we explored a range of theoretical and methodological territories as they relate to children with PMLD, and at each turn we have found ambiguity and complexity. At the level of academic theory we found subjective qualities like "contingency awareness" (Lancioni et al., 2003; Saunders et al., 2007; Schweigert, 1989) and "happiness" (Dillon & Carr, 2007; Green & Reid, 1999a) seeping into behaviourist research (see Chapter Two); we found competing perspectives about the nature and development of infantile intersubjectivity and communication in cognitivism (Schaffer, 1971a; Trevarthen & Aitken, 2001) (see Chapter Three); and in phenomenology we found a radically alternative understanding of embodied subjectivity in the form of "organic thought", which competes with understandings of behaviour, consciousness and cognition found in traditional psychology (Merleau-Ponty, 1963; 2002) (see Chapter Four). In the penultimate chapter we applied lenses informed by these approaches but found that Sam resisted being "read" from a singular perspective. Furthermore, there was ambiguity in relation to Sam's identity—that is, his movement between PMLD and not-PMLD, his shifting manifestations of agency and awareness.

The critical analysis of vignettes made it clear that where the current perspectives taken in the PMLD literature are the only perspectives used to make intelligible children with PMLD, then we limit our understandings of the richness of their being. Sam's resistance to each of the analytical frameworks applied to him speaks volumes. He bursts through the constraints that each perspective places on him. The behaviourist perspective cannot make intelligible Sam's resistance to simple stimulus-response constancies. The cognitivist perspective is troubled by Sam's situated intersubjective discrepancies. The phenomenological perspective offers a theory of embodied subjectivity that accounts for change in behaviour in terms of temporality, but Merleau-Ponty's (1963; 2002) stance on intersubjectivity is unclear. Sam's shifting identities, and the difficulties each perspective has on pinning down "Sam-proper", challenges fixed regimes of interpretation and calls for an alternative approach to thinking about children described as having "PMLD". This alternative approach is one that begins with the sustained encounter of children with PMLD in context.

After encountering Sam in different sets of circumstances (special school/mainstream school, peers/adults, etc.) we negotiated a new pathway through the theoretical and empirical literatures explored in Chapters Two, Three, and Four. It was the encounter that determined which points in the path were connected: Trevarthen and Aitken's (2001) notion of primary intersubjectivity was linked to Merleau-Ponty's (2002) notion of habit-body, which was linked to behaviour states (Foreman et al., 2004), etc. These eclectic hybrids of multiple connections emerged not through a traditional reading, since these connections are never made in the PMLD literature as we demonstrated in Chapter One. Rather, after treading several predetermined pathways during explication of the notion of PMLD and related special educational research and practice, we encountered Sam, and together we charted a new route back, stopping at alternative locations, sometimes moving from point to point in ways that the dominant readings of children with PMLD could not imagine (contingency aware and not-contingency aware, intersubjective and not-intersubjective) and, at times, even creating new points ("proto-secondary-intersubjectivity"). With countless literatures that illuminate human beings in multiple ways, the choice of resources for "reading" Sam could have been very different. Stepping off the predetermined pathway of existing PMLD literature allowed us to foreground alternative viewpoints. However, Sam had demonstrated that there is clearly a need for an emergent encounter to help negotiate the pathways, rather than forcing one particular reading upon him. Different literatures afford different readings, leading to reconfigurations of Sam that allow us to think differently about him. And yet, at the same time, it is Sam's resistance to the readings that allows him to actively reconfigure the encounter and take some control over his own life story. It was through Sam's resistance that a sense of his power and agency emerged. This process allows us to rethink the meaning of PMLD. It suggests that children with PMLD are capable of responding in unpredictable ways. If this is true of children with PMLD generally, then we have to reconsider ways of capturing this individuality in order to tell individual stories. If children with PMLD are "one offs", if they are unique like Sam, then this challenges orthodox accounts of children with PMLD (as children lacking in explicit awareness of themselves, others, and the surrounding world). Individuality resists traditional readings in which children with PMLD form a homogeneous group. To resist the group is also to resist the regimes of practice based on the idea of PMLD. Sam actively resisted his special school provision (by being passive or self-aggressive), and this resistance was illuminated further through Sam's opportunities to engage in a non-PMLD context. It was through his engagement with his mainstream school that Sam emerged in new ways.

The life-world revisited

In the remainder of this chapter we theorise the above interpretive process by drawing from phenomenological theory once more and relating the ambiguity above to previous descriptions of the life-world. Specifically, we will discuss how such ambiguity, far from obscuring the life-world, provides us with rich insight into the lived experiences of Sam. We also consider the meaning of the life-world for children with (and without) PMLD generally, before concluding about future directions for research and practice.

In Chapter Four we drew from Lewis and Staehler's (2010) historical account of the life-world, which is based on Husserl's (1970) evolving thought. This led to two definitions. The first is the life-world in the narrow sense, which is a raw, pre-conceptual experience of the world. The life-world in the broad sense is a more mature concept of Husserl's (1970) and was defined as "the all-encompassing, concrete world of our life … the historical world which contains nature as well as culture" (p. 40). With regards to the life-world in the mature sense, there is said to be a circulation between culture and experience (Varela et al., 1991) insofar as our immediate experience of the world becomes shaped by historical circumstances and cultural projects. For example, whilst we do not experience the abstract world as described by Western sciences, the models, constructs, materials and techniques are experienceable insofar as "their effects flow into the everyday world and become tangibly experienced in the form of technology and social practice" (Thompson, 2007, p. 34).

From Merleau-Ponty's (1963) perspective, the life-world in the "simple sense" is more than just a composite of sensuous materials. We explored in Chapter Four how the experiential world is carved out through the "original activity" (p. 31) of the organism. The nature of the organism's embodiment combined with its preceding motor movements result in the emergence of an *Umwelt*, or environment, for the organism. Furthermore, the meaning of this experience for the organism is such that the world is understood in terms of affordances that relate the organism to the world in terms of motility. The notion of "organic thought" (Merleau-Ponty, 2002, p. 89) that emerges from this description is useful to revisit here since we will relate this to the broader sense of the life-world shortly. From the perspective of Merleau-Ponty's (2002) phenomenology, the body is not simply an object, nor is it something to be abstractly represented by a detached, reflective consciousness. Instead, the body is pre-objective; it is the condition for any form of conscious awareness whatsoever. As a condition for conscious experience it shapes that experience, and in that experience the body itself features in an immediate, implicit and pre-reflective way. The body plays an active role in monitoring and governing movement and posture independently of contemplative awareness; it endows perception with motor significance where what is perceived is pre-cognitively understood in terms of how it can be manipulated (i.e., a practical field); and the body lends itself to action without the need for explicit thought about the coordination of every muscle fibre in the body. Further, the body is not static but dynamic—organic thought grows in complexity through sustained opportunities for rich and varied experiences, as expressed by the interplay of the body at this moment and the habit-body. Thus, Merleau-Ponty (2002) articulates different modes of bodily existence, the different ways of being a body, and the different ways of being-in-the-world. The idea of organic thought has direct bearings on areas of practical concern. It reconceptualises cognition as action and resists the passive principles of automated stimulus-response learning (Watson, 1913) and passive neuronal imprinting (Schaffer, 1971a). It suggests new ways of relating to children through intercorporeality, new ways of understanding the many dimensions of children's lived experiences, and motivates exploration of the ways in which agency can manifest.

Thus, the life-world is not something over and above the descriptions we have made in Chapter Five. Rather, those ambiguities exist *as* descriptions of Sam's life-world, as a fluid or dynamic space through which Sam's world is differentially signified depending on where he is and which social milieus he is situated within. The notion of organic thought translates his actions into a positive language which is neither reflexive nor wholly agentic. From this perspective, the life-world is not the assimilation of sensations into a picture in the mind that objectively matches the world. Instead, the life-world is a meaningful experience signified pre-thematically in terms of motility. In trying to articulate the life-worlds of Sam, we would say that different environments afforded him different opportunities to engage in the world. However, to articulate this any further requires us to draw on how such significance is situated—that is, the life-world in the broad sense.

The life-world in the broad sense relates organic thought to historically and culturally situated opportunities for Sam to engage with the world around him, thus forging different senses of self and other through habituated patterns of interactions. These interactions are structured in relation to different social milieus, alternative forms of educational practices and related materiality. Sam's special educational provision was shaped by prevailing understandings of what it means to "be" PMLD that is, pre-intentional, pre-symbolic, pre-intersubjective, pre-contingency aware, etc. (what we may dub the "pre-x symptomology"). The educational experience was thus aimed at fostering the emergence of cognitive and behavioural competencies that would support Sam through the preverbal stages of development. Hence the predominance of switch-based learning activities in his special school to foster contingency awareness, deemed to be a precursor to communication (knowing that you can cause an effect in the environment is needed before you can learn that your actions can cause a social effect). Sam's resistance to these activities is taken as evidence of his inability to master such tasks, his actions are dubbed "stereotyped" and his self-directed activities (performed with varying intensities) lack meaning, or perhaps more appropriately, "adaptation". By contrast, in his mainstream school these stereotyped behaviours take on new signification from the perspective of Sam's peers. It is through those *self-directed* behaviours that Sam engages with *others*; his head-slapping and hand-flapping are part of his repertoire of behaviours that he uses during social interaction. Here, intersubjectivity is not an objective representation of the other or something achieved through a logical act, but a performance or sustained intercorporeality (Dreyfus, On Merleau-Ponty, Part 2/2, www.youtube.com)—the pre-objective communion of bodies, not just organic thought but what we may refer to as "interorganic thought". However, the paradox here is that Sam engages with his social milieu through the same behaviours that are used to define him as PMLD. Sam is denied opportunity to be not-PMLD in his special school insofar as his behavioural repertoire is considered maladaptive and evidence of his being PMLD.

We can also relate the idea of the life-world to our own theoretical activities. Whist we did not explicitly "bracket" our theoretical assumptions during fieldwork or even during the application of lenses to the data, Sam's resistance to being "read" creates antagonisms, which force us to shed our theoretical commitments. We can intellectually wrestle with multiple world views, but the tautology at work here is inescapable. Sam defies *a priori* theorisations of "PMLD". He also resists theorisations through different *post hoc* lenses. His individuality challenges universalising objectifications. Yet he is not alone in this resistance. Arguably, if the theorisations cannot make Sam intelligible then they do not make other children with PMLD intelligible and attempting to do so denigrates their identity. The last thirty years have witnessed critical challenges to how we understand childhood and the need to identify diversities and unique dimensions of childhood experiences (including identities that are complex, fluid, and ever-changing). It is opportune to be foregrounding the most disabled children in society as children first, and as children who deserve to be considered and understood as intentional, communicative and unique individuals and this was something we emphasised as lacking in the current PMLD literature in Chapter One. The new challenge should be to use theoretical tools at our disposal in order to make this paradigmatic shift in thinking, and create the intellectual space to develop nuanced and sophisticated ways of enabling us to see children with PMLD as autonomous beings. This is essential to the wider project of realising rights and respect for all people in society. It means engaging with profoundly disabled children in emotional and relational ways that resist othering processes on the basis of bodily impairment or diversity.

The importance of peers and peer interactions in Sam's communication gains and different behaviour states cannot be overstated as it challenges segregated provisions not on rights bases or equality bases, but on empirically observed effects that relate to *other* children. This relates to basic human needs for interactions and contact with people "like us"—that is, the need to attain recognition, respect, value, and friendship. There are also important insights about childhood and about the importance not just of children learning from experts and elders but of horizontal observational and modelled interactions by other children. Sam's changed behaviour states in different contexts are evidence of this. Essential to children's wellbeing is that individuals can subjectively report their experiences (and have them heard); that wellbeing is contextually located and temporal and that wellbeing exists in relationships with other people (family, friends, community, school, etc.) (Watson et al., 2012). This is what is happening for Sam—it is the unique combination of contexts and relationships—he is being "heard" because of the sensitive and reflexive observations undertaken by Ben; he is observed in different environments that offer different opportunities to act, leading to different insights on his ability to exert control over his life-world, and he is enabled to create meaningful peer relationships in the mainstream setting that are embodied and intercorporeal in nature.

REFERENCES

Abbott, D. (2012). Other voices, other rooms: reflections on talking to young men with Duchenne muscular dystrophy and their families about transition to adulthood. *Children & Society*, 26: 241–250.

Adams, J., Swain, J., & Clark, J. (2000). What's so special? Teachers' models and their realisation in practice in segregated schools. *Disability & Society*, 15: 233–245.

Ainscow, M., & Haile-Giorgis, M. (1998). The education of children with special needs: barriers and opportunities in Central and Eastern Europe. *Innocenti Occasional Papers, Economic and Social Policy, 67*. Florence: UNICEF International Child Development Centre.

Alderson, P. (1999). *Learning and Inclusion: The Cleves School Experience*. London: David Fulton.

Appleton, J. V. (1995). Analysing qualitative interview data: addressing issues of validity and reliability. *Journal of Advanced Nursing*, 22: 993–997.

Armstrong, A. C., Armstrong, D., & Spandagou, I. (2010). *Inclusive Education: International Policy & Practice*. London: SAGE.

Arthur, M. (2000). Behavior states and a half-full glass: a response to Mudford, Hogg, and Roberts. *American Journal on Mental Retardation*, 105: 509–511.

Arthur, M. (2004). Patterns amongst behavior states, sociocommunicative, and activity variables in educational programs for students with profound and multiple disabilities. *Journal of Developmental and Physical Disabilities*, 16: 125–149.

Arthur-Kelly, M., Bochner, S., Center, Y., & Mok, M. (2007). Sociocommunicative perspectives on research and evidence-based practice in the education of students with profound and multiple disabilities. *Journal of Developmental and Physical Disabilities*, 19: 161–176.

Arthur-Kelly, M., Foreman, P., Bennett, D., & Pascoe, S. (2008). Interaction, inclusion and students with profound and multiple disabilities: towards an agenda for research and practice. *Journal of Research in Special Educational Needs*, 8: 161–166.

Arvio, M., & Sillanpää, M. (2003). Prevalence, aetiology and comorbidity of severe and profound intellectual disability in Finland. *Journal of Intellectual Disability Research*, 47: 108–112.

Atkinson, D. (1997). *An Autobiographical Approach to Learning Disability Research*. Milton Keynes: Open University Press.

Austin, J. L. (1962). *How to Do Things with Words*. New York: Oxford University Press.

Aylott, J. (1999). Is the sexuality of people with a learning disability being denied? *British Journal of Nursing*, 8: 438–442.

Baars, B. (1986). *The Cognitive Revolution in Psychology*. New York: Guilford Press.

Baker, J. (2009). Special school headship in times of change: impossible challenges or golden opportunities? *British Journal of Special Education*, 36: 191–197.

Bates, E., Camaioni, L., & Volterra, V. (1975). The acquisition of performatives prior to speech. *Merrill-Palmer Quarterly of Behavior and Development*, 21: 205–226.

Bateson, M. C. (1971). The interpersonal context of infant vocalization. *Quarterly Progress Report of the Research Laboratory of Electronics*, 100: 170–176.

Baylies, C. (2002). Disability and the notion of human development: questions of rights and capabilities. *Disability & Society*, 17: 725–739.

Beebe, B., Knoblauch, S., Rustin, J., & Sorter, D. (2005). *Forms of intersubjectivity in infant research and adult treatment*. New York: Other Press.

Bellamy, G., Croot, L., Bush, A., Berry, H., & Smith, A. (2010). A study to define: Profound and Multiple Learning Disabilities (PMLD). *Journal of Intellectual Disabilities*, 14: 221–235.

Beresford, B. (2012). Working on well-being: researcher's experiences of a participative approach to understanding the subjective well-being of disabled young people. *Children & Society*, 26: 234–240.

British Institute of Learning Disabilities (BILD) (2004). *Factsheet—Intensive Interaction*. Kidderminster: BILD.

Binney, V. (1992). Staff training to run activity groups with people with profound learning disabilities: evaluation of attitude, knowledge and skills changes. *Behavioural Psychotherapy, 20: 267–278.*

Bishop, A., & Jones, P. (2003). I never thought they would enjoy the fun of science just like ordinary children do– exploring science experiences with early years teacher training students and children with severe and profound learning difficulties. *British Journal of Special Education, 30: 34–43.*

Blackmore, R. (2001). Advocacy in nursing: perceptions of learning disability nurses. *Journal of Intellectual Disabilities, 5: 221–234.*

Bogdan, R., & Taylor, S. J. (1989). Relationships with severely disabled people: the social construction of humanness. *Social problems, 36: 135–148.*

Bolton, D., & Hill, J. (1996). *Mind, Meaning and Mental Disorder: The Nature of Causal Explanation in Psychology and Psychiatry.* Oxford: Oxford University Press.

Boxall, K., & Ralph, S. (2010). Research ethics committees and the benefits of involving people with profound and multiple learning disabilities. *British Journal of Learning Disabilities, 39: 173–180.*

Brazelton, T. B. (1984). *Neonatal Behavioral Assessment Scale* (2nd edn). Philadelphia: J. B. Lippincott Co./Spastics International Medical Publications.

Brennan, J. F. (2003). *History and Systems in Psychology* (6th edn). Delhi: Pearson Education.

Brett, J. (2002). The experience of disability from the perspective of parents of children with profound impairment: is it time for an alternative model of disability? *Disability & Society, 17: 825–843.*

Brewster, S. J. (2004). Putting words into their mouths? Interviewing people with learning disabilities and little/no speech. *British Journal of Learning Disabilities, 32: 166–169.*

Brewster, S. J., & Coleyshaw, L. (2010). Participation or exclusion? Perspectives of pupils with autistic spectrum disorders on their participation in leisure activities. *British Journal of Learning Disabilities, 39: 284–291.*

Brodin, J. (2005). Diversity of aspects on play in children with profound multiple disabilities. *Early Child Development and Care, 175: 635–646.*

Bruner, J. (1975). The ontogenesis of speech acts. *Journal of Child Language, 2: 1–19.*

Burchardt, T. (2004). Capabilities and disability: the capabilities framework and the social model of disability. *Disability & Society, 19: 735–751.*

Burford, B. (1988). Action cycles: rhythmic actions for engagement with children and young adults with profound mental handicap. *European Journal of Special Needs Education, 3: 189–206.*

Burke, J. (2012). Some kids climb up; some kids climb down: culturally constructed play-worlds of children with impairments. *Disability & Society, 27*: 965–981.

Burtner, P. A., & Dicks, J. L. (1994). Providing oral health care to individuals with severe disabilities residing in the community: alternative care delivery systems. *Special Care in Dentistry, 14*: 188–193.

Cannella, H. I., O'Reilly, M. F., & Lancioni, G. E. (2005). Choice and preference assessment research with people with severe to profound developmental disabilities: a review of the literature. *Research in Developmental Disabilities, 26*: 1–15.

Carlson, L., & Bricker, D. D. (1982). Dyadic and contingent aspects of early communicative intervention. In: D. D. Bricker (Ed.), *Interventions with At-risk and Handicapped Infants*. Baltimore: University Park Press.

Carman, T. (2008). *Merleau-Ponty*. Abingdon: Routledge.

Carnaby, S. (2004). People with profound and multiple learning disabilities: a review of research about their lives. A report commissioned by Mencap.

Carnaby, S. (2007). Developing good practice in the clinical assessment of people with profound intellectual disabilities and multiple impairment. *Journal of Policy and Practice in Intellectual Disabilities, 4*: 88–96.

Carpenter, B. (2004). The mental health needs of young people with profound and multiple learning disabilities. *PMLD Link, 16*: 9–12.

Carpenter, B. (2007). Changing Children—Changing Schools? Concerns for the Future of Teacher Training in Special Education. *PMLD Link, 19*: 2–4.

Carter, B., McArthur, E., & Cunliffe, M. (2002). Dealing with uncertainty: parental assessment of pain in their children with profound special needs. *Journal of Advanced Nursing, 38*: 449–457.

Carter, E. W., & Hughes, C. (2005). Increasing social interaction among adolescents with intellectual disabilities and their general education peers: effective interventions. *Research and Practice for Persons with Severe Disabilities, 30*: 179–193.

Cartwright, C., & Wind-Cowie, S. (2005). *Profound and Multiple Learning Difficulties*. London: Continuum.

Cerbone, D. R. (2006). *Understanding Phenomenology*. Durham: Acumen.

Chesley, G. M., & Calaluce, P. D. (1997). The deception of inclusion. *Mental Retardation, 35*: 488–490.

Christensen, P. H., & James, A. (2008). *Research with Children: Perspectives and Practices*. London: Routledge.

Clement, T. A., & Bigby, C. (2009). Breaking out of a distinct social space: reflections on supporting community participation for people with severe and profound intellectual disability. *Journal of Applied Research in Intellectual Disabilities, 22:* 264–275.

Cocks, A. (2008). Researching the lives of disabled children: the process of participant observation in seeking inclusivity. *Qualitative Social Work, 7:* 163–180.

Connors, C., & Stalker, K. (2007). Children's experiences of disability: pointers to a social model of childhood disability. *Disability & Society, 22:* 19–33.

Cormany, E. E. (1994). *Enhancing Services for Toddlers with Disabilities: A Reverse Mainstreaming Inclusion Approach.* Ed.D Practicum Report, Nova Southeastern University.

Coupe O'Kane, J., & Goldbart, J. (1998). *Communication Before Speech: Development and Assessment* (2nd edn). London: David Fulton.

Croll, P., & Moses, D. (2000). Ideologies and utopias: education professionals' views of inclusion. *European Journal of Special Educational Need, 15:* 1–12.

Crotty, M. (2003). *The Foundation of Social Research.* London: SAGE.

Dahlberg, G., & Moss, P. (2005). *Ethics and Politics in Early Childhood Education.* Oxford: Routledge Falmer.

Davies, D., & Evans, L. (2001). Assessing pain in people with profound learning disabilities. *British Journal of Nursing, 10:* 513–516.

Davis, P. K., Young, A., Cherry, H., Dahman, D., & Rehfeldt, R. A. (2004). Increasing the happiness of individuals with profound multiple disabilities: replication and extension. *Journal of Applied Behavior Analysis, 37:* 531–534.

Dawkins, B. (2009). Valuing Tom: will valuing people now change the lives of people with profound and multiple learning disabilities? *Tizard Learning Disability Review, 14:* 3–12.

DCSF. (2009). Schools, pupils and their characteristics. Child and Maternal Health Intelligence Network: www.chimat.org.uk/resource/item.aspx?RID=77411 [last accessed January 2009].

De Geeter, K. I., Poppes, P., & Vlaskamp, C. (2002). Parents as experts: the position of parents of children with profound multiple disabilities. *Child: Care, Health and Development, 28:* 443–453.

Denis, J., Van Den Noortgate, W., & Maes, B. (2011). Self-injurious behavior in people with profound intellectual disabilities: a meta-analysis of single-case studies. *Research in Developmental Disabilities, 32:* 911–923.

Department of Health. (2001). *Valuing people: a new strategy for learning disability for the 21st century.* London: Department of Health (DH).

Department for Education and Skills (DfES). (2001). *Special Educational Needs Code of Practice.* Annesley: DfES Publications.

Diesfeld, K. (2001). Disability matters in medical law. *Journal of Medical Ethics*, 27: 388–392.

Dillon, C. M., & Carr, J. E. (2007). Assessing indices of happiness and unhappiness in individuals with developmental disabilities: a review. *Behavioral Interventions*, 22: 229–244.

Dillon, M. C. (1997). *Merleau-Ponty's Ontology* (2nd edn). Evanston: Northwestern University Press.

Downing, J. E. (2005). Inclusive education for high school students with severe intellectual disabilities: supporting communication. *Augmentative and Alternative Communication*, 21: 132–148.

Downs, C., & Craft, A. (1996). Sexuality and profound and multiple impairment. *Tizard Learning Disability Review*, 1: 17–22.

Downs, C., & Farrell, S. (1996). A practical response to masturbation: working with people with profound and multiple disabilities. *Tizard Learning Disability Review*, 1: 23–26.

Dreyfus, H. On Merleau-Ponty, Part 2/2. www.youtube.com/watch?v=JgbEnvVfqaU [last accessed 08.07.2013].

Edgerton, R. B. (1993). *The Cloak of Competence* (Revised and Updated). Berkeley: University of California.

Education & Skills Committee. (2006). RE: Select Committee on Education and Skills Third Report on Special Educational Needs. House of Commons, London: The Stationery Office.

Ellis, P. (1997). The music of sound: a new approach for children with severe and profound and multiple learning difficulties. *British Journal of Music Education*, 14: 173–186.

Emerson, E. (2005). Underweight, obesity and exercise among adults with intellectual disabilities in supported accommodation in northern England. *Journal of Intellectual Disability Research*, 49: 134–143.

Emerson, E. (2009). Estimating future numbers of adults with profound multiple learning disabilities in England. *Tizard Learning Disability Review*, 14: 49–55.

Emerson, E., Robertson, J., Gregory, N., Kessissoglou, S., Hatton, C., Hallam, A., Knapp, M., Järbrink, K., Netten, A., & Linehan, C. (2000). The quality and costs of community-based residential supports and residential campuses for people with severe and complex disabilities. *Journal of Intellectual and Developmental Disability*, 25: 263–279.

Ephraim, G. W. (1979). Developmental process in mental handicap: a generative structure approach. PhD thesis, Brunel University.

Eriksson, L., & Granlund, M. (2004). Conceptions of participation in students with disabilities and persons in their close environment. *Journal of Developmental and Physical Disabilities*, 16: 229–245.

Farrell, A. (2005). *Ethical Research with Children*. Maidenhead: Open University Press.
Farrell, M. (2004). *Inclusion at the Crossroads*. London: David Fulton.
Fava, L., & Strauss, K. (2010). Multi-sensory rooms: comparing effects of the Snoezelen and the stimulus preference environment on the behavior of adults with profound mental retardation. *Research in Developmental Disabilities, 31: 160–171.*
Felce, D., & Emerson, E. (2001). Living with support in a home in the community: predictors of behavioral development and household and community activity. *Mental Retardation and Developmental Disabilities Research Reviews, 7: 75–83.*
Fergusson, A., Howley, M., & Rose, R. (2008). Responding to the mental health needs of young people with profound and multiple learning disabilities and autistic spectrum disorders: issues & challenges. *Mental Health and Learning Disabilities Research and Practice, 5: 240–251.*
Finch, H., & Lewis, J. (2003). Focus Groups. In: Ritchie J., & Lewis, J. (Eds.), *Qualitative Research Practice—A Guide for Social Science Students and Researchers*. London: SAGE.
Firth, G. (2006). Intensive interaction: a research review. *Mental Health and Learning Disabilities, 3: 53–62.*
Fitton, P., O'Brien, C., & Willson, J. (1995). *Home at Last: How Two Young Women with Profound Intellectual and Multiple Disabilities Achieved their Own Home*. London: Jessica Kingsley.
Fodor, J. A. (1975). *The Language of Thought*. New York: Thomas Y. Crowell.
Foreman, P., Arthur-Kelly, M., Pascoe, S., & Smyth King, B. (2004). Evaluating the educational experiences of students with profound and multiple disabilities in inclusive and segregated classroom settings: an Australian perspective. *Research & Practice for Persons with Severe Disabilities, 29: 183–193.*
Forster, S., Gray, K. M., Taffe, J., Einfeld, S. L., & Tonge, B. J. (2011). Behavioural and emotional problems in people with severe and profound intellectual disability. *Journal of Intellectual Disability Research, 55: 190–198.*
Gadamer, H. G. (1976). *Philosophical Hermeneutics*. Berkeley: University of California Press.
Gallagher, S. (1986). Body image and body schema: a conceptual clarification. *Journal of Mind and Behavior, 7: 541–554.*
Gallagher, S., & Zahavi, D. (2008). *The Phenomenological Mind: An Introduction to Philosophy of Mind and Cognitive Science*. Abingdon: Routledge.
Ganesh, S., Potter, J., & Fraser, W. (1994). An audit of physical health needs of adults with profound learning disability in a hospital population. *Mental Handicap Research, 7: 228–236.*

Garcia, M. J., & Matson, J. L. (2008). Akathisia in adults with severe and profound intellectual disability: a psychometric study of the MEDS and ARMS. *Journal of Intellectual and Developmental Disability, 33*: 171–176.

Gardner, H. (1987). *The Mind's New Science: A History of the Cognitive Revolution*. New York: Basic Books.

Germain, R. (2004). An exploratory study using cameras and talking mats to access the views of young people with learning disabilities on their out-of-school activities. *British Journal of Learning Disabilities, 32*: 170–174.

Giangreco, M. F., Edelman, S. W., Broer, S. M., & Doyle, M. B. (2001). Paraprofessional support of students with disabilities: literature from the past decade. *Exceptional Children, 68*: 45–63.

Glick, N. R., Fischer, M. H., Heisy, D. M., Leverson, G. E., & Mann, D. C. (2005). Epidemiology of fractures in people with severe and profound developmental disabilities. *Osteoporosis International, 16*: 389–396.

Goldbart, J. (1994). Opening the communication curriculum to students with PMLDs. In: Ware, J. (Ed.), *Educating Children with Profound and Multiple Learning Difficulties*. London: David Fulton.

Goldbart, J. (2002). Commentary on: Melanie Nind and Mary Kellett. Responding to individuals with severe learning difficulties and stereotyped behaviour: challenges for an inclusive era. *European Journal of Special Needs Education, 17*: 283–287.

Goodley, D. (2001). Learning difficulties, the social model of disability and impairment: challenging epistemologies. *Disability & Society, 16*: 207–231.

Goodley, D., Lawthom, R., Clough, P., & Moore, M. (2004). *Researching Life Stories: Method, Theory and Analyses in a Biographical Age*. London: Routledge Falmer.

Gordon, M., Rosenman, L., & Cuskelly, M. (2007). Constrained labour: maternal employment when children have disabilities. *Journal of Applied Research in Intellectual Disabilities, 20*: 236–246.

Green, C. W., & Reid, D. H. (1996). Defining, validating, and increasing indices of happiness among people with profound multiple disabilities. *Journal of Applied Behavior Analysis, 29*: 67–78.

Green, C. W., & Reid, D. H. (1999a). A behavioral approach to identifying sources of happiness and unhappiness among individuals with profound multiple disabilities. *Behavior Modification, 23*: 280–293.

Green, C. W., & Reid, D. H. (1999b). Reducing indices of unhappiness among individuals with profound multiple disabilities during therapeutic exercise routines. *Journal of Applied Behavior Analysis, 32*: 137–147.

Green, C. W., Gardner, S. M., & Reid, D. H. (1997). Increasing indices of happiness among people with profound multiple disabilities: a program replication and component analysis. *Journal of Applied Behavior Analysis*, 30: 217–228.

Green, C. W., Middleton, S. G., & Reid, D. H. (2000). Embedded evaluation of preferences sampled from person-centered plans for people with profound multiple disabilities. *Journal of Applied Behavior Analysis, 33:* 639.

Green, C. W., Gardner, S. M., Canipe, V. S., & Reid, D. H. (1994). Analyzing alertness among people with profound multiple disabilities: implications for provision of training. *Journal of Applied Behavior Analysis, 27:* 519.

Green, C. W., Reid, D. H., Canipe, V. S., & Gardner, S. M. (1991). A comprehensive evaluation of reinforcer identification processes for persons with profound multiple handicaps. *Journal of Applied Behaviour Analysis,* 24: 537–552.

Green, C. W., Reid, D. H., Rollyson, J. H., & Passante, S. C. (2005). An enriched teaching program for reducing resistance and indices of unhappiness among individuals with profound multiple disabilities. *Journal of Applied Behavior Analysis, 38:* 12.

Green, C. W., Reid, D. H., White, L. K., Halford, R. C., Brittain, D. P., & Gardner, S. M. (1988). Identifying reinforcers for persons with profound handicaps: staff opinion verses systematic assessment preferences. *Journal of Applied Behavior Analysis, 21: 31–43.*

Green, D. W. (1996). *Cognitive Science: An Introduction.* Oxford: Blackwell Publishing.

Gregory, R. L., & Zangwill, O. L. (1987). *The Oxford Companion to the Mind.* Oxford: Oxford University Press.

Grove, D. N., Dalke, B. A., Dredericks, H. D., & Crowley, R. F. (1975). Establishing appropriate head positioning with mentally and physically handicapped children. *Behavioral Engineering, 3:* 53–59.

Grove, N. (2007). Exploring the absence of high points in story reminiscence with carers of people with profound disabilities. *Journal of Policy and Practice in Intellectual Disabilities,* 4: 252–260.

Grove, N. (2012). Story, agency and meaning making: narrative models and the social inclusion of people with severe and profound intellectual disabilities. *Journal of Religion, Disability and Health,* 16: 334–351.

Guess, D., Roberts, S., Behrens, G. A., & Rues, J. (1998). Response to Mudford, Hogg, and Roberts on continuous recording of behavior state. *American Journal on Mental Retardation,* 103: 75–77.

Guess, D., Roberts, S., Siegel-Causey, D., & Rues, J. (1993). Replication and extended analysis of behavior state, environmental events and related variables in profound disabilities. *Annual Conference of the Association for Persons with Severe Handicaps. Chicago, Illinois.*

Guess, D., Siegel-Causey, E., Roberts, E., Rues, K., Thompson, B., & Siegel-Causey, D. (1990). Assessment and analysis of behavior state and related variables among students with profoundly handicapping conditions. *Journal of the Association for Persons with Severe Handicaps, 15:* 211–230.

Habermas, J. (1974). *Theory and Practice.* Boston: Beacon Press.

Hakken, N., & Pijl, S. P. (2002). Getting along with classmates in regular schools: a review of the effects of integration on the development of social relationships. *International Journal of Inclusive Education, 6:* 47–61.

Hanley, G. P., Iwata, B. A., & McCord, B. E. (2003). Functional analysis of problem behavior: a review. *Journal of Applied Behavior Analysis, 36:* 147–185.

Hanline, M. F. (1993). Inclusion of preschoolers with profound disabilities: an analysis of children's interactions. *Journal of the Association for Persons with Severe Handicaps, 18:* 28–35.

Harcourt, D., Perry, B., & Waller, T. (2011). *Researching Young Children's Perspectives: Debating the Ethics and Dilemmas of Educational Research with Children.* London: Routledge.

Harding, C., & Halai, V. (2009). Providing dysphagia training for carers of children who have profound and multiple learning disabilities. *The British Journal of Development Disabilities, 55:* 33–47.

Harris, J. (2002). Commentary on: Nind and Kellett (2002). *European Journal of Special Needs Education, 17:* 289–291.

Harrison, J., MacGibbon, L., & Morton, M. (2001). Regimes of trustworthiness in qualitative research: the rigors of reciprocity. *Qualitative Inquiry, 7:* 323–345.

Hatton, C., Emerson, E., Robertson, J., Henderson, D., & Cooper, J. (1995). The quality and costs of residential services for adults with multiple disabilities: a comparative evaluation. *Research in Developmental Disabilities, 16:* 439–460.

Helm, J. M., & Simeonsson, R. J. (1989). Assessment of behavioral state organization. In: Bailey, D. B., & Woolery, M. (Eds.), *Assessing Infants and Preschoolers with Handicaps.* Columbus, O.H: Merrill Publishing.

Henderson, G. E., & Brown, C. (1997). Speech act theory, glossary of literary theory. www.library.utoronto.ca/utel/glossary/Speech_act_theory.html. [last accessed 21.04.2013].

Hermans, H., & Evenhuis, H. M. (2010). Characteristics of instruments screening for depression in adults with intellectual disabilities: systematic review. *Research in Developmental Disabilities, 31:* 1109–1120.

Heslop, P., Blair, P., Fleming, P., Hoghton, M., Marriott, A., & Russ, L. (2013). *Confidential inquiry into premature deaths of people with learning disabilities (CIPOLD).* Bristol: Norah Fry Research Centre, University of Bristol.

Hewett, D. (1996). How to start doing intensive interaction: a summary. In: Collis, M., & Lacey, P. (Eds.) *Interactive Approaches to Teaching: A Framework for INSET*. London: David Fulton.

Hewitt, H. (2000). A life story approach for people with profound learning disabilities. *British Journal of Nursing*, 9: 90–95.

Hiemstra, S. J., Vlakamp, V., & Wiersma, L. A. (2007). Individual focus in an activity centre: an observational study among persons with profound and multiple disabilities. *Education and Training in Developmental Disabilities*, 42: 14–23.

Hinder, S., & Perry, D. (2000). Sodium-valproate-induced pancreatitis in a man with profound intellectual disability: the significance of diagnostic difficulties. *Journal of Applied Research in Intellectual Disabilities*, 13: 292–297.

Hodge, N. (2008). Evaluating lifeworld as an emancipatory methodology. *Disability & Society*, 23: 29–40.

Hogg, J. (1999). People with profound intellectual and multiple disabilities: understanding and realising their needs and those of their carers. *Scottish Executive Review of Services for People with Learning Disabilities*.

Hogg, J. (2002). Commentary on: Nind and Kellett. *European Journal of Special Needs Education*, 17: 293–297.

Hogg, J. (2007). Complex needs and complex solutions: the challenge of profound intellectual and multiple disabilities. *Journal of Policy and Practice in Intellectual Disabilities*, 4: 79–82.

Hogg, J., Cavet, J., Lambe, L., & Smeddle, M. (2001). The use of 'Snoezelen' as multisensory stimulation with people with intellectual disabilities: a review of the research. *Research in Developmental Disabilities*, 22: 353–372.

Hogg, J., Remington, R. E., & Foxen, T. (1979). Classical conditioning with profoundly retarded, multiply handicapped children. *Developmental Medicine and Child Neurology*, 21: 779–786.

Hostyn, I., Daelman, M., Janssen, M. J., & Maes, B. (2010). Describing dialogue between persons with profound intellectual and multiple disabilities and direct support staff using the scale for dialogical meaning making. *Journal of Intellectual Disability Research*, 54: 679–690.

Hostyn, I., Petry, K., Lambrechts, G., & Maes, B. (2011). Evaluating the quality of the interaction between persons with profound intellectual and multiple disabilities and direct support staff: a preliminary application of three observation scales from parent–infant research. *Journal of Applied Research in Intellectual Disabilities*, 24: 407–420.

Hughes, R. P., Redley, M., & Ring, H. (2011). Friendship and adults with profound intellectual and multiple disabilities and English disability policy. *Journal of Policy and Practice in Intellectual Disabilities*, 8: 197–206.

Hulland, S., & Sigal, M. J. (2000). Hospital-based dental care for persons with disabilities: a study of patient selection criteria. *Special Care in Dentistry*, 20: 131–138.

Hussein, H. (2010). Using the sensory garden as a tool to enhance the educational development and social interaction of children with special needs. *Support for Learning*, 25: 25–31.

Husserl, E. (1964). *Cartesian Meditations: An Introduction to Phenomenology*. Abingdon: Routledge.

Husserl, E. (1970). *The Crisis of European Sciences and Transcendental Phenomenology*. Evanston: Northwestern University Press.

Hutchinson, C. (1998). Positive health: a collective responsibility. In: Lacey, P. & Ouvry, C. (Eds.), *People with Profound and Multiple Learning Disabilities—A Collaborative Approach to Meeting Complex Needs*. London: David Fulton.

Imray, P. A., & Hinchcliffe, V. (2012). Not fit for purpose: a call for separate and distinct pedagogies as part of a national framework for those with severe and profound learning difficulties. *Support for Learning*, 27: 150–157.

Ivancic, M. T., & Bailey, J. S. (1996). Current limits to reinforcer identification for some persons with profound multiple disabilities. *Research in Developmental Disabilities*, 17: 77–92.

Ivancic, M. T., Barrett, G. T., Simonow, A., & Kimberly, A. (1997). A replication to increase happiness indices among some people with profound multiple disabilities. *Research in Developmental Disabilities*, 18: 79–89.

Jan, J. E., & Freeman, R. D. (2004). Melatonin therapy for circadian rhythm sleep disorders in children with multiple disabilities: what have we learned in the last decade? *Developmental Medicine & Child Neurology*, 46: 776–782.

Jansen, S. L. G., Van Der Putten, A. A. J., & Vlaskamp, C. (2012). What parents find important in the support of a child with profound intellectual and multiple disabilities. *Child: Care, Health and Development*. Child and Maternal Health Intelligence Network: www.chimat.org.uk/resource/item.aspx?RID=126680 [last accessed].

Janssen, C. G. C., Schuengel, C., & Stolk, J. (2002). Understanding challenging behaviour in people with severe and profound intellectual disability: a stress-attachment model. *Journal of Intellectual Disability Research*, 46: 445–453.

Jaydeokar, S., & Piachaud, J. (2004). Out-of-borough placements for people with learning disabilities. *Advances in Psychiatric Treatment*, 10: 116–123.

Jeannerod, M. (1986). The formation of finger grip during prehension. A cortically mediated visuomotor pattern, *Behavioural Brain Research*, 199: 99–116.

Jenks, C. (2001). *Childhood*. London: Routledge.
Jones, M. C., Walley, R. M., Leech, A., Paterson, M., Common, S., & Metcalf, C. (2007). Behavioral and psychosocial outcomes of a 16-week rebound therapy-based exercise program for people with profound intellectual disabilities. *Journal of Policy and Practice in Intellectual Disabilities, 4: 111–119.*
Jones, P. (2004). They are not like us and neither should they be: issues of teacher identity for teachers of pupils with profound and multiple learning difficulties. *Disability & Society, 19: 159–169.*
Jones, P. (2005). Teachers' views of their pupils with profound and multiple learning difficulties. *European Journal of Special Needs Education, 20: 375–385.*
Jones, P. (2010). My peers have also been an inspiration for me: developing online learning opportunities to support teacher engagement with inclusive pedagogy for students with severe/profound intellectual developmental disabilities. *International Journal of Inclusive Education, 14: 681–696.*
Jones, R. S. P., Walsh, P., & Sturmey, P. (1995). *Stereotyped Movement Disorders*. Chichester: John Wiley and Sons.
Kellett, M. (2000). Sam's story: evaluating intensive interaction in terms of its effect on the social and communicative ability of a young child with severe learning difficulties. *Support for Learning, 15: 165–171.*
Kellett, M. (2005). Catherine's legacy: social communication development for individuals with profound learning difficulties and fragile life expectancies. *British Journal of Special Education, 32: 116–121.*
Kellett, M., & Nind, M. (2001). Ethics in quasi-experimental research on people with severe learning disabilities: dilemmas and compromises. *British Journal of Learning Disabilities, 29: 51–55.*
Kemmis, S., & McTaggart, R. (1998). Participatory action research. In: Denzin, N. K., & Lincoln, Y. S. (Eds.), *Handbook of Qualitative Research* (2nd edn). London: SAGE.
Kemmis, S., & Wilkinson, M. (1998). Participatory action research and the study of practice. In: Atweh, B., Kemmis, S., & Weeks, P. (Eds.), *Action Research in Practice—Partnership for Social Justice in Education*. London: Routledge.
Kennedy, C. H., & Haring, T. G. (1993). Teaching choice making during social interactions to students with profound multiple disabilities. *Journal of Applied Behaviour Analysis, 26: 63–76.*
Klotz, J. (2004). Sociocultural study of intellectual disability: moving beyond labelling and social constructionist perspectives. *British Journal of Learning Disabilities, 32: 93–104.*
Kurani, D., Neruka, A., Miranda, L., Jawadwala, F., & Prabhulkar, D. (2009). Impact of parents' involvement and engagement in a learning readiness programme for children with severe and profound intellectual

disability and complex needs in India. *Journal of Intellectual Disabilities, 13:* 269–289.

Kwok, H., & Cheung, P. W. (2007). Co-morbidity of psychiatric disorder and medical illness in people with intellectual disabilities. *Current Opinion in Psychiatry, 20:* 443–449.

Lacey, P. (Ed.) (1998). *People with Profound and Multiple Learning Disabilities: A Collaborative Approach to Meeting Complex Needs*. London: David Fulton.

Lacey, P. (2001). The role of learning support assistants in the inclusive learning of pupils with severe and profound learning difficulties. *Educational Review, 53:* 157–167.

Lambrechts, G., Kuppens, S., & Maes, B. (2009). Staff variables associated with the challenging behaviour of clients with severe or profound intellectual disabilities. *Journal of Intellectual Disability Research, 53:* 620–632.

Lancioni, G., Bellini, D., Oliva, D., Singh, N., O'Reilly, M., Lang, R., & Didden, R. (2011). Camera-based microswitch technology to monitor mouth, eyebrow, and eyelid responses of children with profound multiple disabilities. *Journal of Behavioral Education, 20:* 4–14.

Lancioni, G. E., Campodonico, F., & Mantini, M. (1999). Promoting mild physical exercise in a person with profound multiple disabilities. *Scandinavian Journal of Behaviour Therapy, 28:* 115–118.

Lancioni, G. E., O'Reilly, M. F., & Emerson, E. (1996). A review of choice research with people with severe and profound developmental disabilities. *Research in Developmental Disabilities, 17:* 391–411.

Lancioni, G. E., O'Reilly, M. F., & Basili, G. (2001). Use of microswitches and speech output systems with people with severe/profound intellectual or multiple disabilities: a literature review. *Research in Developmental Disabilities, 22:* 21–40.

Lancioni, G. E., O'Reilly, M. F., Campodonico, F., & Mantini, M. (2002a). Increasing indices of happiness and positive engagement in persons with profound and multiple disabilities. *Journal of Developmental and Physical Disabilities, 14:* 231–237.

Lancioni, G. E., O'Reilly, M. F., Singh, N. N., Oliva, D., & Groeneweg, J. (2002b). Impact of stimulation versus microswitch-based programs on indices of happiness of people with profound multiple disabilities. *Research in Developmental Disabilities, 23:* 149–160.

Lancioni, G. E., Singh, N. N., O'Reilly, M. F., & Oliva, D. (2005a). Microswitch programs for persons with multiple disabilities: an overview of the responses adopted for microswitch activation. *Cognitive Processing, 6:* 177–188.

Lancioni, G. E., Singh, N. N., O'Reilly, M. F., Oliva, D., & Basili, G. (2005b). An overview of research on increasing indices of happiness of people with severe/profound intellectual and multiple disabilities. *Disability and Rehabilitation,* 27: 83–93.

Lancioni, G. E., Singh, N. N., O'Reilly, M. F., & Sigafoos, J. (2009). An overview of behavioral strategies for reducing hand-related stereotypies of persons with severe to profound intellectual and multiple disabilities: 1995–2007. *Research in Developmental Disabilities,* 30: 20–43.

Lancioni, G. E., Abels, J., Wilms, E. H., Singh, N. N., O'Reilly, M. F., & Groeneweg, J. (2003). Microswitch responding and awareness of contingency in persons with profound multiple disabilities. *Perceptual and Motor Skills,* 96: 835–838.

Lancioni, G. E., Tota, A., Smaldone, A., Singh, N. N., O'Reilly, M. F., Sigafoos, J., Oliva, D., & Montironi, G. (2007a). Extending the evaluation of novel microswitch technology for small responses in children with profound multiple disabilities. *Assistive Technology,* 19: 11–16.

Lancioni, G. E., O'Reilly, M. F., Cuvo, A. J., Singh, N. N., Sigafoos, J., & Didden, R. (2007b). PECS and VOCAs to enable students with developmental disabilities to make requests: an overview of the literature. *Research in Developmental Disabilities,* 28: 20.

Langdridge, D. (2007). *Phenomenological Psychology: Theory, Research, and Method.* Harlow: Pearson Education.

Laverty, S. M. (2003). Hermeneutic phenomenology and phenomenology: a comparison of historical and methodological considerations. *International Journal of Qualitative Methods,* 2: 21–35.

Leahey, T. H. (1994). *A History of Modern Psychology.* New Jersey: Prentice Hall.

Legerstee, M. (2005). *Infants' Sense of People: Precursors to a Theory of Mind.* Cambridge: Cambridge University Press.

Levi-Strauss, C. (1966). *The Savage Mind.* Chicago: Chicago University Press.

Lewis, A. (2002). Accessing, through research interviews, the views of children with difficulties in learning. *Support for Learning,* 17: 110–116.

Lewis, A. (2004). And when did you last see your father? Exploring the views of children with learning difficulties/disabilities. *British Journal of Special Education,* 31: 3–9.

Lewis, A. (2010). Silence in the context of child "voice". *Children & Society,* 24: 14–23.

Lewis, A. (2011). Disabled children's "voice" and experiences. In: Haines, S., & Ruebain, D. (Eds.), *Education, Disability and Social Policy.* Bristol: Policy Press.

Lewis, A., & Porter, J. (2004). Interviewing children and young people with learning disabilities: guidelines for researchers and multi-professional practice. *British Journal of Learning Disabilities,* 32: 191–197.

Lewis, M., & Staehler, T. (2010). *Phenomenology: An Introduction*. London: Continuum.

Lim, W. W. C. (2007). Use of psychoactive medications in Hong Kong institutions for adults with severe to profound learning disabilities: a retrospective study (1988–2003) and economic analysis. *Journal of Applied Research in Intellectual Disabilities, 20:* 529–538.

Lima, M., Silva, K., Magalhaes, A., Amaral, I., Pestana, H., & De Sousa, L. (2012). Can you know me better? an exploratory study combining behavioural and physiological measurements for an objective assessment of sensory responsiveness in a child with profound intellectual and multiple disabilities. *Journal of Applied Research in Intellectual Disabilities, 25:* 522–530.

Lindsay, W. R., Pitcaithly, D., Geelen, N., Buntin, L., Broxholme, S., & Ashby, M. (1997). A comparison of the effects of four therapy procedures on concentration and responsiveness in people with profound learning disabilities. *Journal of Intellectual Disability Research, 41:* 201–207.

Liu, K. P. Y., Lee, T., Yan, A., Siu, C. W. M., Choy, F. W. Y., Leung, K. L. K., Siu, T. Y., & Kwan, A. C. S. (2007). Use of the interact short form as a tool to evaluate emotion of people with profound intellectual disabilities. *Journal of Intellectual Disability Research, 51:* 884–891.

Logan, K. R., & Gast, D. L. (2001). Conducting preference assessments and reinforcer testing for individuals with profound multiple disabilities: issues and procedures. *Exceptionality, 9:* 123–134.

Logan, K. R., Jacobs, H. A., Gast, D. L., Murray, A. S., Daino, K., & Skala, C. (1998). The impact of typical peers on the perceived happiness of students with profound multiple disabilities. *Journal of the Association for Persons with Severe Handicaps, 23:* 309–318.

Logan, K. R., Jacobs, H. A., Gast, D. L., Smith, P. D., Daniel, J., & Rawls, J. (2001). Preferences and reinforcers for students with profound multiple disabilities: can we identify them? *Journal of Developmental and Physical Disabilities, 13:* 97–122.

Lyons, G., & Cassebohm, M. (2012). Student wellbeing for those with profound intellectual and multiple disabilities: same, or same but different? *Journal of Student Wellbeing, 5:* 18–33.

Macann, C. (1993). *Four Phenomenological Philosophers*. Abingdon: Routledge.

Mac Naughton, G. (2005). *Doing Foucault in Early Childhood Studies: Applying Post-Structural Ideas*. London: Routledge.

Male, D. B. (1998). Parents' views about special provision for their child with severe or profound and multiple learning difficulties. *Journal of Applied Research in Intellectual Disabilities, 98:* 129–145.

Malin, M. (2003). Competing interests between researcher, teacher and student in the ethics of classroom ethnography. *Westminster Studies in Education*, 26: 21–31.

Mansell, J. (2006). Deinstitutionalisation and community living: progress, problems and priorities. *Journal of Intellectual and Developmental Disability*, 31: 65–76.

Mansell, J. (2010). *Raising our sights: services for adults with profound intellectual and multiple disabilities.* London: Department of Health.

Matson, J. L., Bamburg, J. W., & Smalls, Y. (2004). An analysis of Snoezelen equipment to reinforce persons with severe or profound mental retardation. *Research in Developmental Disabilities*, 25: 89–95.

Matthews, E. (2006). *Merleau-Ponty: A Guide For the Perplexed.* London: Continuum.

Mechling, L. C. (2006). Comparison of the effects of three approaches on the frequency of stimulus activations, via a single switch, by students with profound intellectual disabilities. *The Journal of Special Education*, 40: 94–102.

Mechling, L. C., & Bishop, V. A. (2009). Assessment of computer-based preferences of students with profound multiple disabilities. *The Journal of Special Education*, 45: 15–27.

Meehan, S., Moore, G., & Barr, O. (1995). Specialist services for people with learning disabilities. *Nursing Times*, 91: 33–35.

Mellstrom, B., Saunders, M., Saunders, R., & Olswang, L. (2005). Interaction of behavioral state and microswitch use in individuals with profound multiple impairments. *Journal of Developmental and Physical Disabilities*, 17: 35–53.

Meltzoff, A. M. (1999). Born to learn: what infants learn from watching us. In: Fox, N., & Worhol, J. G. (Eds.), *The Role of Early Experience in Infant Development*. Skillman, New Jersey: Pediatric Institute Publications.

Mencap. (2001). *No ordinary life—the support needs of families caring for children and adults with profound and multiple learning disabilities.* London: Mencap.

Mencap. (2003). *Breaking point.* London: Mencap.

Mencap. (2004). *Treat me right! better healthcare for people with a learning disability.* London: Mencap.

Mencap. (2006). *Breaking point—families still need a break.* London: Mencap.

Mencap. (2007). *Death by indifference—following up the "treat me right!" report.* London: Mencap.

Mercieca, D. P. (2008). *Living Otherwise. Students with Profound and Multiple Learning Disabilities as Agents in Educational Contexts.* Unpublished PhD thesis, School of Education, Stirling University

Merleau-Ponty, M. (1963). *The Structure of Behavior.* Pittsburgh: Duquesne University Press.

Merleau-Ponty, M. (2002). *Phenomenology of Perception.* London: Routledge.

Michael, J. (2008). *Report of the independent inquiry into access to healthcare for people with learning disabilities.* London: Independent Inquiry into Access to Healthcare for People with Learning Disabilities.

Middleton, D., & Hewitt, H. L. (1999). Remembering as social practice: identity and life story work in transitions of care for people with profound learning disabilities. *Narrative Inquiry,* 9: 97–121.

Mitchell, W. (2010). I know how I feel: listening to young people with life-limiting conditions who have learning and communication impairments. *Qualitative Social Work,* 9: 185–203.

Mitra, S. (2006). The capability approach and disability. *Journal of Disability Policy Studies,* 16: 236–247.

Moir, L. (2010). Evaluating the effectiveness of different environments on the learning of switching skills in children with severe and profound multiple disabilities. *The British Journal of Occupational Therapy,* 73: 446–456.

Moore, J. (2008). *Playing, Laughing and Learning with Children on the Autism Spectrum: A Practical Resource of Play Ideas for Parents and Carers* (2nd edn). London: Jessica Kingsley.

Moore, M., Beazley, S., & Maelzer, J. (1998). *Researching Disability Issues.* Maidenhead: Open University Press.

Moran, D. (2000). *Introduction to Phenomenology.* Abingdon: Routledge.

Moran, D. (2002). Editor's Introduction. In: Moran, D., & Mooney, T. (Eds.), *The Phenomenology Reader.* London: Routledge.

Morris, C. (2009). Measuring participation in childhood disability: how does the capability approach improve our understanding? *Developmental Medicine and Child Neurology,* 51: 92–94.

Morris, J. (2003). Including all children: finding out about the experiences of children with communication and/or cognitive impairments. *Children & Society,* 17: 337–348.

Morris, K. J. (2012). *Starting with Merleau-Ponty.* London: Continuum.

Mount, H., & Cavet, J. (2007). Multi sensory environments: an exploration of their potential for young people with profound and multiple learning difficulties. *British Journal of Special Education,* 22: 52–55.

Mudford, O. C., Hogg, J., & Roberts, J. (1997). Interobserver agreement and disagreement in continuous recording exemplified by measurement of behavior state. *American Journal on Mental Retardation,* 102: 54–66.

Mudford, O. C., Hogg, J., & Roberts, J. (1999). Readers reactions: behaviour states: now you see them, now you don't. *American Journal on Mental Retardation,* 104: 385–391.

Muir, D., & Slater, A. (2003). The scope and methods of developmental psychology. In: Slater, A., & Bremner, G. (Eds.), *An Introduction to Developmental Psychology*. Oxford: Blackwell Publishing.

Munde, V., Vlaskamp, C., Ruijssenaars, W., & Nakken, H. (2011). Determining alertness in individuals with profound intellectual and multiple disabilities: the reliability of an observation list. *Education and Training in Autism and Developmental Disabilities, 46*: 116–123.

Munde, V. S. (2011). *Attention Please! Alertness in individuals with profound intellectual and multiple disabilities*. PhD thesis, School of Behavioural and Cognitive Neurosciences, University of Groningen.

Munde, V. S., Vlaskamp, C., Maes, B., & Ruijssenaars, A. J. J. M. (2012a). Catch the wave! Time-window sequential analysis of alertness stimulation in individuals with profound intellectual and multiple disabilities. *Child: Care, Health and Development, 1365–2214*.

Munde, V., Vlaskamp, C., Post, W. J., Ruijssenaars, A. J. J. M., Maes, B., & Nakken, H. (2012b). Observing and influencing alertness in individuals with profound intellectual and multiple disabilities in multisensory environments. *Journal of Cognitive Education and Psychology, 11*: 5–19.

Munde, V. S., Vlaskamp, C., Ruijssenaars, A. J. J. M., & Nakken, H. (2009). Alertness in individuals with profound intellectual and multiple disabilities: a literature review. *Research in Developmental Disabilities, 30*: 462–480.

Murdoch, H. (1997). Stereotyped behaviours: how should we think about them? *British Journal of Special Education, 24*: 71–75.

Murphy, E., Clegg, J., & Almack, K. (2010). Constructing adulthood in discussions about the future of young people with moderate-profound intellectual disabilities. *Journal of Applied Research in Intellectual Disabilities, 24*: 61–73.

Murphy, K. M., Saunders, M. D., Saunders, R. R., & Olswang, L. B. (2004). Effects of ambient stimuli on measures of behavioral state and microswitch use in adults with profound multiple impairments. *Research in Developmental Disabilities, 25*: 355–370.

Murphy, R., Doughty, N., & Nunes, D. (1979). Multielement designs: an alternative to reversal and multiple baseline evaluation strategies. *Mental Retardation, 17*: 23–27.

Murray, L., & Trevarthen, C. (1986). The infant's role in mother–infant communication. *Journal of Child Language, 13*: 15–29.

Nakken, H., & Vlaskamp, C. (2007). A need for a taxonomy for profound intellectual and multiple disabilities. *Journal of Policy and Practice in Intellectual Disabilities, 4*: 83–87.

Neilson, A., Hogg, J., Malek, M., & Rowley, D. (2000). Impact of surgical and orthotic intervention on the quality of life of people with profound intellectual and multiple disabilities and their carers. *Journal of Applied Research in Intellectual Disabilities, 13:* 216–238.

Ng, J. S. W. (2011). *Knowing the patient well: learning disability nurses' experiences of caring for terminally ill people with profound learning disabilities in residential care settings.* PhD thesis, University of Greenwich.

Nind, M. (2007). Supporting lifelong learning for people with profound and multiple learning difficulties. *Support for Learning, 22:* 111–115.

Nind, M. (2008). *Conducting qualitative research with people with learning, communication and other disabilities: methodological challenges.* University of Southampton: ESRC: National Centre for Research Methods.

Nind, M., & Hewett, D. (1988). Interaction as curriculum. *British Journal of Special Education, 15:* 55–57.

Nind, M., & Hewett, D. (1994). *Access to Communication: Developing the Basics of Communication with People with Severe Learning Difficulties through Intensive Interaction.* London: David Fulton.

Nind, M., & Hewett, D. (2001). *A Practical Guide to Intensive Interaction.* Kidderminster: British Institute of Learning Difficulties (BILD) Publications.

Nind, M., & Kellett, M. (2002). Responding to individuals with severe learning difficulties and stereotyped behaviour: challenges for an inclusive era. *European Journal of Special Needs Education, 17:* 265–282.

Nind, M., & Powell, S. (2000). Intensive interaction and autism: some theoretical concerns. *Children & Society, 14:* 98–109.

Nind, M., & Thomas, G. (2005). Reinstating the value of teachers' tacit knowledge for the benefit of learners: using intensive interaction. *Journal of Research in Special Educational Needs, 5:* 97–100.

Novak, G. D., & Pelaez, M. (2004). *Child and Adolescent Development: A Behavioral Systems Approach.* London: SAGE.

Nussbaum, M. (1992). Human functioning and social justice: in defence of Aristotelean essentialism. *Political Theory, 20:* 202–247.

Nussbaum, M. (2000). *Women and Human Development: The Capabilities Approach.* Cambridge: Cambridge University Press.

Nussbaum, M. (2003). Capabilities as fundamental entitlements: Sen and social justice. *Feminist Economics, 9:* 33–59.

Nussbaum, M. (2007). Frontiers of justice. disability, nationality, species membership. *Scandinavian Journal of Disability Research, 9:* 133–136.

Nussbaum, M., & Sen, A. (1993). *The Quality of Life.* Oxford: Clarendon Press.

Ockelford, A., Welch, G., Zimmermann, S., & Himonides, E. (2005). Sounds of intent: mapping, assessing and promoting the musical development

of children with profound and multiple learning difficulties. *Elsevier: International Congress Series, 1282, 898–902.*
Odman, P. J., & Kerdeman, D. (1999). Hermeneutics. In: Keeves, J. P., & Lakomski, G. (Eds.), *Issues in Educational Research.* Oxford: Elsevier Science.
Office of Public Sector Information" (OPSI). (2001). *Special Educational Needs and Disability Act* (ch.10).
Ouvry, C. (1986). Integrating pupils with profound and multiple handicaps: in a school for children with severe learning difficulties. *Journal of the British Institute of Mental Handicap (APEX), 14: 157–160.*
Ouvry, C. (1987). *Educating Children with Profound Handicaps.* Kidderminster: British Institute of Mental Handicap (BIMH) Publications.
Pace, G. M., Ivancic, M. T., Edwards, G. L., Iwata, B. A., & Page, T. J. (1985). Assessment of stimulus preference and reinforcer value with profoundly retarded individuals. *Journal of Applied Behavior Analysis, 18: 249–255.*
Parfit, D. (1984). *Reasons and Persons.* Oxford: Clarendon Press.
Park, K. (1998). Dickens for all: inclusive approaches to literature and communication with people with severe and profound learning disabilities. *British Journal of Special Education, 25: 114–118.*
Pawlyn, J., & Budd, S. (2009). Continence. In: Pawlyn, J., & Carnaby, S. (Eds.), *Profound Intellectual and Multiple Disabilities: Nursing Complex Needs.* Oxford: Wiley-Blackwell.
Pawlyn, J., & Carnaby, S. (2009). *Profound Intellectual and Multiple Disabilities: Nursing Complex Needs.* Oxford: Wiley-Blackwell.
Petry, K., & Maes, B. (2006). Identifying expressions of pleasure and displeasure by persons with profound and multiple disabilities. *Journal of Intellectual and Developmental Disability, 31: 28–38.*
Petry, K., & Maes, B. (2007). Description of the support needs of people with profound multiple disabilities using the 2002 AAMR system: an overview of literature. *Education and Training in Developmental Disabilities, 42: 130.*
Petry, K., Maes, B., & Vlaskamp, C. (2005). Domains of quality of life of people with profound multiple disabilities: the perspective of parents and direct support staff. *Journal of Applied Research in Intellectual Disabilities, 18: 35–46.*
Petry, K., Maes, B., & Vlaskamp, C. (2007). Support characteristics associated with the quality of life of people with profound intellectual and multiple disabilities: the perspective of parents and direct support staff. *Journal of Policy and Practice in Intellectual Disabilities, 4: 104–110.*
Petry, K., Maes, B., & Vlaskamp, C. (2009a). Measuring the quality of life of people with profound multiple disabilities using the QOL-PMD: first results. *Research in Developmental Disabilities, 30: 1394–1405.*

Petry, K., Maes, B., & Vlaskamp, C. (2009b). Psychometric evaluation of a questionnaire to measure the quality of life of people with profound multiple disabilities (QOL-PMD). *Research in Developmental Disabilities*, 30: 1326–1336.

Pfister, A. A., Roberts, A. G., Taylor, H. M., Noel-Spaudling, S., Damian, M. M., & Charles, P. D. (2003). Spasticity in adults living in a developmental center. *Archives of Physical Medicine and Rehabilitation*, 84: 1808–1812.

Phelvin, A. (2013). Getting the message: intuition and reflexivity in professional interpretations of non-verbal behaviours in people with profound learning disabilities. *British Journal of Learning Disabilities*, 41: 31–37.

Piaget, J. (1952). *The Origins of Intelligence in Children*. New York: International Universities Press.

PMLD Network (2001). *Valuing people with profound and multiple learning disabilities*. PMLD Network.

Poppes, P., Van Der Putten, A. J., & Vlaskamp, C. (2010). Frequency and severity of challenging behaviour in people with profound intellectual and multiple disabilities. *Research in Developmental Disabilities*, 31: 1269–1275.

Porter, J. (2005). Awareness of number in children with severe and profound learning difficulties: three exploratory case studies. *British Journal of Learning Disabilities*, 33: 97–101.

Pratchett, G. B. (2004). *It's a matter of understanding: a study of movement behaviour patterns in children with profound, complex and multiple learning disabilities*. PhD thesis, University of Exeter.

Preece, D., & Jordan, R. (2009). Obtaining the views of children and young people with autism spectrum disorders about their experience of daily life and social care support. *British Journal of Learning Disabilities*, 38: 10–20.

Punch, S. (2002). Research with children: the same or different from research with adults? *Childhood-a Global Journal of Child Research*, 9: 321–341.

Radcliffe, J. (2007). Distress in children with learning disabilities at a respite unit: perspectives on their experiences. *British Journal of Learning Disabilities*, 36: 91–101.

Radnor, H. A. (2002). *Researching Your Professional Practice: Doing Interpretative Research*. Buckingham: Open University Press.

Rayner, M. (2011). The curriculum for children with severe and profound learning difficulties at Stephen Hawking School. *Support for Learning*, 26: 25–32.

Realon, R. E., Favell, J. E., & Dayvault, K. A. (1988). Evaluating the use of adapted leisure materials on the engagement of persons who are profoundly, multiply handicapped. *Education and Training in Mental Retardation*, 23: 228–37.

Reber, A. S. (1995). *Penguin Dictionary of Psychology*. London: Penguin Reference.

Regnard, C., Reynolds, J., Watson, B., Matthews, D., Gibson, L., & Clarke, C. (2007). Understanding distress in people with severe communication difficulties: developing and assessing the Disability Distress Assessment Tool (DisDAT). *Journal of Intellectual Disability Research, 51:* 277–292.

Reid, D. H., & Hurlbut, B. (1977). Teaching nonvocal communication skills to multihandicapped retarded adults. *Journal of Applied Behavior Analysis, 10: 591–603.*

Reid, D. H., Everson, J. M., & Green, C. W. (1999). A systematic evaluation of preferences identified through person-centered planning for people with profound multiple disabilities. *Journal of Applied Behavior Analysis, 32: 467–477.*

Reid, D. H., Phillips, J. F., & Green, C. W. (1991). Teaching persons with profound multiple handicaps: a review of the effects of behavioral research. *Journal of Applied Behavior Analysis, 24: 319–336.*

Reid, D. H., Parsons, M. B., McCarn, J. E., Green, C. W., Phillips, J. F., & Schepis, M. M. (1985). Providing a more appropriate education for severely handicapped persons: increasing and validating functional classroom tasks. *Journal of Applied Behavior Analysis, 18: 289–301.*

Remington, B. (1996). Assessing the occurrence of learning in children with profound intellectual disability: a conditioning approach. *International Journal of Disability, Development and Education, 43: 101–118.*

Richardson, M. (1997). Reflection and celebration—Neal (1960–1987): narrative of a young man with profound and multiple disabilities. *Journal of Intellectual Disabilities, 1: 191–195.*

Robertson-Malt, S. (1999). Listening to them and reading me: a hermeneutic approach to understanding the experience of illness. *Journal of Advanced Nursing, 29: 290–297.*

Robinson, D. N. (1981). *An Intellectual History of Psychology*. New York: Macmillan.

Romdenh-Romluc, K. (2011). *Merleau-Ponty and Phenomenology of Perception*. London: Routledge.

Roper, S. O., & Jackson, J. B. (2007). The ambiguities of out-of-home care: children with severe or profound disabilities. *Family Relations, 56: 147–161.*

Ross, E., & Oliver, C. (2003). The assessment of mood in adults who have severe or profound mental retardation. *Clinical Psychology Review, 23: 225–245.*

Ross, S. M. (1972). Trace and delay classical eyelid conditioning in severely and profoundly retarded subjects as a function of interstimulus interval. *American Journal of Mental Deficiency, 77: 39–45.*

Ryan, W. G., & Bernard, R. H. (1994). Data management and analysis methods. In: Denzin, N. K. & Lincoln, Y. S. (Eds.), *Handbook of Qualitative Research*. London: SAGE.

Salt, T. (2010). *Salt review: independent review of teacher supply for pupils with Severe, Profound and Multiple Learning Difficulties (SLD and PMLD)*. Nottingham: Crown Copyright.

Samuel, J., & Pritchard, M. (2001). The ignored minority: meeting the needs of people with profound learning disability. *Tizard Learning Disability Review, 6: 34–44*.

Saunders, M. D., Smagner, J. P., & Saunders, R. R. (2003a). Improving methodological and technological analyses of adaptive switch use of individuals with profound multiple impairments. *Behavioral Interventions, 18: 227–243*.

Saunders, M. D., Timler, G. R., Cullinan, T. B., Pilkey, S., Questad, K. A., & Saunders, R. R. (2003b). Evidence of contingency awareness in people with profound multiple impairments: response duration versus response rate indicators. *Research in Developmental Disabilities, 24: 231–245*.

Saunders, R. R., Saunders, M. D., Struve, B., Munce, A. L., Olswang, L. B., Dowden, P. A., & Klasner, E. R. (2007). Discovering indices of contingency awareness in adults with multiple profound disabilities. *American Journal on Mental Retardation, 112: 246–260*.

Scanlon, T. (1993). Value, desire, and quality of life. In: Nussbaum, M. C., & Sen, A. (Eds.), *The Quality of Life*. Oxford: Clarendon Press.

Schaffer, H. R. (1971a). *The Growth of Sociability*. Harmondsworth: Penguin.

Schaffer, H. R. (1971b). *The Origins of Human Social Relations*. London: Academic Press.

Schaffer, H. R. (1977a). Early Interactive Development. In: Schaffer, H. R. (Ed.), *Studies in Mother–Infant Interaction*. London: Academic Press.

Schaffer, H. R. (1977b). *Studies in Mother–Infant Interaction*. London: Academic Press.

Schaffer, H. R. (1984). *The Child's Entry into a Social World*. New York: Academic Press.

Schaffer, H. R., & Emerson, P. E. (1964). Patterns of response to physical contact in early human development. *Journal of Child Psychology and Psychiatry, 5: 1–13*.

Schaffer, H. R., & Liddell, C. (1984). Adult-child interaction under dyadic and polyadic conditions. *British Journal of Developmental Psychology, 2: 33–42*.

Schweigert, P. (1989). Use of microswitch technology to facilitate social contingency awareness as a basis for early communication skills. *Augmentative and Alternative Communication, 5: 192–198*.

REFERENCES

Schweigert, P., & Rowland, C. (1992). Early communication and microtechnology: instructional sequence and case studies of children with severe multiple disabilities. *Augmentative and Alternative Communication, 8:* 273–286.

Scope. (2013). Profound and Multiple Learning Disabilities/Difficulties (PMLD). www.scope.org.uk/services/education-and-learning/schools/meldreth-manor/pmld [last accessed 10.02.2013].

Sen, A. K. (1985). Well-being, agency and freedom. *Journal of Philosophy, 82:* 169–221.

Sen, A. K. (1993). Capability and well-being. In: Nussbaum, C., & Sen, A. K. (Eds.), *Quality of Life.* Oxford: Clarendon Press.

Sheehy, K., & Nind, M. (2005). Emotional well-being for all: mental health and people with profound and multiple learning disabilities. *British Journal of Learning Disabilities, 33:* 34–38.

Silverman, D. (1993). *Interpreting Qualitative Data—Methods for Analysing Talk, Text and Interaction.* London: SAGE.

Simmons, B., & Bayliss, P. (2007). The role of special schools for children with profound and multiple learning difficulties: is segregation always best? *British Journal of Special Education, 34:* 19–24.

Simmons, B., Blackmore, T., & Bayliss, P. (2008). Postmodern synergistic knowledge creation: extending the boundaries of disability studies. *Disability & Society, 23:* 733–745.

Singh, N. N., Lancioni, G. E., Winton, A. S., Wahler, R. G., Singh, J., & Sage, M. (2004). Mindful caregiving increases happiness among individuals with profound multiple disabilities. *Research in Developmental Disabilities, 25:* 207–218.

Skinner, B. F. (1986). Interview with Bernard Baars. In: Baars, B. (1986). *The Cognitive Revolution in Psychology.* New York: The Guildford Press.

Smith, A. D. (2007a). The flesh of perception: Merleau-Ponty and Husserl. In: Baldwin, T. (Ed.), *Reading Merleau-Ponty: On Phenomenology of Perception.* Abingdon: Routledge.

Smith, B. A. (2007b). *Increasing the comfort level of teachers toward inclusion through use of school focus groups.* Ed.D, thesis Nova Southeastern University.

Smith, P. D., Gast, D. L., Logan, K. R., & Jacobs, H. A. (2001). Customizing instruction to maximize functional outcomes for students with profound multiple disabilities. *Exceptionality, 9:* 135–145.

Sokolowski, R. (2000). *Introduction to Phenomenology.* Cambridge: Cambridge University Press.

Spevack, S., Yu, C. T., Lee, M. S., & Martin, G. L. (2006). Sensitivity of passive approach during preference and reinforcer assessments for

children with severe and profound intellectual disabilities and minimal movements. *Behavioral Interventions, 21: 165–175.*
Sternberg, L., Pengatore, L., & Hill, C. (1983). Establishing interactive communication behaviors with profoundly mentally handicapped students. *Journal of the Association for Persons with Severe Handicaps (JASH), 8: 39–46.*
Stickley, T., Crosbie, B., & Hui, A. (2011). The stage life: promoting the inclusion of young people through participatory arts. *British Journal of Learning Disabilities, 40: 251–258.*
Strogilos, V., Lacey, P., Xanthacou, Y., & Kaila, M. (2011). Collaboration and integration of services in Greek special schools: two different models of delivering school services. *International Journal of Inclusive Education, 15: 797–818.*
Tadema, A. C., & Vlaskamp, C. (2010). The time and effort in taking care for children with profound intellectual and multiple disabilities: a study on care load and support. *British Journal of Learning Disabilities, 38: 41–48.*
Tang, J. C., Patterson, T. G., & Kennedy, C. H. (2003). Identifying specific sensory modalities maintaining the stereotypy of students with profound multiple disabilities. *Research in Developmental Disabilities, 24: 433–451.*
Taylor, S. J., & Bogdan, R. (1989). On accepting relationships between people with mental retardation and non-disabled people: towards an understanding of acceptance. *Disability & Society, 4: 21–36.*
Terzi, L. (2005a). Beyond the dilemma of difference: the capability approach to disability and special educational needs. *Journal of Philosophy of Education, 39: 443–459.*
Terzi, L. (2005b). A capability perspective on impairment, disability and special needs: towards social justice in education. *Theory and Research in Education, 3: 197–223.*
Thompson, E. (2007). *Mind in Life: Biology, Phenomenology and the Sciences of Mind.* London: The Belknap Press of Harvard University Press.
Tisdall, K. (2012). The challenge and challenging of childhood studies? Learning from disability studies and research with disabled children. *Children & Society, 26: 181–191.*
Tisdall, K., Davis, J., & Gallagher, M. (2008). *Researching with Children and Young People: Research Design, Methods and Analysis.* London: SAGE.
Trevarthen, C. (1979). Communication and cooperation in early infancy: a description of primary intersubjectivity. In: Bullowa, M. (Ed.), *Before Speech.* Cambridge: Cambridge University Press.
Trevarthen, C. (1998). The concept and foundations of infant intersubjectivity. In: Braten, S. (Ed.), *Intersubjective Communication and Emotion in Early Ontogeny.* Cambridge: Cambridge University Press.

Trevarthen, C., & Aitken, K. J. (2001). Infantile intersubjectivity: research, theory and clinical applications. *Journal of Child Psychology and Psychiatry, 42:* 3–48.

Trevarthen, C., & Hubley, P. (1978). Secondary intersubjectivity: confidence, confiding and acts of measuring in the first year. In: Lock, A. (Ed.), *Action, Gesture and Symbol*. London: Academic Press.

Trevarthen, C., Kokkinaki, T., & Fiamenghi, C. A. J. (1999). What infants' imitations communicate: with mothers, with fathers, and with peers. In: Nadel, J., & Butterworth, G. (Eds.), *Imitation in Infancy*. Cambridge: Cambridge University Press.

Tullis, C. A., Cannella-Malone, H. I., Basbigill, A. R., Yeager, A., Fleming, C. V., Payne, D., & Wu, P. (2011). Review of the choice and preference assessment literature for individuals with severe to profound disabilities. *Education and Training in Autism and Developmental Disabilities, 46:* 576–595.

Tyrer, F., Smith, L. K., McGrother, C. W. (2007). Mortality in adults with moderate to profound intellectual disability: a population-based study. *Journal of Intellectual Disability Research, 51:* 520–526.

United Nations (UN) (1990). *United Nations Convention on the Rights of the Child*. Geneva: Office of the United Nations High Commissioner for Human Rights.

Van Der Heide, D. C., Van Der Putten, A. A. J., Van Den Berg, P. B., Taxis, K., & Vlaskamp, C. (2009). The documentation of health problems in relation to prescribed medication in people with profound intellectual and multiple disabilities. *Journal of Intellectual Disability Research, 53:* 161–168.

Van Der Putten, A., & Vlaskamp, C. (2011). Pain assessment in people with profound intellectual and multiple disabilities; a pilot study into the use of the pain behaviour checklist in everyday practice. *Research in Developmental Disabilities, 32:* 1677–1684.

Van Der Putten, A., Vlaskamp, C., & Schuivens, E. (2011). The use of a multisensory environment for assessment of sensory abilities and preferences in children with profound intellectual and multiple disabilities: a pilot study. *Journal of Applied Research in Intellectual Disabilities, 24:* 280–284.

Van Oort, R. (1997). Performative-constative revisited: the genetics of Austin's theory of speech acts. *Anthropoetics, 2:* 2.

Varela, F. J., Thompson, E. T., & Rosch, E. (1991). *The Embodied Mind: Cognitive Science and Human Experience*. Cambridge: The MIT Press.

Verdonschot, M. M. L., De Witte, L. P., Reichrath, E., Buntinx, W. H. E., & Curfs, L. M. G. (2009). Community participation of people with an intellectual disability: a review of empirical findings. *Journal of Intellectual Disability Research, 53:* 303–318.

Veugelers, R., Benninga, M. A., Calis, E. A., Willemsen, S. P., Evenhuis, H., Tibboel, D., & Penning, C. (2010). Prevalence and clinical presentation of constipation in children with severe generalized cerebral palsy. *Developmental Medicine & Child Neurology, 52:* 216–221.

Vlaskamp, C., & Cuppen-Fonteine, H. (2007). Reliability of assessing the sensory perception of children with profound intellectual and multiple disabilities: a case study. *Child: Care, Health and Development, 33:* 547–551.

Vlaskamp, C., De Geeter, K. I., Huijsmans, L. M., & Smit, I. H. (2003). Passive activities: the effectiveness of multisensory environments on the level of activity of individuals with profound multiple disabilities. *Journal of Applied Research in Intellectual Disabilities, 16:* 135–143.

Vlaskamp, C., Hiemstra, S. J., & Wiersma, L. A. (2007a). Becoming aware of what you know or need to know: gathering client and context characteristics in day services for persons with profound intellectual and multiple disabilities. *Journal of Policy and Practice in Intellectual Disabilities, 4:* 97–103.

Vlaskamp, C., Hiemstra, S. J., Wiersma, L. A., & Zijlstra, B. J. H. (2007b). Extent, duration, and content of day services' activities for persons with profound intellectual and multiple disabilities. *Journal of Policy and Practice in Intellectual Disabilities, 4:* 152–159.

Vlaskamp, C. A., & Nakken, H. (2008). Therapeutic interventions in the Netherlands and Belgium in support of people with profound intellectual and multiple disabilities. *Education and Training in Developmental Disabilities, 43:* 8.

Vorhaus, J. (2005). Citizenship, competence and profound disability. *Journal of Philosophy of Education, 39:* 461–475.

Vorhaus, J. (2013). Capability, freedom and profound disability. *Disability & Society, 28:* 1047–1058.

Vos, P., De Cock, P., Petry, K., Van Den Noortgate, W., & Maes, B. (2010). Do you know what I feel? A first step towards a physiological measure of the subjective well-being of persons with profound intellectual and multiple disabilities. *Journal of Applied Research in Intellectual Disabilities, 23:* 366–378.

Wacker, D. P., Wiggins, B., Fowler, M., & Berg, W. K. (1988). Training students with profound or multiple handicaps to make requests via microswitches. *Journal of Applied Behavior Analysis, 21:* 331–343.

Wacker, D. P., Berg, W. K., Wiggins, B., Muldoon, M., & Cavanaugh, J. (1985). Evaluation of reinforcer preferences for profoundly handicapped students. *Journal of Applied Behavior Analysis, 18:* 173–178.

Wallis, C. (2009). Respiratory health of people with profound intellectual and multiple disabilities. In: J. Pawlyn, & S. Carnaby (Eds.), *Profound Intellectual and Multiple Disabilities: Nursing Complex Needs.* Oxford: Wiley-Blackwell.

Ware, J. (1994). Using interaction in the education of pupils with PMLDs (i) creating contingency-sensitive environments.
Ware, J. (Ed.) (1994). *Educating Children with Profound and Multiple Learning Disabilities*. London: David Fulton.
Ware, J. (1996). *Creating a Responsive Environment for People with Profound and Multiple Learning Difficulties*. London: David Fulton.
Ware, J. (2003). *Creating a Responsive Environment for People with Profound and Multiple Learning Difficulites* (2nd edn). London: David Fulton.
Ware, J. (2004). Ascertaining the views of people with profound and multiple learning disabilities. *British Journal of Learning Disabilities, 32*: 175–179.
Ware, J., Julian, G., & Mcgee, P. (2005). Education for children with severe and profound general learning disabilities in Ireland: factors influencing teachers' decisions about teaching these pupils. *European Journal of Special Needs Education, 20*: 179–194.
Warnock, M. (2005). *Special Educational Needs—A New Look, Impact No. 11*. London, Philosophy of Education Society of Great Britain.
Watson, D. L., Emery, C., & Bayliss, P. D. (2012). *Children's Social and Emotional Wellbeing in Schools: A Critical Perspective*. Bristol: Policy Press.
Watson, J. B. (1913). Psychology as the behaviorist views it (first published in *Psychological Review, 20*, pp. 158–177). www.psychclassics.yorku.ca/Watson/views.htm. [last accessed 12.04. 2013].
Watson, J. B. (1930). *Behaviorism* (Revised edition). New York: Harper's.
Watson, N. (2012). Theorising the lives of disabled children: How can disability theory help? *Children & Society, 26*: 192–202.
Wellington, J. (2000). *Educational Research—Contemporary Issues and Practical Approaches*. London: Continuum.
Whitehurst, T. (2007). Liberating silent voices—perspectives of children with profound & complex learning needs on inclusion. *British Journal of Learning Disabilities, 35*: 55–61.
Wilder, J. (2008). *Proximal Processes of Children with Profound Multiple Disabilities*. Stockholm: Stockholm University.
Wilder, J., Axelsson, C., & Granlund, M. (2004). Parent–child interaction: a comparison of parents' perceptions in three groups. *Disability and Rehabilitation, 26*: 1313–1322.
Williams, J. (2005). Achieving meaningful inclusion for people with profound and multiple learning disabilities. *Tizard Learning Disability Review, 10*: 52–56.
Wilson, F. C., Harpur, J., & McConnell, N. (2007). Vegetative and minimally conscious states survey: attitudes of clinical neuropsychologists and speech and language therapists. *Disability and Rehabilitation, 29*: 1751–1756.

Withers, P., & Bennett, L. (2003). Myths and marital discord in a family with a child with profound physical and intellectual disabilities. *British Journal of Learning Disabilities, 31*: 91–95.

Wolf, D. E. (1980). The effect of automated interrupted music on head positioning of cerebral palsied individuals. *Journal of Music Therapy, 17*: 184–206.

Wolff, P. H. (1959). Observations on newborn infants. In: Stone, J., Smith, H. T., & Murphy, L. B. (Eds.), *The Competent Infant*. New York: Basic Books.

Woodruff Smith, D. (2008). **Phenomenology**. www.plato.stanford.edu/entries/phenomenology/. [last accessed 11.06.2010].

Young, H., & Lambe, L. (2011). Multi-sensory storytelling for people with profound and multiple learning disabilities. *PMLD Link, 23*: 29–31.

Young, H., Fenwick, M., Lambe, L., & Hogg, J. (2011). Multi sensory storytelling as an aid to assisting people with profound intellectual disabilities to cope with sensitive issues: a multiple research methods analysis of engagement and outcomes. *European Journal of Special Needs Education, 26*: 127–142.

Zelic (2008). On the phenomenology of the life-world. *Synthesis Philosophica, 46*: 413–426.

Zijlstra, H. P., & Vlaskamp, C. (2005). The impact of medical conditions on the support of children with profound intellectual and multiple disabilities. *Journal of Applied Research in Intellectual Disabilities, 18*: 151–161.

INDEX

Indexer: Dr Laurence Errington

acceptance theory 16
adaptive skills development 34
adult support (in special school) and Sam 166–171
advocacy and nurses 14
agency 107–108
akathisia 7
alertness 39–43
    microswitch-pressing and 45–46, 49
amputee phantom limb 120–127
anti-reductionism 136–137, 150, 157
asleep-active (behaviour state) 40
asleep-inactive (behaviour state) 40
assessment 5–6, 84–85
    behavioural state 13
    cognitivism and its influence in 66–78
atomism 103–105, 108
Austin's speech act theory 63–64, 66, 70

autonomy 14–15, 19
awake-active state 41
awake-active state/stereotypy state 41
awake-inactive state 41

Bates, Camaioni and Volterra 54, 63–68, 70–71, 82, 84, 173, 177–178
Behavior State Observation Schedule (BSOS) 40
behaviour
    carers role in monitoring changes in 7
    cognitivism in study of 22
    definitions/types 40–41
    observing 147–148
    rejecting mechanistic models of 97–102
    responding to 79–80
behaviour states 39–43, 160–163

assessing 13
microswitch-pressing and 45–46, 165–179
Sam 166–196
see also specific states/types
behaviourism (behavioural psychology) 21–50, 96–97, 117, 124, 164, 186
body and 96–97
early research in PMLD 28–35
education and 11–14
history/rise of 23–24
new wave of research in PMLD 35–48
Sam and 167–173, 175, 178–179, 182–183
summary of theory 22–23
being-in-the-world (notion of) 109, 112, 114–120, 126–128, 178, 194, 201
Sam and 178, 184–186, 194
Bekhterev, Vladimir 24–25
blinking 31
body
as object 95–102, 107, 109, 117, 127, 176
"at-this-moment" 120–127, 129, 194–195, 200
existentially/globally poised 112–113, 116
experience of 108–109
habitual *see* habitual body
image 109–110, 127–128, 176
mechanistic (mechanistic physiology) 94–102, 104–107, 116, 119, 127, 186
pre-objective *see* pre-objective body
schema 109–111, 113, 127–128
bricoleur (of Levi–Strauss) 134

capabilities 17–19
carers, role in monitoring changes in behaviour 7
see also family; parents
Carlotta (the infant) and Bates 64–66
Carman, T. 94, 96, 102–103, 106, 110–112, 122, 124–125
causality
circular 99
linear 97, 99
third person 121
worldly 117, 186
cause and effect 73, 118–119
cerebral palsy, Sam's 131, 134, 156
children, other
education of 10
Sam and 152, 156, 169, 190–191, 202–203
see also friends; peers
circular causality 99
cognitive development 8, 13, 51–85
profoundly delayed/severely impaired 3
relatively advanced 125
cognitivism (cognitive psychology) 22, 124, 176, 183
defining 52–54
education and 11–14
phenomenology and 93
PMLD interventions/assessment 66–76
responsive environments and 82–83
Sam and 173, 174–175, 198
summary of theory 52–66
collective construction 135
colour perception 98
communication 58–85
early (newborns/infants) 58–85
assessment 67–72
in learning environment 42

intentional *see* intentionality
lack (non-communication) 5, 140–141, 143, 157
non-verbal 64, 66, 69–70, 139–140
of symptoms *see* symptoms
see also interviews; "voices"
symbolic 12, 63, 84, 177, 184
community-based services as alternatives to institutional care 8–9
concurrent operant preference assessment 36
conditioning 24–28, 30–33, 164
choosing alternative responses to condition 37–39
classical 23–24, 27–28, 30, 48, 164
in PMLD 30–31, 48
operant *see* operant conditioning
constructionism (in research) 135–137, 140–141
contact, physical *see* touch
continental philosophy 87
contingency awareness 12–13, 30, 35, 37–39, 50, 79–80, 104, 114, 119, 197, 201
Sam 164–165, 167, 178, 186
contingency manipulation with stereotyped behaviours 47
contingent reinforcement 47
conversations, starting, and giving chances to reply 80–81
see also protoconversations
Coupe O'Kane and Goldbart 63, 67–68, 70–72, 82–83, 174, 177–178, 183–184
Crotty, M. 132–136, 152
crying/agitated state 41
cue cards 144–145

daze (behaviour state) 40
definitions of PMLD 2–4
deinstitutionalisation 8–9

depression 6
development (infant/child)
cognitive *see* cognitive development
Nussbaum's theory 18
differential reinforcement
of an alternative behaviour (DRA) 47
of other behaviour (DRO) 47
doctors, parents/experiences of ways they question quality of life 6
drowsy (behaviour state) 40

education 9–14
inclusive *see* inclusive education
see also mainstream school; special school; teachers
embodied subjectivity 197–198
embodiment (organism's) 92–94, 108, 126–128, 192, 200
multiple 125
time and 128
environment(s)
learning, and behaviour state 42
Merleau-Ponty's (=*Umwelt*) 99, 108, 178, 200
multisensory 5, 13–14, 43
responsive 78–83
epistemology 132–136, 150
constructionist 135, 139
ethics in research 137, 147–148
ethnographic approach 138–139
European (continental) philosophy 87
experience(s)
of body 108–109
PMLD 108, 137–141
external perception 111
externalism 30, 97

extinction with stereotyped
    behaviours 47
eye blinking 31

face (head) slapping 47, 157,
    179, 202
family, role 7–8
    see also parents
focus groups, pre-observation
    145–153
free operant preference assessment
    36
friends and friendship 9
    Sam at mainstream school
        190–192
    see also peers
functional analysis of conditions
    maintaining stereotyped
    behaviours 46–47

Goodley, D. 138–139
grip (notion of) 111

habitual body (body-habit) 120–129
    Sam 194–195, 198, 200
happiness 17, 49
    indices 43–45
    states of 161–162, 166, 171–179,
        180–181, 189, 192
    see also mutual pleasure
head (face) slapping 47, 157, 179, 202
health
    mental 6–7
    physical 4–6
healthcare
    barriers 6
    needs 4–5
hermeneutic phenomenology,
    philosophy of 150–152
human rights 133
humanness 16
Husserl, E. 88–90, 199

idealism (odontological) 136–137, 154
identity 2, 14–16
illocutions (performatives prior to
    speech) 63–66, 70, 84
image, body 109–110, 127–128, 176
imitation 76–77
imprinting, social (perceptual
    learning in early social
    development) 63, 83–84, 193,
    201
    acquired intersubjectivity
        through 54–58
inclusive education 9–11, 131
    Sam 141
    see also mainstream school
individual mind 135
infants see development; neonates
insects, limb substitution 114–120
institutional care, community-based
    services as alternatives to
    8–9
intensive interaction (intervention)
    12, 51, 67, 72–76, 79, 82–84
    contact/touch in 77
    interactive style of 74–75
    Sam 145–146
intentionality (intentional
    communication) 64,
    66–68, 70–71, 75–76, 78,
    82–83, 119
    Sam 136–137, 141, 155, 158,
        174–177, 183, 185, 193
interactions (social) 42, 44, 68, 74,
    80–83
    allowing him/her to take the
        lead in 81–82
    interactive interaction as a
        style of, see also intensive
        interaction
    mutually satisfying and
        reciprocal 11
    perceptual 55

Sam 154, 183–184, 187–188, 194
sharing control in 81
interactive style of intensive interaction (intervention) 74–75
internal states (concept) 49
internal variable, theorising 39–45
intersubjectivity 54–63, 67, 136–137, 193, 195, 197–198, 202
  acquired, via social imprinting 54–58
  primary/innate 60–62, 84, 132, 162–163, 175, 177–178, 183–184, 188–190, 192, 194–195, 198
  Sam's 178, 184, 188, 192–194, 198
  secondary/emergent 54, 58–59, 61–63, 84, 132, 136, 163, 175, 177–178, 183–184, 188, 192
interviews 139, 142–145
  Sam 149, 151

kinaesthesis 110, 113, 127

lead in interaction, allowing him/her to take the 81–82
learning, perceptual *see* imprinting
learning environment and behaviour state 42
learning support assistants (LSAs) with Sam 132, 153, 157, 166–167, 169–172, 179–181, 189, 191
Levi-Strauss, C. 134
Lewis and Staehler 89–90, 199
life stories 16, 144
life world 89–92, 199–203
  explored in Chapter Four 91–92, 199–200
  in broad sense 90–91, 200–201
  in narrow sense 89–90, 200

limb
  phantom 120–127
  substitution (insects) 114–120
  see also restless leg syndrome
linear causality 97, 99
locutionary stage (in emergence of speech) 63, 66, 71, 84
longitudinal research 149

mainstream school 9–11, 13, 15, 42
  behavioural states in 161–163
  Sam in 137, 150, 152–154, 156–159, 161–162, 170–179, 190–196
  see also inclusive education
maladaptive behaviours 29, 46, 50
  Sam 168–170, 179, 202
manipulanda 112, 128, 176
mechanical restraints with stereotyped behaviours 47
mechanistic physiology/mechanistic body 94–102, 104–107, 116, 119, 127, 186
Merleau-Ponty, M. 89, 92–129, 176–178, 184, 186–188, 194–195, 197–198, 200, 202
microswitch-pressing 12–13, 17, 29, 37–39, 49
  alertness and 45–46, 49
  behaviour states and 45–46, 165–179
  Sam 163–179, 187, 189
  with stereotyped behaviours 47
mind, representational *see* representation
mood 6
Moore M. et al. (1998) 139
Moran, D. 87–88
  and Mooney, T. 88
Morris, K. J. 18–19, 140–141, 149, 153
mothering 73
Müller-Lyer illusion 106–107

multiple stimulus preference format (MS)
  with replacement (MSW) 36
  without replacement (MSWO) 36
multisensory environments 5, 13–14, 43
muscle contraction 101–102
music and postural control 33
mutual pleasure and dependence 60, 78, 147, 149

negative reinforcement 47, 72
Neonatal Behavioral Assessment Scale 40
neonates/newborns
  cognitive development 40
  communication 58
newborns *see* neonates
Nind and Hewett 12, 72–79, 82–85, 118–119, 145, 186
non-contingent stimulation with stereotyped behaviours 47
non-participatory observation (vignettes) 145–146, 149, 154–158, 166–196, 198
non-verbal communication 64, 66, 69–70, 139–140
nurses 6, 14
Nussbaum's theory of human development 18

object(s)
  awareness of *see* other-object awareness
  body as 95–102, 107, 109, 117, 127, 176
  exploring 163
  perception 105–106, 112
objectivism 133–136
observation 145–149
  focus groups before 145–153
  non-participatory (vignettes) 145–146, 149, 154–158, 166–196, 198
  participatory 145, 148–149, 153–154
ontology 136–137, 150, 152, 154
operant conditioning 12, 23, 26–28, 30
  in PMLD 31–33, 36, 47, 49, 51, 164–165
oppression 14
original activity (of organism) 98–99, 107, 127, 200
other-active-happy state 162
  Sam 171–179, 192
other-active state, Sam 181–182
other-active-unhappy state 163
othering 14–15
other-object awareness 163
  Sam 171–179, 192–196

parents 16
  experiences of ways doctors question quality and value of life 6
  interactions with 81
  physical and emotional demands 8
  see also family
participatory observation 145, 148–149, 153–154
passive-distant state 161
  Sam 189
passive-focused state 161
  Sam 189
passive-happy state 161
  Sam 189
passive-unhappy state 161
  Sam 166–171
Pavlov, Ivan 25–26, 28, 164
peers and Sam 203
  at mainstream school 171–179, 187–189, 190–192

at special school 187–192, 196
see also friends
perception 98–100, 102–103, 108–109, 112, 116
    colour 98
    external 111
    interaction and 55
    learning in early social development *see* imprinting
    object 105–106, 112
    rejection of mechanistic model of 104–107
performatives (illocutions prior to speech) 63–66, 70, 84
perlocutions 63–64, 66, 70, 82, 84
phantom limb 120–127
phenomenology 16, 87–129
    Merleau-Ponty's 89, 92–129, 176–178, 184, 186–188, 194–195, 197–198, 200, 202
    PMLD and 92–97, 102–104, 108, 114–115, 117–120, 122, 124–126, 128–129
    rationale for 92–93
    Sam and 176–177, 184, 187–188, 194–195, 197, 200, 202
    summary of theory 87–95
philosophy
    atomistic 103–105, 108
    continental 87
    of hermeneutic phenomenology 150–152
physical contact *see* touch
physical health 4–6
pointing gesture 66, 70, 84, 101
    Carlotta's 65–66
positive reinforcement 32–34, 47
postural control, improving 33–34
pre-communicative state, Sam 178, 184
preferred awake states 41
preferred stimuli 35–37, 44–45, 48

preintentional communication 67–70, 76, 79, 82–83
    Sam and 132, 140, 174
pre-objective body 108–114
    examples 114–120
pre-observation focus groups 145–153
preverbal development 63
    Sam 136
proactive communication 68–70
proprioception 110–111, 113, 127
protoconversations 60–62, 84, 183
protodeclaratives 54, 64, 66, 68, 70–71, 83–84
    Carlotta's 65
    Sam's 173–175, 177, 183
protoimperatives 54, 63, 66, 70–71, 83–84
    Carlotta's 65
    Sam's 173–175, 177, 183
proto-secondary-intersubjectivity 177–178, 198

quality of life and wellbeing 2, 17–19, 203
    parents/experiences of doctors question 6

reach-for-real behaviour/action 71
    Sam 174
reactive communication/behaviour 68–69
realism (odontological) 136–137
reductionism 136–137, 140, 146, 157
    see also anti-reductionism
reflex response 100–102
reflexive communication/behaviour 68–70
reflexology 24–25
reinforcement 27–28, 47
    contingent 47
    negative 47, 72

positive 32–34, 47
  with stereotyped behaviours 47
representation 53, 102–104, 108, 118–119, 128, 140
  acquisition 55, 57–58, 124
  Sam and 152, 179, 186–187, 193, 202
research project (with Sam) 131–158
  background 131–133
  design 133–136
  methods 145–158
  search for methodology 141–149
residential care, community-based services as alternatives to 8–9
response(s)
  blocking, with stereotyped behaviours 47
  choosing alternative responses to condition 37–39
  conditioned 25–26, 31
  environments providing 78–83
  reflex 100–102
  stimulus causing *see* stimulus
  unconditioned 25–26, 31
restless leg syndrome 7
rights, human 133
Romdenh-Romluc, K. 91
Russian physiology and conditioning theory 24–25

Sam 131–203
  interpreting 131–158
  research project *see* research project
Schaffer, H. R. 52, 54–58, 63, 67, 75–77, 82–85, 104, 193
schema, body 109–111, 113, 127–128
schooling 9–11
  see also mainstream school; special school; teachers
Sechenov, Ivan 24

self-active-happy state 162
  Sam 166, 180–181
self-active-unhappy state 162
  Sam 166–171
self-harming/injury 4, 7, 46–47, 50
  Sam 157–158, 169–170, 179
SENDA (Special Educational Needs and Disability Act) 9
sensory abilities, assessment 5
  see also multisensory environments
single stimulus (SS) preference assessment 36
Skinner, Burrhus Frederic 26–28, 164
slapping oneself 166, 169, 179, 184
  head/face 47, 157, 179, 202
sleep states 40
Smith, A. D. 109–110, 112–113
social cognitivism 12, 58
social development
  interactions in *see* interactions
  perceptual learning in *see* imprinting
social imprinting *see* imprinting
social interactions *see* interactions
Sokolowski, R. 89–90
special educational needs 9
special schools 9–11, 13, 42
  behavioural states in 161–163
  Sam at 132, 137, 150, 156–163, 166–173, 176–196, 198–199, 201–202
speech
  Austin's speech act theory 63–64, 66, 70
  locutionary stage in emergence of 63, 66, 71, 84
  performatives (illocutions) prior to 63–66
stereotyped behaviours 46–48, 50
  Sam 158, 168, 179–181, 184, 187–188, 202

stimulus (stimuli) 97–100
    conditioned 25–26, 30–31, 48, 164
    non-contingent stimulation with stereotyped behaviours 47
    preferred 35–37, 44–45, 48
    response to 26–28, 30–31, 35
    unconditioned 25–26, 28, 30–31, 48, 164
stories, life 16, 144
stress 7
subjectivity (and subjectivism) 59, 62, 93–94, 119, 133–136
    embodied 197–198
    primary 62, 84
    Sam and 135, 138, 183, 187, 192–196
    secondary 62, 192–196
successive choice procedure 35–36, 44, 48
switch-pressing *see* microswitch-pressing
symbolic communication 12, 63, 84, 177, 184
symptoms, communicating/reporting 6
    difficulties 5, 143

talking mats 142, 144
teachers 10–11, 13, 15, 47
    Sam and 132, 143, 157, 169–171, 179–180, 188
terminology 2–3
third person causality 121

Thompson, E. 90–91, 110, 126, 200
touch (physical contact) 77–78, 110
    Sam and Ben 184
Trevarthen and Aitken 54, 58–63, 84, 132, 160, 174–178, 183–184, 188, 193–195, 198

Umwelt 99, 108, 178, 200
unconditioned response 25–26, 31
unconditioned stimulus 25–26, 28, 30–31, 48, 164
unhappy states 161–163
    Sam 166–171
United Nations Convention on the Rights of the Child (UNCRC) 133

vignettes (non-participatory observation) 145–146, 149, 154–158, 166–196, 198
visual methods of research 142–144
"voices" (of people with PMLD), accessing/hearing 137–143, 148

Ware, J. 3, 12, 15, 72, 78–84, 125, 140
Watson, John B. 23–26, 28, 93, 117, 201
wellbeing *see* quality of life and wellbeing
Woodruff Smith, D. 87
worldly causality 117, 186